PUBLIC LAW AND POLITICS

The Edinburgh Centre for Law and Society
Series Editor: Professor Emilios A. Christodoulidis

Titles in the Series

Transformations of Policing
Edited by Alistair Henry and David J. Smith

The Universal and the Particular in Legal Reasoning
Edited by Zenon Bankowski and James MacLean

Law and the Politics of Reconciliation
Edited by Scott Veitch

Public Law and Politics
The Scope and Limits of Constitutionalism

Edited by

EMILIOS CHRISTODOULIDIS
University of Glasgow, UK

STEPHEN TIERNEY
University of Edinburgh, UK

Routledge
Taylor & Francis Group
LONDON AND NEW YORK

First published 2008 by Ashgate Publishing

2 Park Square, Milton Park, Abingdon, Oxon OX14 4RN
711 Third Avenue, New York, NY 10017, USA

Routledge is an imprint of the Taylor & Francis Group, an informa business

First issued in paperback 2016

British Library Cataloguing in Publication Data
Public law and politics : the scope and limits of
constitutionalism. - (The Edinburgh Centre for Law and
Society series)
1. Public law - Philosophy 2. Public law - Political
aspects
I. Christodoulidis, Emilios A. II. Tierney, Stephen
III. University of Edinburgh. Centre for Law and Society
342'.001

Library of Congress Cataloging-in-Publication Data
Christodoulidis, Emilios A.
Public law and politics : the scope and limits of constitutionalism / by Emilios Christodoulidis and Stephen Tierney.
p. cm. -- (Edinburgh Centre for Law and Society series)
Includes index.
ISBN 978-0-7546-7363-7
1. Public law--Philosophy. 2. Public law--Political aspects. I. Tierney, Stephen. II. Title.

K3150.C49 2008
342.001--dc22

2007046432

ISBN 13: 978-0-7546-7363-7 (hbk)
ISBN 13: 978-1-138-25565-4 (pbk)

Contents

List of Contributors *vii*

1 Public Law and Politics: Rethinking the Debate 1
Emilios Christodoulidis and Stephen Tierney

PART 1: ON 'THE IDEA OF PUBLIC LAW'

2 Sovereignty and the Idea of Public Law 15
Stephen Tierney

3 Authority, Exploitation and the Idea of Public Law 27
Scott Veitch

4 Public Law as Political Jurisprudence:
Loughlin's 'Idea of Public Law' 35
Emilios Christodoulidis

5 Reflections on *The Idea of Public Law* 47
Martin Loughlin

PART 2: PUBLIC LAW AND IMPERIALISM

6 On Law, Democracy and Imperialism 69
James Tully

7 Democracy, Political Reflexivity and Bounded Dialogues:
Reconsidering the Monism-Pluralism Debate 103
Hans Lindahl

8 The Reframing of Law's Imperial Frame:
A Comment on Tully 117
Neil Walker

9 Imperialism and Constitutionalism 129
Gavin W. Anderson

PART 3: PUBLIC LAW AND PROCEDURALISM

10 Constitutionalism as Proceduralism: A Glance at the Terrain 141
Frank Michelman

11 The Crisis of Im/purity 163
Johan van der Walt

12 Between Engagement and Disengagement:
Two Concepts of Civility 189
Ioannis A. Tassopoulos

13 Enabling Proceduralism 205
Victor Tadros

Index *219*

List of Contributors

Gavin W. Anderson is Senior Lecturer in Law at the University of Glasgow

Emilios Christodoulidis is Professor of Legal Theory at the University of Glasgow

Hans Lindahl is Professor of Philosophy at Tilburg University

Martin Loughlin is Professor of Public Law at the London School of Economics

Frank Michelman is Robert Walmsley University Professor at Harvard Law School

Victor Tadros is Professor of Law at Warwick University

Ioannis A. Tassopoulos is Reader in Public Law at the University of Athens

Stephen Tierney is Reader in Law at the University of Edinburgh

James Tully is the Distinguished Professor of Political Science, Law, Indigenous Governance and Philosophy at the University of Victoria

Scott Veitch is Reader in Law at the University of Glasgow

Neil Walker is Professor of Public Law and the Law of Nature and Nations at the University of Edinburgh

Johan van der Walt is Professor of Law at the University of Glasgow

Chapter 1

Public Law and Politics: Rethinking the Debate

Emilios Christodoulidis and Stephen Tierney

I Framing the Debate

This volume seeks to arrive at a better understanding of how the relationship between public law and politics is conceptualised by constitutional theorists today. And to this end we asked the contributors in this volume to take issue with the following question: Should constitutionalism be envisaged as a discrete sphere, hermeneutically closed off or self-standing, subject to its own proper logic which can be described without the deployment of categories of political theory? The book brings together three leading constitutionalists: Frank Michelman from the American constitutionalist tradition which has its emphasis on internal constitutional debates surrounding the substance and processes of a long-settled and popularly endorsed written constitutional settlement. Martin Loughlin who, in *The Idea of Public Law*,[1] articulates a relational account of public law as a phenomenon that has developed in close synergy with its political environment; an account steeped in classical European thinking from the age of modernity to the present. And James Tully, whose radical philosophy presents one of the most startling challenges to orthodox constitutional thinking today, asking questions of liberal constitutionalism in an age where people and peoples call for constitutional recognition of the pluralism which, for Tully, both defines our time *and* is obscured in the hegemonic structures of established constitutional theory and practice. This project was organised by the Centre for Law and Society within the University of Edinburgh through three day-long workshops in 2006, each involving one of the main contributors and a number of papers offered in commentary by members of the Edinburgh Law School and colleagues working in the area of constitutional and political theory either in Scotland or abroad. This collection comprises a selection of these commentaries.

The relationship between politics and public law is a vexing one. In essence, the issue our principal contributors were asked to engage with was the interplay between the legal and the political, exposing the possibility for critical engagement with the function of public law and with constitutionalism in its political dimensions, and searching for the multiple ways in which public law is implicated (per Loughlin) in the logic of rule. This logic of rule seems to operate, on the one hand, in maintaining and underwriting relative patterns of power and weakness through political structures and

---

1 (Oxford: Oxford University Press, 2003).

processes. On the other hand, public law may be considered to contain the potential to redress these patterns through the use of constitutional authority, for example in the application of social and economic as well as civil and political rights, in the redistribution of political power through the development of new sites of territorial governance that reflect sub-state identity patterns, and in moves to supra-state levels of authority. The book tries to reproduce in a succinct way the insights we arrived at which help both expose the limitations and suggest the potentialities of public law within its political setting.

The book begins with four chapters focused upon *The Idea of Public Law* which, both in the UK and elsewhere, has triggered extensive debate in recent years concerning the nature of our discipline. In his chapter, Loughlin takes the opportunity to re-explain the purpose of the book and to answer critics who, in reviewing the book have, in his view, misunderstood its foundational purpose and intellectual contribution. He also responds directly to the commentaries by Stephen Tierney, Scott Veitch and Emilios Christodoulidis. The other two parts of the book have a slightly different format. The chapters by James Tully and Frank Michelman constitute new work, and therefore these chapters are themselves the subject of responses by three commentators. In reference to Tully's chapter, Hans Lindahl, Neil Walker and Gavin Anderson offer a diverse range of comment and critique, while Frank Michelman's chapter is scrutinised by Johan van der Walt, Ioannis Tassopoulos and Victor Tadros.

What is especially fascinating about the contributions from each of the central participants is that they are so varied. Loughlin, Tully and Michelman come from different intellectual and disciplinary backgrounds and, as such, present distinctive understandings of the very nature of public law as a discipline, its empirical foundations, the scope of its application in respect of the state and beyond, and whether or not it has any essential normative content. But although each engages with the relationship between law and politics in particular ways, a central theme that emerges is that central to this relationship is the nature of power relations within (Loughlin and Michleman), and extending beyond (Tully), the polity. Politics is of course about relations of power, and in this context, per Loughlin, we might usefully define public law as the set of rules that provides public authority with legitimacy for the exercise of political power through the practice of governing.[2] In many established formulations (for example, Michelman's) this legitimacy is to be found in the way public law both divides power among a number of public authorities, and constrains the mode of its exercise.

Finally, by way of introduction, a note on terminology. All three of the main contributors seem to treat public law as synonymous with constitutional law: indeed Tully notes explicitly that he and Loughlin do so, while it is common in American legal scholarship to do so, and such an approach seems to be implicit in Michelman's chapter. In the context of this volume not much hangs on this distinction. Since the book is concerned with broad, conceptual issues concerning the very nature of higher order legal authority within the polity, the concepts with which it engages

2 In the book important distinctions are drawn between the notion of 'politics' and that of 'the political'. See chapters by Christodoulidis and Loughlin.

cover principally this constitutional sense of public law rather than the details of administrative regulation.

II Public law, power and governance

With the concept of 'power' as a key to understanding the nature of the relationship with which we are concerned, it is possible to draw out linkages in terms of how the contributors address the issue of power throughout the book in relation to two of its important vehicles: governance and the state. The latter will be considered in the next section. For now let us concentrate on the relationship between public law and governance.

It is the mapping work of Loughlin that first focuses our attention on this issue as central to an understanding of the function of public law. In *The Idea of Public Law* he sets out to articulate the conceptual foundations of public law, an empirical exercise which, in his chapter in this volume, he argues has been badly misconstrued by several reviewers. His book has been charged either with constituting a normative (in the moral sense) exercise, which he argues it does not, or alternatively for failing to be a normative exercise, which again he contends it never purported to be. In short, it is Loughlin's contention that his critics have created a straw man to burn. Loughlin takes these reactions to his book as in themselves an important example of how the discipline of public law has become conceptually weakened by a general assumption that public law scholarship must combine empirical analysis and normative aspiration. This impoverished mindset has made it all the more necessary to excavate the discipline's conceptual underpinnings. However, at the same time it also makes it all the more difficult for readers to appreciate this empirical exercise for what it is. 'The most basic objective of the book … was to retrieve a subject that seems to have fallen off contemporary maps of knowledge. For want of a better term, I call this subject public law. But by public law I do not mean a categorical division within positive law, as is often intended when drawing a distinction between public law and private law. I mean something much more basic: the "law" by which public authority is established and maintained'. For Loughlin then, public law is the normative (in a rule-based sense) structure concerned with the creation and ongoing dynamics of public authority. It is about power, but power with a public face, granted legitimacy by a constitutional system: 'Public law is concerned with those precepts of "political right" that establish and maintain public authority'.

This raises various issues concerning the connection between public law and governance, in particular whether this relationship is sufficient to provide public law with a conceptual autonomy separable from politics and other mechanisms of power, such as economics. Is public law really a discrete idea, or is it so implicated in other relations of power that it cannot be understood as a free-standing concept? In this context Veitch and Christodoulidis ask, respectively, whether in addressing governmental authority, Loughlin neglects economic power and other modes of governance, and whether, in short, his claim that public law is an autonomous discipline lacks coherence. It seems that the purported autonomy of public law is also questioned by Tully in his assessment of public law as deeply implicated in the structures of imperialism. In a way similar to Veitch, Tully raises questions about the pervasive nature of economic power and hence of a continuum of modes of governance across the public *and* private spheres (on the issue of a continuum within Loughlin's account see also Christodoulidis's contribution and Loughlin's reply to this chapter). In short, Tully poses the difficult question whether public law, and with it international public law, are unavoidably co-opted to serve dominant interests through imperial relations of power.

Loughlin's reply in the context of Veitch's critique is interesting in that it initiates a broader (albeit indirect) conversation between Loughlin and Tully. He begins by defending his approach as scientific: in empirical terms it describes what public law does. In practice Loughlin concedes that it is of course the case that public law can act oppressively; governing as we know from history and from contemporary experience can represent the triumph of the powerful over the weak. Indeed, this dynamic 'is not confined to imperialism; it is inherent in the logic of rule'. But this is not the whole story. Public law in a *conceptual* sense, if not necessarily in practice, does not permit exploitation; and in this sense, for Loughlin, it seems to have some democratic or normative content: 'Public law (the precepts of political right) emerged in modern European practice as the explanatory and justificatory language of a particular mode of ruling. This was founded on basic ideas of sovereignty and citizenship and, later, on notions of democracy and rights. It is a mode of rule that claims to be law (*droit*)-governed ... The achievement of a system of public law does not mean that exploitation is eliminated from the world. But it does mean that exploitation is eliminated *conceptually* from the world of public law'.

At this point it seems that on one level we can explain the potential contradiction between Loughlin and Tully by the fact that each is addressing public law in functional terms according to different models of analysis. Loughlin, as has been observed, addresses public law in terms of its role in *constituting* governance/public authority within a polity/state. Tully, however, applies a wider and deeper frame of enquiry. His sociological lens has wider scope in seeking out those other power structures beyond municipal public law that serve the *functional role* of 'governance' (a question also raised by Christodoulidis); and it goes deeper in searching for what governance does in practice and the power relations it both reflects and helps shape. Loughlin addresses public authority as a discrete concept, while recognising that it is an idea that is conditioned by the reality of that authority in practice ('the task for public law is … to understand the ways in which existing constitutional arrangements can be said to work'). Nonetheless, Loughlin does not see his analytical role as one that necessarily extends to addressing in detail the practical ramifications that result from how public law is in fact exercised. But for Tully this is a major concern, and for him public law does, and it seems *can only*, work oppressively in practice: 'The old and new features [of public law] … , whether we like it or not, play imperial roles in what Martin Loughlin calls the "governance" of contemporary legal and political associations. We are not "entrapped" in these fields of imperial relationships, but, to use Wittgenstein's alternative phrase, we are "entangled" in them, and not so sure of our way out as the critics of imperialism lead us to believe'.

It still seems, however, that even in light of these possible tensions between them, in another sense there need be no necessary contradiction between Loughlin and Tully if we address their approaches as constituting different modes of enquiry.

Loughlin's is a strictly limited (in an entirely unpejorative sense) enquiry into the regulatory function of law, describing its component parts and how these come together to form the body of the constitution and its legal structure. Tully's is a sociological enquiry into the uses to which this regulatory framework – and its equivalent international law framework – are put. As Tully states: 'I follow Martin Loughlin … in taking public law to be the basic laws that juridicalize or legalize the distribution, institutionalization and exercise of the political powers of governing, including governing the economy, in any form of legal and political association. Like Loughlin, who follows Foucault on this, I call the basic legal and political institutions "practices of governance"'.[3] And conversely, Loughlin's account does not preclude space for a radical political critique of public law: 'Just as Kelsen claimed that even an anarchist could accept his pure theory of law, so too does the pure theory of public law work irrespective of one's personal political convictions'.

By Tully's account, public law and international public law provide the regulatory mechanisms and purported legitimacy for imperialism, a point brought out in an even more radical form of critique in Anderson's commentary. Is it the case, for Tully, that this is not simply a consequence of malpractice, but rather, in its conceptual essence, the idea of public law is inherently implicated in sustaining oppression? Tully does seem to see structures of oppression as intrinsic to the public law model and as such his account can be termed deeply critical – that is, one that does not disaggregate a functional account of public law from the oppressive practices which, by its nature, it necessarily portends. Tully sets out his work in the context of other anti-imperialist theorists, thereby locating himself within an overtly normative terrain. In doing so he identifies 'five sets of presumptively or allegedly anti-imperial theorists' who examine and criticise 'a range of political and legal phenomena they take to be imperial'. Although they each present an alternative model that they take to be non-imperial, in every case Tully argues that 'features of both the languages and practices they presume to be external to imperialism (non-imperial) turn out on closer examination to be internal to, or play a role in, contemporary imperialism'.

This is a strong critique indeed, and in his commentary Walker observes that Tully's analysis might be seen as nominalist and fatalistic. In terms of the former charge 'the price of a redefinition as radical as that offered by Tully is the loss of precisely that common sense of the zone of plausible contestation around the concept of empire which would make any such redefinition potentially persuasive and so worth making in the first place. On this view, the criticism is that Tully, armed with a stipulative definition that few share, may end up talking only to these converted few. In the second place, there is the charge of *structural fatalism*. According to this argument, the new definition of empire and of empire's law offered by Tully may be so encompassing that it becomes difficult if not impossible to imagine how law is ever to escape the clutches of empire and operate in the service of an alternative geopolitical vision'. Walker concludes that the former charge is in fact ill-founded given the depth of Tully's analysis in highlighting a '*causal* relationship between old and new – between colonial and post-colonial imperialism' and also in the way it identifies and describes 'a close *analogy* between classical and contemporary imperialism'.

---

3 In his chapter Tully cites *The Idea of Public Law*, 5–31, especially 29–31.

And even if we think his diagnosis unduly pessimistic about an alternative anti-imperial role for law, Walker reads Tully's account as, in part, a normative challenge. Although Tully sees (as Walker puts it) 'the deep rules of the game … skewed in favour of empire' and is sceptical of 'the capacity of the subalterns to challenge imperial relations from within in a manner which attacks their very imperial logic and form', what he has done, according to Walker, is formulate new theoretical and practical challenges for those committed to an idea of global justice. We will return to this in the final section.

III Public law: The state and identity

To search further for an answer as to whether Tully's account denies even the possibility of a conceptualisation of public law as non-oppressive, let us turn to the issue of the nation-state and its identity. In Loughlin's sense public law is both a universal and a particular phenomenon. It is universal in that everywhere 'public' power, as it is understood in the modernist sense, is exercised within an authority structure we can call public law. It is particular in that these structures of authority are spatially contained. And it is in this latter fact that the state is so central to Loughlin's account, as he confirms in his responses to both Tierney and Christodoulidis. This reminds us that his is an empirical attempt to understand how public law has served the function of sustaining the link between state and nation – those key constructs of modernity – by giving the former authority – legitimate authority – in the management of the latter.

Tully's focus, although looking beyond the state, also has important things to say about the state in terms of relations of power. One of Tully's critiques of the state system is that powerful states acting both alone, and also in concert through the international order of states which they have built to suit their interests, have acted to control weak states. Here Tully seems to challenge the scope of Loughlin's account: 'While Martin Loughlin presents what is in many respects a classic Westphalian theory of public law and political theory, he does explicitly respond to the imperial hypothesis, but only in the specific form presented by Hardt and Negri in *Empire*, and only with respect to their challenge to the traditional state-centred account of sovereignty, which is very different from the histories of imperialism I am drawing on here'. Tully appears to suggest more explicitly than before that, even conceptually, the modernist construct of public law is oppressive, given the role this idea (as well as its practice) plays in sustaining and legitimising state power. The state, and its homogenising social glue 'the nation', are homogenising theoretical constructs and, therefore, by definition they deny pluralism and act to enhance the role of powerful interests. What is more, the international order of states has acted from the outside to reinforce the idea of the state and the nation within territories where each has been so ill-fitting.

And so we seem to see in Tully's chapter a sense that public law, by its nature, supports structures of order and oppression, and in doing so tends to foreclose political action rather than empower it. Or as Anderson puts it: 'The historic mission of modern constitutionalism, as Tully's work has helped establish, has been to prevent key aspects of constitutional knowledge being opened to debate'. But this in turn causes us to return to Loughlin with the question, if public law is oppressive, is this simply an unavoidable consequence of its role in providing identity and normative authority for a polity, which by definition will contain imbalanced relations between the weak and the powerful? Loughlin's claim that 'exploitation' is eliminated conceptually from the world of public law does not mean that a polity can avoid the inherent power relations that come with the reality of governance and a concept of constitutional unity. In fact, Loughlin seems to view these features as inherent in the logic of rule. They are essential components of a polity with a public law structure and should not by that mere fact alone be cast as inherently exploitative. Let us turn to Lindahl's analysis that the demos is a necessary condition of the polis in exploring this tension between the Loughlin and Tully accounts further.

Lindahl explores the implications of Tully's call for the full constitutional accommodation of deep societal pluralism both as it appears in his chapter in this book and elsewhere, most notably his seminal monograph *Strange Multiplicity: Constitutionalism in an Age of Diversity*.[4] Lindahl suggests that the essence of imperialism for Tully is indeed the denial of pluralism. In this sense empire can in effect be defined as monism, the denial of difference, and even the possibility of difference. But Lindahl argues that there is a core form of monism that is inherent in any legal system and this revolves around the need for some form of demotic unity which is essential to build and sustain a genuine idea of the polis.

In this sense he echoes Loughlin, both in relation to the latter's contention that in empirical terms there is an inherent unity or monism within the methodology of public law, and in his idea of sovereignty as an inherent component of a state constitutional order. For example, in his reply to Tierney, Loughlin states: 'Governmental authority can be divided or shared, but sovereignty cannot. Sovereignty is constitutive of public law; it is an authoritative expression of a particular way of being'. This notion of sovereignty is tied to the notion of 'the people' or 'the nation' as an essential building block of the modern public law state.

In a similar vein Lindahl suggests that the 'we' is an essential element in any theory of democracy: 'To put it another way, the "self" of self-legislation entails the reflexive stance of a collective, the stance whereby individuals refer to themselves as the members of a group that creates norms in its own interest'. But, he argues, this notion seems to be missing, or at least to be understated, in Tully: 'Tully opposes any attempt to view the people that engage in self-rule in terms of "one nation" or the like'. A new or alternative unity may be envisaged that can replace the nation but we can't do without such an idea altogether: 'it makes no sense to simply play off plurality against unity. To be intelligible as a defence of political self-rule, legal pluralism is not simply an argument against the unity of a legal order, as one might be led to believe, but rather a thesis about how legal order is to be constituted as a unity'.

This analysis seems to echo Loughlin's notion of the sovereign state as the necessary institutional vehicle for the modernist conception of public law. As Lindahl continues: 'this is, indeed, the crucial question: how does a political

4 (Cambridge: Cambridge University Press, 1995).

association constitute itself as a legal unity? In particular, what sense are we to make of political self-determination as the act by which a plurality of individuals – and a fortiori of political associations – constitute themselves as a legal collective?' And indeed he concludes that Tully, if his approach is genuinely a dialogical rather than an agonistic one, is also logically committed to an idea of unity. 'Tully's concern is not merely to conserve plurality, but to achieve a form of unity in which a plurality of perspectives can recognize themselves as being part of a whole. The task of a politics of cultural recognition is to *overcome* plurality, albeit provisionally, in a constitution that is culturally – and politically – "neutral", as Tully puts it'. Agonism is genuinely pluralistic but the kind of dialogical approach that Tully wants, according to Lindahl, is not. 'What makes politics agonistic is the experience of *irreducible* plurality, a plurality that cannot be overcome by way of a dialectical mediation of the particular and the general, the many and the one. The strange, in a radical sense of the term, is what resists integration into the dialectic of the self and the other. On this strong reading of plurality, Tully cannot have it both ways: he must choose between an agonistic and a dialogical conception of politics'.

Lindahl seems to endorse the uncomfortable conclusion that Loughlin draws about the logic of rule. It requires some form of unity that will supplant, at least in the foundational moment of the polity, its social pluralism. In Lindahl's 'Gadamerian' analysis of Tully's 'dialogue', the possibilities of destabilising, disrupting and revising understandings are forever thwarted in the face of what installs itself as a *hermeneutical* horizon of possible commonalities – Habermas' famous 'inclusion' of the other is forever an 'integration' of the other. If Lindahl and Loughlin are correct, are we then left with the unsettling conclusion that public law, as the functional vehicle of the state in the modern era, has by necessity acted in a homogenising way, legitimising the denial of pluralism in the name of unity and representation? If so, it is small wonder that Tully's critique extends from the practice to the very concept of public law itself, and that his work endeavours to find a route out of this malaise for the voiceless. In his work, it seems more likely that what we see is not in fact an empirical misunderstanding of the reality of public law, but rather a normative critique that asks the radical question whether the modernist conception of public law is a viable mechanism with which to continue to structure the (legal) normative foundations of human society, particularly in a 'globalising' age.

IV Public law: Beyond the age of the nation-state?

If it is important to appreciate the heft of Loughlin's empirical account, it is equally vital that we do not neglect the normative challenge that lies at the epicentre of Tully's. As noted above, Walker observes how Tully has formulated new theoretical and practical challenges for those committed to an idea of global justice. This is all the more central to analyses of public power today as we address our discipline in an age of constitutional flux. Loughlin remains wedded to the normative strength of the state as receptacle of sovereignty, but even so he is aware that things may change and that new concepts may be needed for a new age. His challenge is simply to point out that such concepts have not yet been developed.

However, Tully's critique of public law and international public law raises the issue of whether the Westphalian state model is still an appropriate one through which to try to understand comprehensively the nature of governance today. Tully asks what the future will bring: 'The traditional struggle of liberation and self-determination against colonization was the classic model for transformation throughout the twentieth century, but we now know, as Fanon first pointed out … , that even this form of contestation did not overcome imperialism but only led to its modification into informal imperialism. So, we do not know if post-colonial forms of individual and collective anti-imperial contestation will lead to modifications that only reproduce the hegemony of the informal imperial features I have enumerated, or if they might lead to its transformation'.

Tully offers some signs of optimism towards the end of his chapter. Pluralism is a reality in the world today: 'These old and new alternative ways of living in the present survive and continue to develop in their own complex and creative ways, in relation to their own traditions, because imperialism has always depended for its very existence on indirect and informal rule, leaving local alternative worlds in operation to some constrained extent, and building its relationships of control and exploitation on them'. In a similar vein Walker engages with the place for public law in a globalising world and is more hopeful than Tully for the non-oppressive potentialities of public law in the age of 'late sovereignty'. In particular, he sees potential for the transformation of institutions from within, especially given the fact that we now have a wide network of 'governing' institutions at the international level, and indeed a set of complex tensions between them. Walker argues that 'plurality also offers transformative possibilities. The absence of a single citadel also means the lack of a monolithic power with the capacity and co-ordination to design and defend "formally" what alternatively may evolve "informally" … And it means that the odds are not so formidably stacked against any such particular transformations as they would be against the removal of a single monolithic structure – something of which we have current cause to remind ourselves as we see in the early years of the new century increasingly intense democratic challenges to the constitutional legitimacy of the Security Council, the WTO and, most acutely of all at present, the EU'.

The task set by Tully is a challenging one and the demands he makes are high. But in the last resort he does seem to see at least the feasibility that public law might escape the conceptual link to oppression which it has occupied in the age of the nation-state.

V Circumventing Politics: The procedural turn

The radical pluralist critique presented by Tully could possibly come up against a 'Loughlin-type' response that power is inevitable within a public law structure. But this also leaves open the argument that within that structure there are internal possibilities for the reconciliation, or at least for the fair co-existence, of conflicting values and identities. Frank Michelman's contribution tests this hypothesis, that pluralism and irreducible disagreement over substantive values might find a 'home' of sorts in a procedural form of constitutionalism. Johan van der Walt explains this well in his contribution: 'The pluralist or multi-cultural societies in which we live lack substantive criteria that can unite all their members in a free consensus regarding the merits of the laws by which we are governed. Coercion of compliance can therefore not be justified with reference to substantive considerations. The only justification available to those who collaborate in the state coercion of compliance must therefore be sought in the fact that the laws that require coerced compliance are the outcomes of procedures that are worthy of the respect of all the members of these pluralist societies, the respect of the coerced members included'. Note the emphasis here on the concern with justified collaboration in state coercion. It is a key concern to which all our contributors, Tadros, Tassopoulos and van der Walt will return. Suffice it to say here that for the advocates of the procedural turn, it is not the justness of the laws themselves, on substantive grounds, that justify the coercion, but the justness of procedure. This is, of course, the Rawlsian heritage, the proceduralism that underlies public reason according to Rawls which must, while maintaining a distance from comprehensive and deeply controversial, but passionately held world views, guarantee political coexistence through the integrity of a procedure that in some crucial sense remains equi-distant from these world views if it is to guarantee the recognition of all citizens as free and equal. In a crucial sense this guarantee is precisely what Tassopoulos also asks of Smith's 'thicker' account of civility, but one that might accommodate a more 'passionate' political subjectivity.

Such then is the weight and significance of the distinction between procedure and substance. Above all what must be avoided if procedural solutions are to carry the day is a mutual infection between substance and procedure, let alone a mutual folding of the two into each other. And it is in this context too that the question of the 'continuity' between political and legal disagreement, that was discussed at length in connection to Loughlin's chapter, poses a threat. Can the procedural logic proper to constitutional law be insulated from the normative speculation characteristic of political theory and political practice?

Perhaps the first important step in Michelman's argument is to build in a certain complexity at the very start. He will avoid any easy reduction of law to politics, eschew any simplistic 'law-as-politics' solution, while acknowledging all the time the unavoidably political role for the judge. The nuance of his position here is picked up by van der Walt and Tadros in different ways. But let us take this a step at a time. The question whether the logic of constitutionalism is or can be strictly procedural is, as both van der Walt and Tadros also acknowledge, the cue that Michelman follows throughout his chapter. There are views, he says, in which 'pure procedural justice is the telos of constitutionalism rightly understood'. Do these theories give us a clear sense of logic proper to constitutionalism? At this formative stage of the chapter his answer 'is going to be no, or at any rate not yet'. The analysis of proceduralism takes him to the theories of Habermas, Rawls (early and later) and Waldron; in all cases the incision is drawn with acuity and always on the side of generosity. But in the end the analyses are found wanting, procedural liberalism in each case falling back in the final instance on substantive criteria of liberty. But what is this substantive and therefore political proceduralism that keeps procedure pivotal while conceding that it can never be pure? Is there a 'bridging' solution, is it productive, and if we think that perhaps it is not, does that inevitably lead us to solutions 'irretrievably suffused with political theory' and if they are thus 'compromised' what leverage can they still gain from procedural, outcome-indifferent, justifications? In the end, how much mileage is left in ambivalence?

The problem that ensues from the procedural turn, as identified by van der Walt, is that it guarantees constitutionalism a level of independence only by rendering it incapable of answering most of the really pertinent questions that it is supposed to answer. 'What are the impurities that might tempt constitutionalism?' is the driving question asked by van der Walt. He asks of Michelman a further concession than the mere acknowledgement of its 'impurity' in the face of political/substantive values. Michelman's response, he claims, is not only that constitutionalism cannot be insulated from political theory, but that political theory itself cannot be insulated from the concerns, even more 'impure' at that, of other fields of theoretical inquiry that would at first glance appear to have little to do with it. He argues: 'The insight that I wish to bring to bear on Michelman's essay with these suggestions is ultimately this: The regard for the "impossibility of pure constitutionalism" ultimately leads to a regard for the impossibility of purity as such. It leads to an understanding of the disciplinary confines of scholarly disciplines as nothing more than markers that theoretical inquiry lays down in its traversal of a vast field of tensions between purity and impurity. This field of tensions, moreover, is not merely traversed by various disciplines of theoretical inquiry, but constituted or co-constituted by these theoretical traversals'.

If van der Walt's strategy is to push Michelman's dissatisfaction with a pure proceduralism to the point at which the 'impure temptations' force constitutional understandings to confront their dangerous supplements, Tadros and Tassopoulos in different ways ask him to rethink the formative distinctions and the mapping itself of the terrain. For Tassopoulos the emphasis is on what Michelman takes from Rawls, a conception of 'civility' that underlies any account of constitutionalism that is to remain faithful to the requirements of equal concern and respect. With this he contrasts an account of civility that taps the moral sentiments, that he takes from Smith, and the implications of which have a significant impact on our understanding of proceduralism. Tadros contests the ways in which the binarism pure/imperfect carve up the terrain to offer competing justifications for coercing those who disagree. Pure procedural solutions, he says, are only justified if procedure commands greater agreement than substantive issues; if coercion rather than punishment is what demands justification; and if we see pure and imperfect proceduralism as exhaustive of the field of procedural solutions. Tadros argues against each of these assumptions and for a theory of 'enabling' proceduralism, that relies on a more complex, and intricate, connection of procedure and substance.

V Conclusion

Constitutionalism, to paraphrase MacIntyre,[5] is an index of how much conflict a society is able to suppress. This may be a highly controversial formulation for most of our contributors. But it captures something very important about how disagreement is channelled into constitutional solutions, what remains in excess of such channelling, to tempt, invoke or necessitate further constitutional responses. Sometimes these are experienced as requiring a move from procedure to substance, sometimes as 'temptations' to 'impure' solutions, sometimes as constitutional crises. In all these cases political theory supports, informs and undergirds constitutional responses. It 'suffuses', to use Michelman's phrase, constitutional solutions and informs substantive priorities. But above all, at a meta-level and both in ordinary and extraordinary times, it directs the allocation of what is and what is not constitutionally negotiable; what is and is not open to constitutional question. In that above all perhaps, in determining what is properly political, what properly constitutional, what properly procedural or substantive, political theory is irretrievably and crucially implicated in constitutional law.

5 MacIntyre, A., *After Virtue: A Study in Moral Theory* (London: Duckworth, 1981).

PART 1
On 'The Idea of Public Law'

Chapter 2

Sovereignty and the Idea of Public Law

Stephen Tierney

1. Introduction: Sovereignty and public law

In this chapter I argue that Martin Loughlin's account of sovereignty as an essentially relational enterprise is a highly adaptable device with which to understand the complex relations of power and authority between citizens and government in the contemporary state. In particular, this flexibility is helpful as we apply the concept of relationality to explain the transformation in these relations of power and identity across a range of increasingly diffuse sites of territorial governance today. Loughlin's idea helps us bypass two caricatures prominent within public law scholarship which have rendered otiose much of the debate over the nature of the discipline in recent times. In the UK, these caricatures are drawn by the 'law as politics' reductionists on the one hand, and the 'pure theorists of positive law' on the other. The reductionist approach, by seeking to collapse public law into politics, misses Loughlin's important explication of public law as 'the third order of the political'; while the rigid positivist approach, in repeating simple mantras about the 'sovereignty' of Parliament as an abstract higher norm, becomes increasingly irrelevant in ontological terms as the normative significance of Westminster's legislative supremacy is upturned by political plate changes which re-order the constitutional landscape beneath the surface of legal formalism. The ways in which Loughlin's relational conception of sovereignty offers a better model with which to understand public law both in terms of UK constitutional practice and in a broader conceptual sense are explored in Section 2.

The new insights Loughlin provides are particularly important as the nature of the state changes. Today external and internal forces, including the sectoral pressures of economic globalisation, the increasingly expansive institutions of international organisations and international law, and the internal resilience of sub-state nationalism each act to constrict the *modus operandi* of state power in ways that question fundamental assumptions about the very nature of that power. In Section 3 I will consider how Loughlin's relational theory, the primary focus of which is relations of political power at the state level, might also help explain the impact of new forces which restrict state power. I will address the extent to which the concept of sovereignty can continue to be mapped exclusively onto the modern idea of the state, and in doing so will suggest ways in which Loughlin's theory might be further adapted to help explain relations of power in a time when the exercise of the state's competence and capacity are in flux. It will be asked to what extent different sets of 'sovereignty relationships' between people and government can overlap within the one territorial space, either within the multinational state or as a result of the state's membership of a suprastate body such as the European Union.

2. Sovereignty: the relationship between people and government

The Idea of Public Law illustrates how narrow positivism has tended to foreclose debates about sovereignty by applying a restrictive focus to the broader interaction between public law and the political process. In contrast, Loughlin's book offers a rich analytical structure for those who seek to move beyond this limited framework in attempting to understand public law in a wider context. The positivist tradition in its most rigid manifestations has constrained a proper understanding of the discipline by means of a pseudo-scientific approach which posits public law simply as a system of legal rules and, therefore, as part of a more general system of civil or private law. Loughlin argues that such an exercise is shown to be inadequate when the legal scientist turns in an empirical way to address the *practice* of public law; because it is in this observational process that we cannot but note the close interaction between the legal and the political which pervades all areas of public law praxis, including the idea of sovereignty; indeed this relationship is inherently symbiotic and cannot be suppressed by asserting the supposed supremacy of formalistic legal rules. In the penultimate chapter of the book which is specifically concerned with method, Loughlin suggests that the error certain positivists have made is to focus only on the regulatory aspects of public law, thereby relegating the equally important constitutive aspects to the realm of positive morality.[1] This is not an unbridled assault upon positivism per se, but rather a carefully directed exposure of the inadequacies of a particular strain of rigid public law legalism. What is needed then is a more fluid approach to the interplay between law and politics which will take us beyond strict juridification to those spheres of public life which even in legal terms often depend 'on social dimensions of normative authority'.[2] This interplay between law and politics, and his focus upon the social as well as the formal institutional dimensions of normative authority, are important building blocks in Loughlin's construction of the concept of sovereignty, as will be discussed throughout this chapter.

In searching for the roots of a modernist conception of public law, Loughlin turns to early-modern writers such as Machiavelli, Bodin and Hobbes each of whom, in attempting to understand the nature of governmental authority and its ultimate manifestation – sovereignty – addressed law as part of the political realm; and it is from them that he attempts to retrieve often forgotten European politico-constitutional concepts such as prudence. For Loughlin, the essential method of public law is encapsulated in this notion of prudence and judgement. The particular task of public law is governing, but this is not achieved simply by following strict rules and procedures (although following procedures and adhering to traditions is

1 *The Idea of Public Law*, 131.

2 Ibid.

a large part of the activity of governing), but also by making prudent judgements in response to unique situations which present themselves in the political realm. Prudence is a virtue rooted in experience and the activity of governing prudently will enable the negotiation of the brokenness of politics and the handling of tensions within the state. Therefore, the measure of a successful constitutional system is whether it accommodates or manages political and other differences in a prudent way, and not whether it conforms with idealistic models of the perfect constitution.

In explaining the functions which public law performs, a central and largely implicit connection drawn throughout the book is between the activity of public law and the existence of the state, and it is in the exercise of describing the state that Loughlin draws upon the core element which links public law to politics within the modern polity – namely the ways in which citizens are represented by and have influence over the state and its governing apparatus. The centrality of the interconnection between state and citizen is apparent from the outset in Loughlin's account; governing the state is cast as the singular object of public law, and the basic identity of the modern state is declared as that institution which 'claims the ultimate allegiance of its citizens'.[3] And so we see another component of Loughlin's conception of sovereignty emerge: in addition to the connection between law and politics, a central feature of this idea is the relationship between state and citizen encapsulated in the notion of allegiance.

This centrality of allegiance to the idea of the modern state brings Loughlin to address a constant tension of sovereignty theory within modern constitutionalism: that between constituent power – the unbridled, democratic power of the sovereign people, every moment reinvented anew – and the constituted power of the state, wherein fundamental constitutional norms consecrated in the constitution's foundational moment are elevated beyond the reach of temporal majorities. Loughlin addresses this paradox, inherent in the constitution which at once offers both democracy yet also legal certainty, through the interplay of representation and sovereignty. Representation, like politics and constituent power, is another component role which public law plays within the state. Indeed, this idea of representation has developed within modern political thought in conjunction with that of sovereignty, whereby the sovereign is envisaged as agent of the commonwealth. Here Loughlin draws upon Sieyes's idea that the constituent power embodied in the people gives to the government constituted power. And in this idea of the commonwealth, the associated notion of 'the people' takes on a collective persona possessed of political agency and hence distinguishable from the pre-political or apolitical concept of 'the crowd'. Therefore, it is in the foundation of the sovereign state that the concept of 'the people' as a collective political actor takes life; and it is in this foundation that people and sovereign are bound together by the concept of representation. In this connection between representation and sovereignty Loughlin once again distinguishes his theory of public law from narrow positivist accounts. For it is in relation to sovereignty that positivists are at their most strident in asserting the existence of a normative legal authority which transcends the political; the vision of a free-standing legal realm is built upon the possibility of an identifiable unitary receptacle of absolute authority

3 Ibid. 153.

within the state (be that a written constitution or 'sovereign' legislature) which acts as the clearly identifiable higher legal source for the affirmation and legitimation of lower order rules and norms.

Loughlin dismisses the idea that 'sovereign' power can be crystallised in this way – again recalling his focus upon social dimensions of normative authority. But on the other hand neither does he argue that modern constitutionalism is a mere chimera, readily supplanted at any moment by the untrammelled constituent power of 'the people'. For Loughlin the truth is more complex, and it is in this complexity that we find another manifestation of the autonomy of public law and another layer of complexity in his concept of sovereignty. Central to Loughlin's thesis is the deep connection he sees between public law and politics, but this does not lead him to embrace the simplicity of 'law as politics' reductionism that seeks to collapse public law into politics. Such an approach misses the role performed by public law as the 'third order of the political'. The first order is politics as conflict; secondly, politics is seen as statecraft, that is, the development of techniques to control or manage these conflicts. Constitutional law is established in this context 'as a continuation of the political engagement' by creating a governing framework for the state. In drawing this connection between – while not simply eliding – constitutional law and politics, Loughlin is reminding us that contestation is in a broader sense the essence of the political. Despite the best efforts of narrow positivist constitutionalism, political conflict will not be resolved far less suppressed, and therefore constitutional law is simply part – albeit a discrete and in some ways autonomous part – of the ongoing political apparatus of the state, designed for the management of political conflict through the application of 'prudence'.

Certainly constituent power remains important even after the constitution is established: 'Constituent power is the power that gives constitutions their open, provisional, and dynamic qualities, keeping them responsive to social change and reminding us that the norm rests ultimately on the exception. Constituent power expresses a belief that the interdependence of democracy and constitutionalism is a paradox not a contradiction, and recognises the need for agencies of the state to work actively to maintain the allegiance of their citizens'.[4] But constituent power coexists with constituted power. Therefore, sovereignty is a complex web embracing both constituted and constituent power; sovereignty within a constitutional system is not a deracinated version of the people as mob, instead it is a more intricate conception which is, from the foundational moment of the state, inherently relational.

And so it is in the concept of sovereignty as relational that Loughlin arrives at his understanding of the interplay between the constituted and the constituent; the fluid and the fixed; thereby distancing himself from the extremities of both legal and political positivism. We also see the different relational components which were gradually delineated above, come together. To grasp this relational idea in its entirety it is important to note that for Loughlin the state and the people exist in symbiosis, whereby neither pre-dates the other. This frees the story of the state and the story of sovereignty from an all-embracing positivisation. Instead law itself – even higher law – is contingent and comes from the initial representational moment of state creation.

4 Ibid. 113.

Sovereignty is released from a purely legalistic conceptualisation and becomes an essentially relational activity emerging from the state's foundation and encapsulated not only in the relationship between 'government' and 'the people' but also that between 'law' and 'politics'. 'Sovereignty is both an expression of official power and is the product of a political relationship ... These legal and political conceptions of sovereignty in turn reflect concerns about the issues of competence and capacity, of authority and power'.[5] These two components – authority and power – interact, making sovereignty a highly political activity, leaving the power structures of the polity open to change as the relationships between people and government and between legal competence and political capacity change: 'the issue of capacity must be drawn into an appropriate relation to that of competence; the political aspects of sovereignty must not be suppressed'.[6] In other words, we must be attentive to the relations of identity and loyalty between people and government upon which the viability of state sovereignty also rests. One consequence of these relational conceptualisations is that the political fluidity behind sovereignty frees it from another positivist assumption – that it has a specific locus. For Loughlin, political power cannot be found in one fixed place, but rather it 'ultimately inheres in the form which the political relationship takes'.[7] And this draws us back to Loughlin's initial point: the centrality of allegiance to governmental authority. 'Once support is withdrawn, the authority of governors dissipates'.[8] Political sovereignty is 'real sovereignty'; dependent ultimately upon citizen loyalty, 'on opinion and belief'.[9]

3. Modern sovereignty and the nation-state

For Loughlin, sovereignty is 'a function of the institutional arrangements established as a consequence of the formation of the modern state',[10] and, therefore, a central feature of this conception is its symbiotic relationship with the institutional fact of a state-centred constitutional order. Sovereignty within the state encapsulates the legal consolidation of the social and political process of 'nation'-building, meaning also 'state'-building. It is this connection to the state – the political unit which so characterises modernity – that distinguishes the modernist concept of sovereignty from its medieval meaning. To explain this point, Loughlin adapts Oakeshott's notion that there are three basic features of the modern state: i) internal coherence, ii) external independence, and iii) supremacy of law. As such, establishing and maintaining the state is 'the singular undertaking of public law'.[11] Section 2 above was largely concerned with the supremacy of law within Loughlin's theory of sovereignty. In the context of the institutional reality of state power today it is now useful to address the two other components of the modern state – freedom from

5 Ibid. 84.
6 Ibid. 91.
7 Ibid. 83.
8 Ibid. 82.
9 Ibid. 78.
10 Ibid. 80.
11 Ibid. 91.

external influence and singular internal power – as it is precisely these aspects that, according to many commentators, are being compromised by other powerful forces in our time.

Although emphasising the continuing importance of the state, Loughlin is aware of challenges to it as a vehicle for the relational idea of sovereignty today and argues that although these are not institutional challenges to the competence of the state, they are still highly significant: 'they are threats to capacity which are directed at the political conception of sovereignty. This is a much more serious threat, one that presents a challenge to the continuing viability of the modern political project'.[12] It is, therefore, important to observe how Loughlin's theory might be applied to situations where the linkage between the state on the one hand and the sovereign relationship between government and people on the other is in fact coming under pressure – at least when we consider sovereignty from the perspective of political capacity. In other words, while it is certainly the case that the state remains in many respects institutionally resilient today, we need to ask whether we can in all cases consider the state to be performing all of the roles it has traditionally performed for the citizen, or whether by continuing to rely upon a modernist conception of the state as a unitary receptacle of sovereignty we under-estimate the essential fluidity of relations of sovereignty, and in doing so may even fall back upon a locus-centred conception of sovereignty which is where many legal formalists go wrong. I will now explore two situations of shifting political and constitutional power today, asking to what extent they challenge in new and important ways the freedom from external influence and the singular internal power of the state; in doing so I will explore ways in which Loughlin's relational theory of sovereignty offers us insights with which to understand these dynamics better.

Freedom from external influence

There are at least two external challenges to the modernist or 'Westphalian' model of absolute sovereignty. These are in fact rival sites of authority which today contest constructions of the nation-state as the exclusive site within which the relations of sovereignty operate. Firstly, is the emergence of supra-state political and legal orders – most prominently the European Union. Although operating at the supra-state level, entities such as the EU remain territorial in their remit. For example, the EU has been described as a 'post-state' polity in that it operates above the state but remains a fully territory-based polity. Secondly, at a 'sectoral' level, there exists a primarily economic challenge to state power through the extra-territorial dynamic of what is often loosely termed 'economic globalisation', but which also embraces a net-worked and powerful system encompassing political and legal dimensions. This process, although consisting primarily of an economic imperative, can impact on legal authority through regulatory devices (for example, in the practices of the World Trade Organisation), and becomes in many respects politically, if not strictly legally, authoritative. In a sense, therefore, the sectoral challenge is a functional one, affecting more the state's 'capacity' than its 'competence'. As Marks puts it,

12 Ibid. 95.

globalisation 'changes the context in which state functions are exercised'.[13] Since it operates on a largely extra-territorial or deterritorialised basis, some have viewed it as a new form of territorially intangible empire which is progressively incorporating the globe within open and expanding frontiers.[14]

A body of literature has built up analysing the implications of these new sites of challenge for the independent operation of municipal constitutional systems. Questions have been raised concerning the continuing capacity and competence of the state to manage social and economic relations; and these have led in turn both to theoretical deconstructions of established notions of statal authority (in particular, reified visions of the state as *the* receptacle of absolute sovereignty),[15] and to radical revisions in the study of constitutions and constitutionalism itself.[16] Although there is undoubtedly a changing environment within which states operate, it is important in light of Loughlin's work to distinguish carefully these two dynamics. Turning first to the sectoral challenge it would seem to be a category mistake to consider sovereignty, as Loughlin explains it, to be affected by economic globalisation. There may well be economic and even institutional ramifications flowing from expanding economic internationalism that affect respectively the capacity and even the competence of the state, but it seems highly unlikely that these developments are diluting the other key aspect of state sovereignty identified by Loughlin, namely the relations of identity and loyalty between citizens and the state. In this sense relations of allegiance to the state remain strong and may indeed be strengthened by a sense that the state can act as an institutional bulwark against the unaccountable processes of globalisation.

The supra-state challenge, taking the EU as the most important example, is potentially a different matter. Certainly it has now become hackneyed to talk of post-sovereignty in the context of the EU, and again in this context Loughlin's relational concept of sovereignty serves to expose sloppy thinking here. Sovereignty when taken to embody the relationship between citizens and their polity has not disappeared in the age of globalisation and suprastate polities. But it does seem that the relationships which characterise sovereignty now have the opportunity to multiply and thereby also to relocate to new sites as the polities which affect people's lives multiply. To use an analogy with energy in the natural world, physics students know that energy cannot be destroyed but that it can relocate and take on new forms. Might we say a similar thing about the relational dynamics of sovereignty? Turning first to the issues of competence and capacity, the state as a site wherein relations

---

13 S. Marks, *The Riddle of all Constitutions: International Law, Democracy, and the Critique of Ideology* (Oxford: Oxford University Press, 2000) at 76.

14 M. Hardt and A. Negri, *Empire* (Cambridge, Mass.: Harvard University Press, 2000) at xii.

15 E. Christodoulidis, *Law and Reflexive Politics* (Dordrecht: Kluwer, 1998); N. MacCormick, *Questioning Sovereignty: Law, State And Nation in the European Commonwealth* (Oxford: Oxford University Press, 1999).

16 K. H. Ladeur, 'Towards a Legal Theory of Supranationality – The Viability of the Network Concept', 3 *European Law Journal* (1997) 33–54; J. Tully *Strange Multiplicity: Constitutionalism in an Age of Diversity* (Cambridge: Cambridge University Press, 1995); and D. Chalmers, 'Postnationalism and the Quest for Constitutional Substitutes', 27 *Journal of Law and Society* (2000), 178–217.

of sovereignty are established retains considerable resilience, but there seem to be two issues which complicate this. Traditional state competences have to some extent shifted to the EU, and with this process the real space within which the capacity of state sovereignty might be exercised is compromised. A state can withdraw from the EU, but the economic, diplomatic and other impediments to doing so make citizens within the state increasingly aware that their sovereign capacity as a self-determining people is becoming reduced. But the implications of this for Loughlin's theory should not be over-stated. This development is simply a more significant loss of state capacity and competence than occurs through the sectoral challenge; it does not undermine the fundamental linkage between people and polity that is the essence of Loughlin's state-based notion of sovereignty.

A second and more significant question to ask, however, is whether European integration is also affecting or has the potential to affect the second element of the relational model, namely the linkage in terms of identity and loyalty between people and government, transferring some of these relational aspects of the state towards new sites. In other words, while it seems clear that the nation-state still embodies a fundamental relationship between people and government, we need to ask are there or in time might there be significant shifts in identity patterns within EU Member States? This chapter, like Loughlin's book, is a piece on constitutional theory and neither purports to analyse recent empirical work by political scientists and political sociologists on this issue nor on related research which argues that there have been some developments towards the building of a European civil society. And indeed here Loughlin's relational conception offers another important note of caution. As he has shown, the sovereign authority of the state 'depends upon loyalty' and here we need to ask just how strong is the emerging evidence from sociologists that throughout Europe people's notions of their nationality is changing; that many *feel* more European? Certainly there is evidence that in a more complex way many have shared identities;[17] but at the same time the referendums in France and the Netherlands in 2005 on the proposed Constitution of the European Union seem to offer a salutary reminder that the state is for many citizens still a very resilient focal point. As yet there are no real signs that proto-polities such as the EU have the potential to offer alternative reference points for both the identity and the loyalty of the citizen comparable to those of the state.[18]

However, we must remain alive to the possibility of further change over time. Certainly, although the state may still command the exclusive or at least dominant allegiance of citizens, it is at least possible that the essential building blocks of a state's sovereign capacity – the identity and loyalty of its citizens – will gradually weaken or variegate, relocating into patterns of shared identity with and loyalty to a new suprastate polity. And if we accept this possibility we must also be prepared to envisage the potential for more than one set of sovereign relationships between people and government – state government and EU government, for example, in

17 L. Moreno, 'Mesogovernments and Territorial Identities', *Nationalism and Ethnic Politics*, 5 (1999), 61–75 at 71.

18 N. Walker, 'The Idea of Constitutional Pluralism', *Modern Law Review*, 65 (2002), 317–359 at 347.

respect of different spheres of activity within the same territory. One strength of the relational theory is that we don't need to look for a finite moment when sovereignty might pass from the locus of the state to the locus of the EU. Instead the process can be more complex and organic; and while sovereignty in such a situation would not be shared, but would in fact be deeply contested between these two sovereigns, it may be possible for them to co-exist over the same territorial space. As Loughlin argues, sovereignty does not mean absolute power vested in one place. Since sovereignty ultimately inheres in the form which the political relationship takes, if the political relationship in fact becomes a plurality of such relationships then we may also need to account for multiple sets of sovereign relationships.

Singular internal power

A growing phenomenon of recent times, which in this context might be seen as a third site of challenge – this time to the state's 'singular internal power' – is sub-state nationalism within multinational or plurinational states such as Belgium, Canada, India, Spain and the UK. The constitutionally crucial trait of plurinational states is the existence within them of a plurality of territorially concentrated, potentially self-governing societies, which are possessed of a desire for specific constitutional recognition as such.[19] In other words, these societies position themselves in a relational way to the state not as internal minorities – in the sense of being simply a particular sub-set of a common demotic whole – but rather as polities which are in fact comparable to the state in the way they offer, or have the potential to offer, an effective site for many if not all of those functional and indentificatory roles which the state plays in the life of the citizen. Therefore, central to the challenge presented by sub-state national societies both to their own host states, and in the context of this chapter, to traditional assumptions about the nature of sovereignty, is a call for the disaggregation of the terms 'state' and 'nation'. While most nation-states do indeed contain but one national society, it is nonetheless the case that a minority of states are characterised by societal, and hence demotic or constituent, plurality. This call for a more accurate representation of the state in sociological terms is also a call for a reconceptualisation of the nature of sovereignty within the state insofar as this is premised upon an exclusively monistic vision of the demos.

The relational idea of sovereignty contained within *The Idea of Public Law* can help us move beyond formalistic approaches to the governmental institutions of these states and to understand that there can in fact be different sets of relationships between *peoples* and polities within the one state. But to do so it needs to be able to conceive of sovereignty relationships in diverse ways and not be tied definitively, at least in the context of these states which have multiple national societies within them, to a 'monistic conception of the state' per Bodin. In Loughlin's modernist construction of the state it seems that each state can only accommodate one set of relationships between one people and one government in terms of the state's 'singular internal power'; but need this be so? Cannot different peoples build

19 W. Kymlicka, *Multicultural Citizenship* (Oxford: Oxford University Press, 1995), at 76.

sovereign relationships both with their sub-state governments and with the central government of the state? In historical terms nation-building within these states was not a unitary activity; in fact in certain situations multiple processes of nation-building commenced and have continued within the one state (and therefore, an associated conceptual task is to disaggregate the modern process of 'state-building' from its usual elision with 'nation-building'). The socio-historical fact, and the contemporary resilience, of demotic pluralism within one state therefore begs the question whether a concomitantly pluralised set of relations of sovereignty can be built within such a state. Loughlin observes that: 'The relational aspects of the political conception of sovereignty is mainly concerned with elaborating the ways in which constitutional arrangements serve state-building purposes'.[20] But perhaps there are different ways to build a state. To do so around a monistic conception of the demos is the clearest and most successful way to date, but today, with the reality of multinational identities, it is also important to discover whether sovereignty might be adapted to the building of the plurinational state: the alternatives being forced assimilation or separatism.

In seeking to hive off this aspect of Loughlin's relational account I am asking, in other words, whether it is possible to appropriate the relational aspects of Loughlin's account of sovereignty without necessarily adopting also the indivisibility thesis. As we have seen, Loughlin's relational conception of sovereignty balances different tensions: between the legal and the political, and between the people as free and the state as constituted. We have also observed that this is a complex, multi-layered conceptualisation even in the context of a unitary notion of the demos. But it seems that this relational model, although perhaps not intended for the purpose, and despite acquiring further layers of complexity in the process of such an application, also translates well to the context of the plurinational state. The notion of sovereignty as expressing a political relationship between the people and the state is very attractive to contemporary sub-state nationalist movements in their conceptualisation of popular constituent power within a constitutional framework, but they adapt it in a radical way by suggesting that within the plurinational state the 'people' are plural and so, concomitantly, are the political relationships between these peoples and the state, negotiated as these relationships are through the different levels of governance which affect their lives and to which they relate through variegated pathways of identity and loyalty.[21]

The particularly interesting aspect of this challenge to unitary conceptions of state sovereignty is that, although often neglected in the literature, it may in fact be stronger than those challenges presented by sectoral or supranational sites of authority. I argued above that the sectoral challenge, while limiting the state's competence and capacity, does not affect the relations of identity and loyalty within the state that are so central to Loughlin's account of sovereignty. The latter challenge was seen to have the potential to affect the state's competence and capacity and also relations

20 85–6.

21 Tierney, '*We the Peoples*: Balancing Constituent Power and Constitutionalism in Plurinational States', in M. Loughlin and N. Walker (eds), *The Paradox of Constitutionalism* (Oxford: Oxford University Press, 2007).

of identity and loyalty, but in terms of offering an alternative site for relations of identity and loyalty today it seems that there is a long way to go before existing attachments to the state are seriously shaken by supra-state organisations. The sub-state nationalist phenomenon, therefore, perhaps offers the most complete challenge to monistic conceptions of state sovereignty. Radical institutional developments in Canada, the UK and most recently Spain represent very extensive reductions in the competence and capacity of central organs of the state. What is more, these changes, unlike EU integration, reflect and are indeed led by dynamics of popular identity and loyalty. These of course do not challenge a monistic conception of state sovereignty when sub-state nationalism is separatist in intent. Separatism simply seeks to create a new state within which a monistic conception of sovereignty can grow. The real challenge emerges in non-separatist models of sub-state nationalism. What is notable about recent radical demands for enhanced autonomy, representation and recognition is that many sub-state nationalist movements do not seek independent statehood in the Westpahalian sense, but instead the reinvention of the state along plurinational lines which will be capable of containing within it deep societal pluralism and the patterns of shared and disaggregated sovereignty which are required to make it viable. In practice of course these processes are difficult to achieve and in conceptual terms they face equally strong challenges. It seems, however, that the insights contained within, and the flexibility offered by, the relational theory of sovereignty makes it a vital tool in any such process towards re-thinking the plurinational state and its constitutional apparatus.

Chapter 3

Authority, Exploitation and the Idea of Public Law

Scott Veitch

In *The Idea of Public Law*, Martin Loughlin defends the argument that the political sphere is autonomous. He claims there are three orders of the political: at root *the political* itself is based on the antagonism between friend and enemy which finds its ultimate expression in violence; in turn, *politics* is the negotiation of conflict for the sake of the strength of the state; and finally *public law* is the prudential deployment of laws for the purpose of governing, 'a form of political jurisprudence that incorporates no transcendental or metaphysical ideas of justice and goodness'.[1] The art of governing and managing populations through the practice of ruling thus requires no necessary engagement with substantive principles of justice or democracy and instead operates according to the idea that the state acts for everyone's benefit: *salus populi suprema lex esto*. There is no persuasive power in a transcendental rationalism for the justification of politics, or public law, nor for the possibility that law can be the foundation for politics. Indeed, the reverse is true: the state has its reasons, we might say, that reason – including legal reason – does not know.

I am sympathetic to Loughlin's determination to put politics and the question of political conflict at the heart of the study of jurisprudence. At a time when the mediatised practice of domestic and regional politics in Europe has all the intellectual lure of sloth-watching, when the legal establishment has somehow managed to achieve the impression – how on earth did this happen? – that it is an engine of progressivism, and when what passes as mainstream jurisprudential analysis is rightly decried by the majority of students for its anodyne, not to say soporific, qualities, then at such impasses a political re-invigoration is just the tonic. It is in the spirit of sympathetic critique then that I want to consider the claims about the autonomy of the political sphere in order to explore further the ways in which we might think productively about the aspirations of a more thoroughly political jurisprudence.

So let me begin by asking two questions: Firstly, what is the political sphere autonomous from? Secondly, what is the status of this claim about autonomy? I will consider these in two forms, though these are not exhaustive.

Firstly, in a general way, the political sphere might be seen as autonomous from the judicial sphere. But according to Loughlin such autonomy is not guaranteed. In *Sword and Scales*, Loughlin provides an insightful analysis of the trend he detects occurring in recent years which he neatly identifies as involving, on the one hand,

1 Loughlin, M., *The Idea of Public Law* (Oxford: Oxford University Press, 2004), 163.

the politicisation of law, and on the other, the legalisation of politics. This double movement provides nothing short of a transformation of our understanding of both law and politics, and of the relation between the two. Law, says Loughlin, 'has come to be viewed as establishing a cordon within which politics is conducted', with the consequence that politics 'appears to have been displaced from its traditional role of giving expression to the character of social existence'.[2] The key underlying concern about the autonomy of politics (or its lack) observable in this 'age of rights' is, in my view, with the way in which the prioritisation of law over politics is marked and energised most decisively by the rise of judicial power. This may not amount to the end of politics as such, says Loughlin, but it does raise serious questions about its decline as an autonomous activity.

If this is so, then what is the status of the claim that the political sphere is autonomous? Here, in a nutshell, is the problem: to the extent that Loughlin's coruscating description of the 'new phase of the interpenetration of law and politics'[3] is a persuasive one – which to my mind it is – then the autonomy of the political sphere is threatened as such. Not only that, but what counts as taking place in or as the political sphere has metamorphosed. Yet if this is so, then the claim that the political *is* an autonomous realm is unsustainable – as anything other than a political claim itself. As such it will have to line up against any other political claims and seek its followers where it can. But given the ascendancy of 'legalised politics' as Loughlin has so astutely analysed it, this is a political claim that is, for the moment anyway, one that does not have a great deal of support. Here, in other words, claiming that the political sphere is autonomous might be thought of as a worthy – though currently unpersuasive – way of promoting the claim that it ought to be. But, like other political claims, it has no intrinsic validity.

Consider another sense in which the autonomy of the political sphere may be understood. On this view, it is autonomous through its differentiation from the material and private spheres, and, allied to this, we may note public law's autonomy vis-à-vis that of private law. These lines of thought are unified and underpinned by one central claim: that there is a profound difference between the mode of rule and the mode of exploitation. Here is how Loughlin puts it:

> The distinction between political power generated through collective action and material power acquired through the ownership of resources is central to the claim that politics is an autonomous sphere of activity. It provides the basis for another distinction, that between public and private modes of being. This public/private distinction lies at the root of the modern state, an institution vested through the agency of law with an absolute power.[4]

But there is something else that 'lies at the root' of the modern state that Loughlin fails to dwell on, but which is absolutely crucial to understanding the plausibility of this statement. In order to be a defensible reading of the historical development of the justificatory practices of modern western state-building (as well as, we might note in

2 Loughlin, M., *Sword and Scales: An Examination of the Relationship between Law and Politics* (Oxford: Hart, 2000).

3 Ibid. 233

4 Loughlin 2004, 159

passing, the critique of rationalism which seems particularly well attuned to the British political and constitutional experience), we need to understand how these practices of state-building were inextricably associated with colonial enterprises. That is, the 'idea' of public law was used in the sense Loughlin describes to legitimate the mode of action of colonial powers, on which activities the wealth and influence of states depended in the modern era. It is in this specific context that the claimed distinction Loughlin argues for between the mode of rule and the mode of exploitation was most thoroughly operationalised. On this view colonial exploitation and its harms might be treated as distinct from the autonomous realm of colonial politics and the purity of its public law. The material effects of the former – discrimination, appropriation, and in a few cases genocide – were redeemable by treating the idea of the latter as distinct, autonomous practices. Only in this way could the claim that the state acts for *everyone*'s benefit – that: 'In general, the basic engagement of government has been one of maintaining and enhancing the well-being of the state and its people'[5] – be maintained in the face of the glaringly obvious fact that this was hardly the case in the colonial context, given the bitter realities of exploitation, assimilation and degradation suffered by so many of the populations colonised by the imperial state.

It is a wonder that this is not developed more rigorously in Loughlin's analysis, since it seems to fit with so many aspects of it. For instance, he writes, 'The historical claim I make is of a general nature. In mainstream European thought, for example, the idea of public law evolved in the early modern period, flourished during the late nineteenth and early twentieth centuries, but has since waned'. It is, of course, no coincidence at all that the trajectory of European imperialism corresponds exactly to this historical periodisation. (If public law in Britain had by the end of this long haul taken an idiosyncratic path, as Loughlin suggests, its central role in the global imperialist project had not, perhaps suggesting the discrepancy was a matter of its own self-image.) So what is the status of the claim, made in this context, of the autonomy of the political sphere, of the distinction between mode of rule and exploitation?

I suggest that, not only, as we saw with the first point, should this claim be understood as a political one, but in this instance it is also best understood as one that is profoundly ideological. The lack of attention to the colonial aspects of the development of the modern state itself tends to underplay the enduring and symbiotic relationship between rule and exploitation, and in particular the relationship between the political sphere and the private law sphere, specifically that of property. The fact is that, as Adam Smith had noted, 'property and civil government very much depend on one another. The preservation of property and the inequality of possession first formed it, and the state of property must always vary with the form of government'.[6] So just as the claim about the distinction between political authority and material exploitation had made good sense – for the wealthy citizens – in the slave society in which Aristotle gave life to it, in the modern colonial context it made similarly good sense for the colonisers.

---

5 Loughlin 2004, 7.

6 Smith, A. (1978) *Lectures on Jurisprudence*, R.L. Meek, D.D. Raphael and P.G. Stein (eds) (Oxford: Oxford University Press), 401.

Yet it too was only a claim of course, and in this instance it was a rather dubious one at that. For in its foundational intricacies the colonial state – its sovereign form and public authority – was not simply a handy detachable cover for colonial expropriation and its legitimation, because its mode of acting (its very mode of rule) was in fact constitutively related to the mode of exploitation. One example will suffice. The British invasion of the Australian continent that started in 1788, depended for its authority on instituting a very specific property regime, one whose effects are felt right up to the present day. It is worth quoting in full the acknowledgement of this by Chief Justice Brennan in the Australian High Court's 1992 *Mabo* judgement:

> As the Governments of the Australian Colonies and, latterly, the Governments of the Commonwealth, States and Territories have alienated or appropriated to their own purposes most of the land in this country during the last 200 years, the Australian Aboriginal peoples have been substantially dispossessed of their traditional lands. They were dispossessed by the Crown's exercise of its sovereign powers to grant land to whom it chose and to appropriate to itself the beneficial ownership of parcels of land for the Crown's purposes. Aboriginal rights and interests were not stripped away by operation of the common law on first settlement by British colonists, but by the exercise of a sovereign authority over land exercised recurrently by Governments. To treat the dispossession of the Australian Aborigines as the working out of the Crown's acquisition of ownership of all land on first settlement is contrary to history. Aborigines were dispossessed of their land parcel by parcel, to make way for expanding colonial settlement. Their dispossession underwrote the development of the nation. … [In this way] it is appropriate to identify the events which resulted in the dispossession of the indigenous inhabitants of Australia, in order to dispel the misconception that it is the common law rather than the action of governments which made many of the indigenous people of this country trespassers on their own land.[7]

Was the logic of rule autonomous from the logic of exploitation? Not at all: they were conceptually and practically inseparable. Did the state act for the benefit of itself *and* the common good of all those who came under its authority including the indigenous population? Hardly. Was it true that 'forging of a sense of common identity, which may be based on ethnicity, culture, language, or common history, provide[d] the key to explaining why the political antecedes the state'?[8] Only if one's reading is determinedly assimilationist and ignores the importance of the fact that Brennan candidly identifies that it remains the *dispossession* of indigenous Australians that *underwrites* the development of the Australian nation.

Not only then does it seem implausible that the logic of rule and of exploitation were autonomous of one another, but in this instance it is straightforwardly wrong. It is for this reason that the claim that the 'distinction between political power generated through collective action and material power acquired through the ownership of resources', the distinction that 'is central to the claim that politics is an autonomous sphere of activity' (supra) appears as not just political but also ideological. For it mis-describes the nature of exploitation, it mis-understands the material realm's constituent relation to the political, and yet *despite* these faults maintains that the

7 *Mabo v. State of Queensland* (No.2) (1992) 175 CLR 1.

8 Loughlin 2004, 41.

logic of exploitation is distinguishable from what turns out to be the imperial state's greatest lie: *salus populi suprema lex esto.*

It is important, politically if you like, not to see these observations as merely exceptions. As Marx pointed out when in fact describing systematic colonisation in the context of Australia, what is discovered here 'is not something new *about* the colonies, but, *in* the colonies'.[9] Analogously for our purposes we may take this to be the coincidence of rule *and* exploitation, authority *and* ownership that is, in the British context at least, normalised and given its most glorious foundation in the fabulous figure of 'the Crown'; simultaneously ruling and legitimating exploitation whether 'at home' or abroad.

To maintain in the face of these observations a claim that the pursuit of an understanding and practice of the political sphere as autonomous is worthwhile therefore throws up some further problems. If the logics of rule and of exploitation are – or ought to be seen as – autonomous, does this mean that exploitation is thereby *non*-political? Whether in its high imperial manifestations in the forms of slavery or land expropriation (the land and people grabs so essential to the development of the modern state and some of its most powerful players – well into the nineteenth century and in some cases beyond), or in the current forms of capitalist material exploitation on which our society is conditionally dependent, if these are all indeed part of a 'mode of exploitation', which they clearly are, does that make them *non-political*? Whatever this might mean, while the desire to hold the two apart may remain intact (as that, a desire) the actual relation between the two is far more complex, intriguing and imbricated than the autonomy of the political theory would suggest. That is, the theory or claim to autonomy may remain pure, but it is not a theory of the actual practice. R. H. Tawney succinctly captures this point: 'Political authority is a genuine form of power, and is, both for good and evil, an important form. But it is one form, not the only form. To represent it as unique in kind and unrivalled in degree is to draw a picture which has little relation to the facts of life'.[10] Unless of course, as I have suggested, it is ideologically motivated.

It follows from this that if the historical trajectory of the distinction between the mode of rule and of exploitation is deeply suspect, except as an ideological device, then the claim about the distinction's *decline* is necessarily overstated. The desire to re-establish the autonomy of the political signals nostalgia for a past that never was. So Loughlin's fear about the intrusion of the economic and judicial spheres into the realm of the political is in this specific sense misguided. That said there is a further twist to this that is exceedingly important. These 'intrusions' work best when they are in fact de-politicised; as if material exploitation or the judicial cordoning of politics were not political. The recent successes of the political right and of contemporary corporate capital are largely based on this programmatic politicisation that appears as non-political, and were identified by Pierre Bourdieu as 'a conservative revolution ... that restores the past but presents itself as progressive, transforming regression

9 Marx, K. (1990), *Capital Vol. 1* (London: Penguin, 1990), 932.

10 (Tawney 1964: 59).

itself into a form of progress. It does this so well that those who oppose it are made to appear regressive themselves'.[11]

So let us consider again briefly Loughlin's description of the contemporary relation between law and politics in its sociological context. Loughlin writes that, 'One of the defining features of modern government has been the dramatic increase, over the last 150 years, in the range of its tasks as a consequence of the extension in its administrative responsibilities. This has resulted in an unprecedented degree of interaction between government, economy, and society'.[12] Likewise, he notes, 'In the name of promoting security, liberty, and prosperity, modern governments have greatly expanded the range of their activities, and have now assumed responsibility for furthering economic and social development, managing the economy, and providing for the welfare of their citizens'.[13] He concludes, 'By the end of the twentieth century, there were few areas not only of public but also of personal life in which government performed no role'.[14]

These observations seem incontrovertible. But what are we to make of them *if* we are not persuaded that they signify a *decline* in the autonomy of the political, but rather a reconfiguration of the political's relation to the economic sphere in the context of an expanding administrative state? One possibility is that the demise of the importance of the distinction – the collapse of *worth* of holding on to the distinctions between the public realm and the private, between authority and exploitation – was in fact one of the achievements of the twentieth century's administrative welfare state. According to this view, is it not plausible to argue that public law and politics as practices of government, inextricably bound up with economy and management, in fact led to great *improvements* in matters of social and personal welfare, albeit not unalloyed ones? Would the effort required to divorce political supervision of the private and material realms in order to maintain 'a pure idea' of public law and the political – if public law is to be 'concerned solely with those precepts of conduct that have evolved through political practice to ensure the maintenance of the public realm as an autonomous entity'[15] – would this effort not put in jeopardy the very possibility that the economic realm be made accountable to a democratic polity? Again as Tawney put it, 'If power divorced from responsibility is the poison of states, it is improbable that it is the tonic of economic effort'.[16] Given the drawbacks that came with the putative separation of the two precisely in terms of exploitation, and given the ideological work the distinction did historically, is it not feasible to say that a very strong case indeed would need to be made – made *politically* – to re-establish it?

On the other hand, we might see the recent and omnivorous drive to privatise and dismantle politically what were formerly publicly supervised practices – health

11 Bourdieu, P. (2002), 'The "Progressive" Restoration: A Franco-German Dialogue' (Gunther Grass and Pierre Bourdieu) 14 *New Left Review* 63–77.

12 Loughlin 2004, 25.

13 Loughlin 2004, 8.

14 Loughlin 2004, 11.

15 Loughlin 2004, 163.

16 Tawney, R.H., *Equality* (London: Unwin, 1964), 188.

services, schools, universities, and so on – as providing evidence that that welfare state point of view is already itself in decline, and is so in large part because of the apparent success of those who *do* want to separate in theory the political and the economic. In other words, we might see the neo-liberal revolution of the last few decades as one expression of the claim to get the political out of the economic and allow the latter – in theory at least – to work exclusively according to its logic (the logic of exploitation), without hindrance or supervision from political authority (the logic of rule). (It is ironic, of course, that this *political* project succeeds best by trying to establish a quasi-constitutionalisation of private law and competition rights at the domestic and particularly European levels.)

As such, and here I agree with Loughlin, the question of the status and role of the political sphere in relation to those of the economic and juridical is in dire need of jurisprudential scrutiny. But another way to understand this issue is to see that while Loughlin rightly diagnoses the problem, he mistakes the prognosis. The difficulty faced by those who object to those contemporary practices Loughlin rightly identifies – to the marketisation and juridification of social life, public values and even political ideals – is not so much that it is a problem in need of rectification through establishing the autonomy of the political sphere; rather the problem is that it is the wrong kind of political programmes that are currently succeeding. One is reminded here of Orwell's wonderful description of England in mid-century, perhaps one to which it has already explicitly returned: it 'resembles a family, a rather stuffy Victorian family, with not many black sheep in it but with all its cupboards bursting with skeletons. It has rich relations to be kow-towed to and poor relations who are horribly sat upon, and there is a deep conspiracy of silence about the source of the family income … [It is] a family with the wrong members in control – that, perhaps, is as near as one can come to describing England in a phrase'.[17]

By all means then, we should take Loughlin's advice to be wary of the usurpation by the judicial institutions of political conflicts. Certainly we should be jurisprudentially attentive to the runaway juridification and marketisation – two processes which so often go hand in hand – of public values and goods. But what might be required to counter these developments is not an effort to establish in theory or practice the autonomy of the political sphere, but rather a re-doubled effort to *re-politicise* that which has been already been politicised *as* non-political, namely as economic or juridical. Otherwise, given the current conditions which Loughlin identifies so well, responding by canvassing for a political jurisprudence as a discrete, autonomous subject is unlikely to succeed as an attractive theoretical or practical suggestion at all the various levels of interaction necessary to change current conditions. Worst of all, from my point of view, it is unlikely to succeed as a political response to these corrupting developments. Why? Because its political disengagement rings hollow; it seems too much like trying to learn to swim without getting in the water.

17 Orwell, G. (1979), 'The Lion and the Unicorn: Socialism and the English Genius', Collected Non-Fiction (London: Secker & Warburg/Octopus), 536.

Chapter 4

Public Law as Political Jurisprudence: Loughlin's 'Idea of Public Law'

Emilios Christodoulidis

Martin Loughlin's *The Idea of Public Law* is an important re-statement of *political* constitutionalism in the way John Griffith understood that constitutive dimension of public law in the seminal article that inaugurated a tradition of political-constitutional jurisprudence in England.[1] But there is a crucial ambivalence at the heart of the main 'synthesis' Loughlin attempts and it involves a problematic articulation of law with the political. On the one hand, Loughlin aims to 'restore Public Law as "political jurisprudence (*droit politique*)"' and in that must establish a certain *continuity* between three 'orders' of the political, that he identifies as 'the political', 'politics', and 'constitutional law'. On the other hand, the author is at pains to establish this theory as '*pure*' and I take 'pure' (despite what Loughlin sometimes says against him) to have the meaning that Kelsen gave the term, as underwriting the autonomy of the practice at the level at which it acquires its *objective meaning* as legal; otherwise stated, one that guarantees the distinctiveness of the practice, its values *sui generis*, its meanings autonomous and distinct. Between these two fundamental tenets, between continuity and autonomy, the interplay is – let us say – *improbable*, and their tension – if we can call it that – is forever threatening to undercut the claims made in respect of either of them. I will explore this ambivalence for what it elides and for what it makes possible in that elision.

I

Let us begin with autonomy as underwritten by the 'pure' theory of public law, which is the title that Loughlin gives to his manifesto-type restatement of the 'idea of public law' in the final chapter of the book. Here is the first of the forty theses of the 'Pure Theory of Public Law': 'Public Law is an autonomous subject. Many controversies surrounding the subject have arisen precisely because this claim has been neglected or even suppressed. Unless this autonomy is recognized, public law cannot properly be understood'.[2]

The idea of a *pure* theory connects us back to Hans Kelsen's jurisprudence and his hugely influential attempt to think the legal in terms that are properly its own.

1 J. A. G. Griffith, 'The Political Constitution', in [1979] 42 *Modern Law Review* 1.

2 M. Loughlin, *The Idea of Public Law* (Oxford: Oxford University Press, 2003), 153. All page references in the text, unless otherwise indicated, are to this text.

On the issue of the relationship between law and politics Kelsen draws an internal (in fact mutually constitutive) connection between attribution and imputation. What, asks Kelsen, will give the 'subjective' political act its 'objective' meaning as law? His answer is that the *objective meaning* of the political will of the 'People' is attributed to a people capable of willing because imputed to a legal body whose capacity is underwritten by the law. For the Kantian that he is, the 'juridical condition' (Kant's *rechtlicher Zustand*) is doing all the work here. This is what is interesting in the otherwise exaggerated insistence on his 'Basic Norm'. It is precisely in responding to this need of legal interpretation that Kelsen introduces the *Grundnorm* as hypothetical validation of a founding act that could not be interpreted as such, could not have claimed its objective (legal) meaning for itself but remained an act of politics. Kelsen's Grundnorm does the job of keeping law's founding moment legal: its hypothesis an *a priori* – an 'as-if' – that diffuses the temporal paradox that the supreme legal act of founding a constitution cannot (at the time) be imputed to a body that is capable of law-making. The scheme of interpretation that would have allowed its objective meaning *as* law is not yet in place. But revealing as they are, we should not here confine ourselves to original founding acts alone. It is instead important, both for Kelsen's argument and for Loughlin's, to see how the same logic – of the attribution of legal meaning to political acts – is spread over continuous time, so to speak, in the ordinary acts of law-*making*. In each such instance what keeps law *pure* is that the meaning of the act as legal is conferred onto the political act of creating the law through structures of attribution ('chains of validity' in Kelsen, the deployment of 'coding' and 'programming' in Luhmann, and so on) that are specifically and constitutively its own, that is, legal.

While Kelsen casts his shadow over *The Idea of Public Law* he makes no concrete appearance therein. Instead, remarkably, Loughlin ties the claim to autonomy ('that public law is special') 'to the singular character of its object- the activity of governing' (in thesis 3). But for this, or any other, 'object' to be constitutive of the autonomy of the subject (see thesis 1) one must at least assume the absence of functional equivalents. That is the problem with functional definitions. If what is 'special' about public law is *constitutively* connected to what is singular about its object, 'governing', then it must be *only* public law that performs that function and the existence of functional equivalents – other agents of 'governing' – would erode not just its autonomy but its *very definition and individuation* as a proper sphere. Simply put, it would either collapse all forms of governing (from Aristotle's private governing of the household, 'oiko-nomia', to new management techniques employed by corporate actors) into public law, or at best blur (rather than define) the boundaries between public law and other disciplines of governing, something that Loughlin was careful to address in the analysis of Foucault earlier in the book.

Let us for a moment leave aside these definitional difficulties to return to the question of autonomy and function. In earlier work in which Loughlin explored the possibilities of an adequate understanding of 'public law in the face of the future', he flirted with Niklas Luhmann's 'revitalized functionalist style' as 'firmly anchored in our contemporary experience of law'.[3] In that work Luhmann allowed Loughlin to

---

3 M. Loughlin, *Public Law and Political Theory* (Oxford: Clarendon, 1992), 256.

circumvent the narrowness of a positivism that misses the reciprocities of governing, as well as the varieties of 'normativism' in both its conservative and liberal guises. 'The turn to self-referential systems shifts the focus from control to autonomy'.[4] Because '[w]e must appreciate that the claims to law's autonomy can be understood only in the context of the normative/cognitive (or system/environment) relationship'.[5] What Loughlin endorses in Luhmann's radical restatement of the positivity of law (my formulation, not his) is that it goes furthest in answering 'the critical question facing public law this century': that of 'how law responds to the challenge of providing a normative framework capable of structuring and conditioning the performance of the political-administrative system'.[6]

This is all important and to my mind powerfully stated. But if it is attentive to social complexity and avoids any causal, simple or reductionist law-society mappings of the type that Loughlin correctly rebuts as simplistic expressions within a paradigm of thinking regulation as 'control' of social processes, it is precisely because of Luhmann's insistence on system-boundaries, closure and autonomy-as-autopoiesis. Luhmann's is a radical restatement of the positivity of law and of its radical autonomy vis-à-vis political processes to which it remains – paradoxically – cognitively open through its own normative closure, that is *because* of its own specific mode of handling expectations as singularly *legally* meaningful. Loughlin knows all this because he is a careful reader of Luhmann. But radical closure of this kind radicalises the pure theory of law to the point at which any 'layering' of levels or orders, any continuity or articulation of the political and the legal is radically undercut, re-conceptualised along system-environment boundaries as 'irritation' or 'coupling' but in no case 'continuity'. This is the important point that questions Loughlin's neat account of 'orders', but we will need to look at that analysis carefully again in the next section, and return, in the final section, to its improbability.

In the meantime, let me emphasise again that what underlies the concern with boundaries is not an a priori delineation and maintenance of proper spheres. Instead it is that the closing off of a sphere, through repeated operations of a kind that enable self-observation, allows concepts of public law (or any other representational order) to crystallise and complexity to build up within it. What this might tell us about the specific coupling of law and politics is suggestive. The possibilities of addressing and conceptualising political power, 'structuring and conditioning the performance of the political system' (above), including its most exalted expression as constituent power, acquires *a form* in its constitutional instantiation. This in a crucial sense provides a structure of difference that, in suspending other differences, allows the political to emerge as a unity.

The emergence of this unity – the political system – is hugely important, both for what it actualises and for what it suppresses. It actualises a certain way of thinking the political. But just as crucially in this context, Luhmann's limiting proposal concerning the nature of the political system hedges in the exaggerated aspirations of much constitutional theory today, and I would place Loughlin's imaginative synthesis

4 Ibid. 257.

5 Ibid. 255.

6 Ibid. 258.

of levels in this category. Luhmann's analysis queries a long tradition of political thought that inclines us to see only a unified politico-legal system – evoked to a large extent by the concept of the state which is both political and legal, of precisely the kind that Griffith's 'political constitution' invoked and which Loughlin's thesis renews.

Luhmann will accept that this close dovetailing makes it harder today to distinguish the systems. But there is a response in this to both those who see in constitutionalism the 'co-originality' of law and democracy, and those who seek through 'constitutional authorship' a *legal* means to affect political self-determination. 'It is wholly impossible', Luhmann will respond, 'to see politics as an ongoing interpretation of a legally fixed Constitution'. 'Our proposition will be', he will counter-suggest, 'that there is not one system under the concept of the state, but two distinct systems, both operatively closed, both with different functions, codes and code-dependent programmes'.[7] The concept of the state then becomes one of the concepts that secure the structural coupling of the systems as holding together what emerges, at each step and with every new operation, as the 'self-reinforcing dynamics of the political and legal systems'.

It is this emphasis on the *self*-reinforcing dynamics of each system that Luhmann offers as a sobering reminder to the hyperbole of the recourse to law as panacea for tackling political problems, appeasing political conflict, channelling self-government or substituting for the self-government of a people. Of course it is possible – in fact it is of the essence – to politically exploit the ambiguities of law for political reasons as it is to 'resolve' *political disagreement* through *constitutional interpretation*, and I will return to how urgent this is in the final section. But the latter is rarely going to end the political conflicts, and the former 'exploitation' of legal ambiguities will not affect legality or illegality itself but will register instead in terms of political risk, of political success or failure. 'Of course', Luhmann will stress, 'individual operations may have both a political and legal meaning for an observer … [But] the fact that an observer may see it as a unity says nothing about the unity of systems'.

Perhaps 'unity' of systems overstates Loughlin's claim of the connectedness and continuity of orders. There is nonetheless a crucial price to be paid if one takes autonomy seriously as radical rather than relative, and there is no hint in Loughlin's text that it was ever meant as the latter. The price, as Luhmann reminds us, is that the articulation of the political and legal system, what he conceptualises in terms of 'performance', involves the crossing of boundaries that prevents any direct intertraffic such that would allow 'conditioning' or other ambitious interventions into autonomous processes and dynamics, and in fact can only rely on triggering system-specific responses in the 'receiving' system. These responses ('order from noise')[8] may, perhaps, be picked up and thematised anew in reflexive structures in the conditioning system, though Luhmann warns again that one should not

---

7 All references here are to Chapter 9 of Niklas Luhmann's *Law as a Social System*, (trans. K. Ziegert) (Oxford: Oxford University Press, 2004).

8 N. Luhmann, *Social Systems* (trans. J. Bednarz Jnr) (Stanford: Stanford University Press, 1993), 83.

exaggerate claims made in respect of 'reflexive law'.[9] I do not want to turn this into an esoteric debate within systems theory. Let me merely point out once more what one might borrow from it to put to Loughlin in relation to the first of the two legs of the 'pure theory of public law'. Firstly, that if the definition of public law is to be based on its performing a function, then that function must be uniquely performed by public law; functional equivalents collapse functional definitions. Secondly, if public law is to be defined as autonomous, rather than, say, relatively autonomous, one must be very careful to describe what exactly its connectedness or articulation with the political system or sphere consists in. 'Conditioning' is too loose a term and belies the respective autonomy of spheres. And in any case one cannot have it both ways, the autonomy of public law guaranteed *and* its connectedness underwriting its 'political' nature. With this, let us now turn to this second argument about the layering of orders.

II

If *The Idea of Public Law* is to re-establish Public Law as 'political jurisprudence', retrieve the tradition of the 'political constitution', and restore its internal articulation to politics, Loughlin's key move is to argue the continuity between three levels: that of *the political*, expressed as constituent power and as conflict, understood in a significantly similar way to the way Carl Schmitt analysed it; that of *politics* understood as including the activity of governing; and finally that of *positive law*, where the practice of governing finds its legal-institutional expression. If it is the practice (of governing) that provides the institution of public law with its function, it is in the first abstract realm of the political that it draws, explicitly in the mode of Macintyre's internal criteria of excellence for practices,[10] and implicitly in the mode in which Fuller understands the dialectic of aspiration to duty,[11] its *raison d'etre* and insight. The continuity between the three levels is the book's organising thesis. As succinctly put by Loughlin: 'Only within the frame of a viable system of government are the practices of politics – a mode operating on a different plane to that of "the political" – able to flourish'.[12]

The concept of the political, according to Schmitt, is constitutively tied to difference and the acts that draw it out. For difference to be made visible, a distinction must be drawn. Significantly the operation of drawing out a difference suspends further differences and, through repeated operations, allows unities to emerge. For Schmitt, the concept of the political famously draws on the distinction between friend and foe. He says: '[t]he specific political distinction to which political actions and political motives can be reduced is that between friend and

9 N. Luhmann, 'Some Problems with Reflexive Law' in Teubner, G. and Febbrajo, A. (eds.), *State, Law, Economy as Autopoietic Systems* (Milano: Giuffré, 1985).

10 A. McIntyre, *After Virtue* (London: Duckworth, 1981).

11 L. L. Fuller, *The Morality of Law* (New Haven and London: Yale University Press, 1964), ch. 1.

12 *The Idea of Public Law*, 156. All page numbers in the text refer to this book.

foe (or enemy)'.[13] It is a distinction that consolidates through repetition, creating the world of political meaning and furnishing political action. Schmitt introduces a number of thresholds and qualifications: the political arises with the *decision to act* on the difference, the initiation and termination of conflict being dependent on this; politics invokes collectivities; and a threshold of *intensity* is constitutive of political action. Importantly, for any discussion of Schmitt's 'political', it imports a *reflexivity* into politics, in the sense that the origin of political action is already political: it resides in the contingency of the recognition of what constitutes a political unity in the first place. Of course, this reflexivity sediments into forms of state antagonism, because the resources to undertake political action effectively reside there. For Schmitt, indeed, state sovereignty was the effective carrier of difference against the dangerous 'monist' universalism of the (English) pluralists. But that sedimentation remains contingent, a crystallisation of political antagonism that can be thought otherwise, cast across different configurations of friend and foe.[14]

Like Marx, Loughlin understands conflict as underlying all politics. And like Schmitt he understands the political as autonomous. Bringing the two together he says: 'if "the political" is to be identified as an autonomous activity, it must rest on its distinctions ... It is the ever present possibility of conflict that gives rise to specifically political behaviour' (156). This first, most abstract, order of the political understood in its constitutively conflictual dimension, connects to the second order of institutional practices. 'Conflict may lie at the root of the political – the first order – but this is not the end of the matter. The second order, politics as a set of practices within a state, is as much concerned with devising forms of co-operation as with conflict over them. In this role, the great value of politics lies in its deployment of a range of techniques enabling us to handle these conflicts and enmities constructively' (52). I will have more to say on these 'techniques' and on what 'constructively' means and makes possible in this context. In any case, in making that connection between the level of its abstract conceptualisation and the level of its institutional manifestations, Loughlin re-introduces a differentiation that traditionally finds its expression in political semantics in the distinction between 'la politique' and 'le politique' in French; between 'die Politik' and 'das politische' in German; between 'la politica' and 'il politico' in Italian, although, as Ernest Vollrath comments in an early article,[15] Anglo-American political theory has been more reluctant to draw the distinction (that Loughlin deploys) between 'the political' and 'politics'. In all these cases the first inscription denotes the 'political prescription', so to speak, that is a specific modality according to which one may speak of what is specifically political in practices, events and phenomena; the second inscription denotes these concrete manifestations (practices, events and phenomena) of that 'political prescription'. In a recent paper I have argued how both urgent and difficult it is to keep the

13 Schmitt, *The Concept of the Political* [1932] (trans. George Schwab) (Chicago: University of Chicago Press, 1996), 26.

14 There can be few better readings of Schmitt's thesis than William Rasch's recent *Sovereignty and Its Discontents*. (London: Birkbeck Law Press, 2005).

15 E. Vollrath, 'The "Rational" and the "Political": an Essay in the Semantics of Politics', 13 (1987) *Philosophy and Social Criticism* 17 at 23.

differentiation in sight, the 'double inscription' alive in our political thinking and acting.[16] Claude Lefort, for one, warns that liberal democratic thinking mistakenly runs together the political and its institutional reduction to the societal sub-system of politics. Loughlin is perhaps not typical of the thinking Lefort has in mind, but he is unapologetic about a substantiation of the abstract 'political' in concrete 'politics', and the concrete politics are in turn contained within the state form.

Now for the second articulation of 'orders'. Having argued that 'the distinctive nature of public law is founded on the autonomy of the political realm', (52) he 'will try to show ... that we might best understand the way in which law establishes the governing framework of a state as a continuation of the political engagement' (52). 'Does … constitutional law transcend the political?' he asks. His answer is that it does not. 'The framework must be conceived as a set of formal practices rooted within, and acquiring identity from, a wider body of political practices. The expression "fundamental law" is a reference to these wider political practices' (156–7). 'As an immanent practice that conditions and sustains the activity of governing, public law is best conceived as political jurisprudence' (163). Though, interestingly, 'when touching on core issues relating to the activities of governing, law speaks in a different register' (157). In all this, 'relationality' plays a crucial role, shooting through all three levels. The state is the institutional arrangement through which the practice of governing is organised.

What is the problem with the layering of orders, the neat transition from register to register? It is that each entails an act of substitution. With each crossing of a boundary between layers the meaning of the political is grafted onto a new register, its 'harnessing' a circumscription, a technique of anticipation and substitution. If Loughlin endorses Schmitt's understanding of the political, arguing that '[i]t is the ever present possibility of conflict that gives rise to specifically political behaviour' (156) he will add that '[f]or conflict to be positively harnessed, a less partisan framework of rule needs to be devised'(42). '*Needs*'? Whose need might this be, whose need served? Do we understand 'need' here in line with, say, the management of dissensus in the interests of state-building, or the appeasement of class conflict in the interests of capitalist integration, or the silencing of calls for secession or sub-state self-determination in the interests of nation-building, or the continuation of colonialist and imperialist legacies in the denial to acknowledge indigenous peoples' claims over sovereignty, jurisdiction and property? If we do, then the flipping over of the 'partisan' framework into one conducive to the imperatives of state is an *ideological* move in the most basic terms of social analysis, a move to distort and mis-represent, an act of symbolic simulation. If we don't understand the 'need' in those terms then the pure theory of public law remains facing the impossible task of explaining the obvious contradiction that the 'objective meaning' of partisan conflict be *best* understood in *non*-partisan terms.

Shall we take this more gradually? When Loughlin endorses Schmitt's argument about the autonomous 'political' necessarily resting on its own distinction and from that

16 E. Christodoulidis, 'Against Substitution: the Constitutional Thinking of Dissensus' in M. Loughlin and N. Walker (eds.) *The Paradox of Constitutionalism* (Oxford: Oxford University Press, 2007).

extracts an argument about state 'politics' and the activity of governing that involves techniques of harnessing conflict, in a way similar perhaps to Schmitt's argument about the 'sedimentation' of the political 'into the state form', he over-determines what is crucially a contingent connection in Schmitt. There is in Schmitt's argument, crucially, a reflexivity that involves holding up any sedimentation, harnessing or technique of government to the friend/foe distinction itself, and with it comes the possibility to re-thematise it politically. The political remains a horizon that resists substitution, because in this 'reflexivity', what 'needs' to be done, and what is gained and lost by the 'harnessing' of conflict, remains an irreducibly political question.

With the second 'crossing' from state politics to '*droit positif*' the imperatives of governing acquire their legal institutional form. With it the purposive activity of government registers in terms of legal programmatic structures that are characteristically conditional. Conditionality (the 'if ... then' structure of law) is an expression of the function of the law of maintaining normative expectations in the face of conflict. To secure this function the legal system needs to maintain a relative balance of stability and innovation, or more precisely, to reproduce structures of normative expectations through controlled innovation. This is not an argument about some innate conservatism of the law. It is instead a conceptual point that innovations can only be grafted onto what already exists, and what already exists sets the thresholds of what might count as relevant information, what and under what circumstances may count as a 'surprise' in the system that registers as information that might in turn lead it to vary expectations. But one must appreciate that the balance of variety and redundancy,[17] what is new and what is business-as-usual, can only lean so far in the direction of variety without jeopardising the function of the law that must at some level meet the exigencies of the rule of law, which in this context means that policy imperatives will at some point yield to protected expectations. Maybe this is what Loughlin meant when he talked earlier of the law's 'register'. It is, however, a register that brings with it significant limitations and these limitations are precisely those that stand in the way of connectedness and continuity of orders.

Now the two 'crossings' between 'orders' that are constitutive of the 'continuity thesis' encounter obstacles of a significantly different kind. In the first case the objection to it is normative and political. It is the objection that in maintaining the continuity between the political and politics the argument misses the costs of the reduction of the former to the latter. The harnessing of political conflict, the 'exploitation' of conflict perspectives in the service of governing, involves representing a conflictual situation in terms that are conducive to the logic of government. Those who oppose that logic find their conflict usurped and overdetermined, rendered positive ('constructive' Loughlin tells us earlier) to the business of governing which in this case means the business of suppressing their claim. In the second crossing from politics to positive law the continuity is disrupted because the 'logics' of the two orders are at odds. The imperatives of governing need to instrumentalise a medium that is typically resistant or inert to the programmatic aspect of the logic of administration, and to the frustration of public lawyers of Loughlin's persuasion law makes its inertia known in terms of fundamental rights that 'trump' policies, and in terms of regulatory failures. In the

17 See Luhmann, *Law as a Social System*, above note 7.

face of how differently problematic the two crossings are let me anticipate a possible objection that Loughlin might put to this. The objection goes something like this: the 'pure theory of public law' is not a fully-fledged normative theory but a theory of the hermeneutical kind; its aim is to establish the best internal understanding of public law irrespective of normative political disagreement, to establish its proper grammar so to speak. This defence fails on both grounds. Firstly, because such normative disclaimers are in *all* cases unconvincing. All theory is political because all theory is an intervention in the real; and where it is not explicitly so it performs its function latently. Secondly, because in the absence of the thicker normative claim (that Loughlin's possible objection disowns) those who resist the political instrumentalisation of the law find themselves with the better argument. 'Protect the integrity of the rule of law', Hayek would object to attempts to 'administer' society; 'do not de-differentiate', Luhmann would add in his renewal of that Hayekian argument about the integrity of systems. And if all we are looking for is 'proper grammar', is Loughlin really to say that they got it wrong?

III

The Idea of Public Law is a book in public law *and* political theory and Loughlin has paid political theory the compliment of taking it seriously, and he is truly in the minority in that respect. His thesis has generated a renewed interest in the political underpinnings of public law amongst public lawyers. It is a hugely ambitious book and Loughlin paints on an immense canvas, as he often does. What he has given us is something very rich and controversial in equal measure, which, I suspect, is exactly what he intended.

In my short comment I identified two theses that are constitutive of the pure theory and called them the 'autonomy' thesis and the 'continuity' thesis. I argued that both are somewhat problematic in their own terms and somewhat problematic in their articulation. In terms of the '*autonomy thesis*', I argued with Loughlin that Public Law does indeed involve a certain 'internalisation' of conflict, of the distinction between right and wrong, of permissible violence, and so on, such that indeed establishes the sphere as autonomous. But I also argued against him that if the practice is to rely on a functional definition, such as that proposed by him in relation to 'governing', the autonomy and identity of the practice presupposes the absence of functional equivalents; if not then law would merge with politics, its autonomy eroded. Everything points to a Kelsenian purity here, a call for a categorical scheme of interpretation that bestows an internal, objective meaning to what happens politically, and this purity is never fully accounted for. *Against the continuity thesis*, I argued for keeping alive the disjunction between the levels. Where Loughlin emphasises continuity and the concentric nature of the realms of the political, of politics and of positive law, I see the dangers of homogenisation and substitution. Not because I disagree on the descriptive or normative project of a political constitutionalism, but because I think that in arguing the continuity one too easily misses the dangers of a certain *internalisation of the constituent in the constituted* and with it of a significant loss of the political.

I also argued that the articulation of the two theses is at least improbable, autonomy standing in the way of continuity, the 'objective' meaning of the law dis-continuous, even distorting, of political meanings and imperatives. This, to my mind, is the main stumbling block for most explicitly 'political' theories of law, and I take Loughlin's, in spite of the autonomy thesis, to be one, and one not lacking in ambition. Yet if the demand to see in this 'pure theory' an 'overcoming of the antagonism between democracy and constitutionalism' (thesis 32), an 'expression of democratic impetus' (30), the 'positive management of conflict' (14), or the 'key to the constitutive aspects of governing' (27), the continuity between the political (as an expression of people's genuine aspirations, antagonisms and griefs), 'politics' and public law must be direct, it cannot afford substitution. Loughlin negotiates and elides difficulties, impasses, tautologies and contradictions, his acrobatic effort to maintain both the 'pure' and the 'political' moments of constitutionalism oscillating between their creative tension and their mutual collapse.

Let me finish with a question over the normative stakes of the pure theory of public law and of political constitutionalism, both arguments for which, rather problematically as I have said, Loughlin runs *in tandem*. For me the critical emphasis on governing is the book's most significant contribution in the context of the mass retreat of public law from its political role that we are witnessing, in the face of an economic sphere that sharply delimits itself from other spheres of society and calls for the respect of its autonomy, integrity or proper logic. This differentiation of the economy marks its disarticulation from politics and has allowed it to grow to (what Karl Polanyi referred to as) a 'sociological enormity',[18] subsuming society to the imperatives of the market, subordinating association to accumulation, and allowing the economy, yet again, to emerge as separate from the political state and to the detriment of society. 'Only since the market was permitted to grind the human fabric into the featureless uniformity of selenic erosion has man's institutional creativeness been in abeyance', Polanyi adds in a later paper.[19] Against a mainstream public law courting such 'selenic erosion' in proclaiming the economic sphere as beyond the Constitution's jurisdiction and in retreating from the field of governing, Loughlin re-asserts the field's constitutive connection to that function. It is perhaps in this light too that his earlier insistence that public law be seen as sharply differentiated from private law, both its principles and values distinctly its own and the methodology of its scholarship also distinct, should be interpreted.[20] In all this he renews the old insight that no complex society can exist without organised power at the centre. This is hugely important. And because it is hugely important it is vital that the 'autonomy' of law that prevents direct translation of political imperatives into its register be taken seriously, to counter the danger that it remain unsuccessful before the autonomous logics of the fields it attempts to regulate. This is what my arguments about the continuity and autonomy theses were intended to highlight. If we draw attention

18 K. Polanyi, *The Great Transformation* [1944] (Boston: Beacon Press, 1957), p.113.

19 K. Polanyi, 'Our Obsolete Market Mentality: Civilization Must Find a New Thought Pattern', in 3 [1947] *Commentary* 109–117, at p.115.

20 In *Public Law and Political Theory*, n.3 above. Many thanks indeed to Adam Tomkins for a discussion of this.

to the autonomy of public law, it is emphatically not to maintain and celebrate it as a natural depository of communal value, as a vehicle for our self-determination as a people, or as a substitute for politics. It is because it is vital that we make strategic use of public law to subordinate a self-regulating economy running amok to democratic society and, in the exact words that Polanyi used to describe socialism, to 'endeavour to make society a distinctively human relationship of persons'.[21]

21 K. Polanyi, *The Great Transformation*, 234.

Chapter 5

Reflections on *The Idea of Public Law*

Martin Loughlin

The Idea of Public Law was not conceived as some abstract speculative task, of seeking to discover the foundations of some ideal constitution 'supposed to exist, God knows where …'.[1] Rather, it sought to investigate the conceptual underpinnings of a field of knowledge that had been set to work in modern political life.[2] Elsewhere, borrowing from Nelson Goodman, I have referred to this type of exercise as seeking to understand 'ways of world-making'.[3]

There were, I felt, specific reasons for trying to explain this particular way of world-making. Contemporary governmental arrangements have become highly systematised, a state of affairs which has been reinforced by changes flowing from the phenomenon of globalisation. Since these changes have altered some of its topological features, a review of the field seemed an essential preliminary to moving forward. In particular, the conditions of this way of world-making – that is, of thinking about the constitution of governmental authority in juristic terms – no longer seemed to be widely recognised. Systematisation within the field was leading to juridification of the field, and juridification was leading to the founding assumptions on which the activity of world-making through public law were becoming obscured from view. If a constructive response from within the discipline were possible, renewal of our understanding of the conditions of this field of knowledge seemed a necessary first step.

Droit Politique

The most basic objective of the book, then, was to retrieve a subject that seems to have fallen off contemporary maps of knowledge. For want of a better term, I call this subject public law. But by public law I do not mean a categorial division within

---

1 G.W.F. Hegel, *Philosophy of Right*, T. M. Knox trans. (Oxford: Clarendon Press, 1952), Preface, p.10: 'Since philosophy is the exploration of the rational, it is for that reason the apprehension of the present and the actual, not the erection of a beyond, supposed to exist, God knows where, or rather which exists, and we can perfectly well say where, namely in the error of a one-sided, empty ratiocination'.

2 Martin Loughlin, *The Idea of Public Law* (Oxford: Oxford University Press, 2003); hereafter IPL. Page references in the text refer to this work.

3 Martin Loughlin, *Sword and Scales: An Examination of the Relationship between Law and Politics* (Oxford: Hart, 2000), ch.2; Nelson Goodman, *Ways of World-Making* (Hassocks: Harvester, 1978).

positive law, as is often intended when drawing a distinction between public law and private law. I mean something much more basic: the 'law' by which public authority is established and maintained.

Although my argument is that the subject establishes its autonomy only in the modern period, the questions it throws into relief have puzzled those jurists who have sought to explain the foundations of their discipline. By way of illustration, consider Bracton's celebrated argument that, although the king is the highest legal authority whose will cannot be questioned by another, he remains under God and the law.[4] Unless we consider him a 'blockhead', we are obliged to recognise that Bracton was running together what we would now treat as two different conceptions of law. While a thirteenth-century jurist would not express it in quite these terms, this is the distinction between law as an instrument of the governing authority, vested in the king, and law that is constitutive of governmental authority, the 'law' that makes the king.

In civilian regimes of continental Europe, this distinction is easier to recognise because different terms specify these two conceptions: law in the sense of the rules posited by the constituted authority is *lex*, *la loi* or *das Gesetz*, while the idea of law as expressed in the rules and practices by which authority is constituted is *ius*, *le droit* or *das Recht*. In this account, 'public law' relates to what the Romans called *ius publicum* (public law), the French *droit politique* (political right), and the Germans understood as *allgemeine Staatsrecht* (the general right of the state). Public law is concerned with those precepts of 'political right' that establish and maintain public authority.

During the Middle Ages, a distinction between those two conceptions of law could not easily be made, not least because the idea that law was a human artefact, something made rather than declared by the king, was not part of their world. However, insofar as this distinction was recognised – and certainly as it was subsequently interpreted by modern jurists – it paralleled a distinction between positive law and natural law.[5] Public law, the precepts of political right, emerges from a tradition of natural law thinking. More specifically, public law emerges through the secularisation, historicisation and positivisation of natural law thought. This process can clearly be seen at work in the writings of those early-modern political philosophers who maintained a profound interest in juristic questions, especially Bodin, Hobbes, Spinoza, Locke, Pufendorf – and thence to Rousseau, Kant and Hegel.

Notwithstanding the differences in their writing – whether of method of analysis, historical context or philosophical world-view – a common concern runs through their work: if divine authorisation or customary practice offer inadequate answers, how is the authority of government to be explained and justified? Rousseau provides an elegant illustration of this juristic theme. Consider, for example, *Du Contrat Social*, and note in particular its subtitle: *Principes du droit politique*. The opening sentence

4 Henry de Bracton, *De Legibus et Consuetudinibus Angliae (On the Laws and Customs of England)* [c.1258], George E. Woodbine ed. Samuel E. Thorne trans., (Cambridge, MA: Belknap Press, 1968), ii.33.

5 On the modern formulation see esp. Jürgen Habermas, 'Natural Law and Revolution', in his *Theory and Practice*, John Viertel trans. (Boston: Beacon Press, 1973), ch. 2.

of the first book comes straight to the point: 'My purpose is to consider whether in civil order there can be any legitimate and certain principle of government, taking men as they are and laws as they may be'.[6] That is, are there principles of public law that render government legitimate?

It would be tempting to claim that Rousseau here takes us straight to the heart of the idea of public law. But there is an important caveat. *The Social Contract* is Rousseau's most explicitly normative study and I have already suggested that our task is not that of political philosophy. Rather than elaborating the structure of some ideal constitution, the task for public law is different: it is to understand the precepts through which constitutional ordering makes sense or, to express this slightly differently, to understand the ways in which existing constitutional arrangements can be said to work.

In their own ways, the philosophers mentioned above recognised this issue and this, I would argue, is precisely what makes them jurists. Let us stick with Rousseau. Rousseau expressed considerable scepticism about the possibility of establishing the type of regime he had outlined in *The Social Contract*. In *Emile* he commented that: 'Public law [the science of political right] has not yet been born, and we might presume that it will never be established'.[7] The reason lies precisely in the last phrase of that first sentence of *The Social Contract*: 'taking men as they are and laws as they may be'. The ideal is the achievement of legitimate and stable government under which justice is never sacrificed to utility. But because of the way humans are, that ideal – self-government in a strict sense – can never become a reality.

So the central question in public law concerns the nature of the governing relationship: how is collective life organised to ensure that those entrusted with the tasks of setting the terms of collective association use their authority for the purpose of promoting the public good? Wrapped up in that question are, of course, many others. The book's objective was to try to specify the conceptual building blocks through which these principal questions have been addressed in public law,[8] and through which we have established a specific (that is, autonomous) way of world-making.

For some, the world that this exercise establishes is the world of politics, not of law. But my argument is that public law refers to the juristic method by which this political world is first established and then maintained.[9] Public law extends beyond

---

6 'Je veux chercher si dans l'ordre civil il peut y avoir quelque règle d'administration légitime et sûre, en prenant les hommes tels qu'ils sont, et les lois telles qu'elles peuvent'.

7 Rousseau, *Emile* (1762), Bk 5, para. 1629: 'Le droit politique est encore à naître, et il est à présumer qu'il ne naîtra jamais'.

8 These are: *the activity of governing*: the unique object of the subject (ch. 2); *politics*: the distinctive practice that evolved to manage the activity of governing (ch. 3); *representation*: the foundational element of public law (ch. 4); *sovereignty*: the modern expression of the autonomy of the political realm (ch. 5); *constituent power*: the juristic representation of *collective autonomy* in modern public law (ch. 6); *rights*: the juristic representation of the principle of *individual autonomy* in modern public law (ch. 7).

9 See, for example, Rousseau, *The Social Contract*, Bk.2, ch.12: 'If the whole is to be set in order, and the commonwealth put into the best possible shape, there are various relations

positive law (*la loi*) to encompass the precepts of political right (*le droit*). And being a distinct way of world-making, these precepts are not transcendental but evolve immanently and serve the purpose of sustaining this world. Public law encompasses the principles, customs, habits and practices that establish and maintain a political world.

Critical Reception

The Idea of Public Law outlines the subject as it had emerged in modern thought and practice. It therefore seeks to move beyond the detailed arrangements of particular regimes and to sketch the way in which, in general, this type of world is established. Since several of the reviews are misconceived about its general aim, maybe that objective was not specified with sufficient clarity.

The book has, in particular, received two unfortunate types of criticism: those that claim it is geared towards making a contribution to a set of specifically British debates, and those that suggest it presents a specifically political (that is, ideological) argument. These include claims that my argument fails unless I can adequately specify the distinction between public law and private law;[10] that my argument is founded on a separation of political and the moral considerations;[11] that the book is best seen as a defence of a political rather than a legal conception of the British constitution;[12] that it is a 'sustained counter-offensive ... to the rise of liberal legalism';[13] and that this counter-offensive must be seen to be one from the political left.[14]

Although none of these arguments seems well founded, they have been prominently posted and deserve reasoned answers. But because they are based on a misunderstanding of the nature of the exercise it is difficult to fashion much by way of constructive response. I therefore confine myself to making brief comments on each of these claims.

The argument based on the public law/private law divide can be dealt with easily. It is rooted in an error of logic.[15] More significantly, the claim has force only if public law is treated as a subset of positive law. Since it is clearly stated that although the

to consider. ... The laws which regulate this relation bears the name of political laws, and are also called fundamental laws ...'.

10 N. W. Barber, 'Professor Loughlin's *Idea of Public Law*' (2005) 25 OJLS 157–67; Paul Craig, 'Theory, "Pure Theory" and Values in Public Law', (2005) *Public Law* 440–7.

11 Barber, ibid. esp. 158–63; Craig, ibid., esp. 443–4.

12 Tom R. Hickman, 'In Defence of the Legal Constitution' (2005) 55 *University of Toronto Law Journal* 981–1022.

13 Hickman, ibid. 985.

14 David Dyzenhaus, 'The Left and the Question of Law' (2004) 17 *Canadian Journal of Law & Jurisprudence* 7–30; Robert Shelly, 'Stuntman for the State: Loughlin's *Idea of Public Law*' (2006) 19 *Ratio Juris* 479–88.

15 If an argument is made that *a*, *b* and *c* are the elements that make up the concept *p*, it is open to the criticism that these are not the defining elements, or that they are incompatible or even incoherent. But it is a basic category error to argue that *p* has not correctly been defined because the ways in which it differs from *q* have not been adequately specified. IPL outlines the conceptual framework of public law (*p*). Anything that does not fit is simply not-*p*.

book presents 'a positive theory of public law' this cannot be 'a theory of positive law' (for example, IPL, 155, 29–31), the criticism arises from a failure to recognise the distinction being made between political right and positive law.

The assertion that the book's argument is founded on a separation of political and moral considerations results from an inappropriate conversion of my autonomy claim into a separation claim; in fact, I doubt whether anyone attempting to explain public law as political right can seriously argue for the separation of politics and morality. 'Those who desire to treat politics and morals separately', Rousseau declaimed, 'will never understand anything of either of them'.[16] He is right, but we should nevertheless distinguish between political and moral discourses or, if one prefers, between public and private morality. Neither express eternal truths; both have histories. Morality is a modern creation expressing subjective freedom, and it is precisely because of its invention that the search for a science of political right commences. In this respect, the distinction that Hegel draws between an abstract, subjective morality (*Moralität*) and ethical life (*Sittlichkeit*), the concrete universal, is helpful.[17] But again we are frustrated by language; although in English the terms ethical and moral are generally used interchangeably, significant differences exist in German between *moralisch*, *ethisch* and *sittlich*. While the first connotes a Kantian, universalistic approach to the question of what is right, the other two refer to notions of right or good that remain rooted in the customs of a particular society and express specific ways of being.[18]

Implicit in this argument are some difficult distinctions that have been explored in modern political philosophy between the right and the good, procedural norms and substantive values, principles and dispositions, universal and local, and even the rational and the aesthetic. Without getting involved in these intricacies, the argument of the book is that public law is institutionalised through local ethical practices. Conceptions of political right are based on the established customs of an existing regime. This does not mean that they are arbitrary or irrational. There may even be, as Michael Walzer put it, 'the makings of a thin and universalist morality inside every thick and particularist [public] morality'. The critical point is that universalist minimalism is not foundational; to the extent that it is recognised, it is because we are able to recognise similarities between practices and principles that are reiterated in different times and different places, 'expressed in different idioms and reflect different histories and different versions of the world'.[19]

This point leads directly to the argument that the book is written in opposition to what is sometimes called 'liberal legalism'. But since this has been combined with a claim that the book defends a political rather than a legal conception of the British constitution, I should first mention this latter claim. This reads like an attempt to

16 *Emile*, Bk.4, para. 838.

17 Hegel, above n.1, §.141A.'The unity of the subjective with the objective and absolute good is ethical life'.

18 See Allen W. Wood, *Hegel's Ethical Thought* (Cambridge: Cambridge University Press, 1990) Pts.III (Morality) and IV (Ethical Life).

19 Michael Walzer, *Thick and Thin: Moral Argument at Home and Abroad* (Notre Dame: University of Notre Dame Press, 1994), xi, 17.

press the book into one side of a false debate and thereby distort its argument: since the book's main concern is how, in juristic terms, we conceive the constitution of the polity, explaining this by elaborating the idea of *droit politique*, it obviously is not concerned with drawing a polarised opposition between legal (*droit*) and political (*politique*) discourse.

The argument about liberal legalism is a little more complicated, especially since it sometimes gets transformed into a cruder assertion that my position is that of 'liberalism with a minus sign'.[20] My target is not liberalism in general. Much of the book's argument in fact shows the ways in which liberal philosophies of governing fit the conception of public law I am advocating. It defends a liberal conception of sovereignty as the foundation of modern public law, justifies a political interpretation of basic constitutional rights, and presents an argument for constitutionalism 'neither [as] a set of fundamental moral principles nor the "unpolitical principles of the bourgeois *Rechtstaat*", but [as] "one of the most effective philosophies of state building ever contrived"' (IPL, 69).

The argument is not against liberalism but against the recent tendency to take a particular species of normative liberal theory – liberalism as moral philosophy – and adopt this as some transcendental legal yardstick against which to measure governing practices. This is what some have called 'liberal legalism' and which previously I referred to as the liberal normativist style of public law.[21] *The Idea of Public Law* argues that the principles of *droit politique* must be immanently derived from the practices of existing governing regimes. It therefore suggests that exercises in normative political philosophy, such as Rawls' universal moral claims in *A Theory of Justice*, do not assist in the tasks of identifying the ethical basis of existing practices. If liberal legalism were an explicitly normative enterprise, I could have no objection; like *A Theory of Justice* it would remain irrelevant to an understanding of public law. But this has not generally been the case amongst legal scholars, where an elision has taken place between adherence to a normative theory and the discovery that all along its principles were actually immanent within existing political and legal practices. This tendency has led to the emergence of a group of legal scholars I referred to as the 'new clerisy' (IPL, 145). We see an illustration of its workings in the claim that the enactment of the Human Rights Act marks 'the crowning achievement of a group of legal scholars'.[22]

It may be because some critics have equated my disdain over attempts to convert law into rationalist liberal metaphysics with a rejection of liberalism in general that the book has been seen as an argument from the political left. Otherwise, it is a surprising and unsustainable assertion.[23] Its source can be traced to an account of

---

20 Dyzenhaus, above n.14, at 9.

21 See Martin Loughlin, *Public Law and Political Theory* (Oxford: Clarendon Press, 1992), esp. chs 5 and 9.

22 Hickman, above n.12, at 983.

23 See, esp. Shelly, above n.14: 'the book … claim[s] to be both radical and progressive and indeed radically progressive' (479); 'the way he works out his conception of autonomy ultimately undermines his own left-of-centre pretensions' (480); 'for a theory that supposedly stakes its claim on the left …' (484). The book never once mentions the words 'left' (in the political sense) or 'progressive' and at no point is it suggested that the analysis is radical.

British public law thought that reduces scholarship to ideological struggle, claims that this battle is one that the 'liberal normativists, a.k.a. liberal legalists, appear to have won', and contends that this has generated some sort of crisis on 'the left'.[24] Its author – David Dyzenhaus – goes on to claim not only that I speak from the political left but am 'one of the leading bearers of the left tradition of legal thought'.[25]

It is tempting to dismiss this out of hand as the interpretation of someone unduly swayed by the highly polarised world of contemporary American legal theory. Let me at least try to unravel its genesis. In *Public Law and Political Theory*,[26] I argued that many of the confusions within British public law thought stemmed from a basic division within the subject between what I termed normativist and functionalist styles of thought and I suggested that understanding might be advanced by unpacking the ideological underpinnings of these contrasting styles. But although there was a cultural affinity in British traditions between right and left and normativist and functionalist styles, the styles cannot be reduced to a distinction between right/left ideologies.[27] It is possible to present a normativist account of law in combination with a leftist political position,[28] just as the functionalist method can be used to promote a rightist argument.[29] These styles are attempts to capture in public law thought the ambiguities of modern law's attempt to present itself as a medium of integration. In this sense, the styles reflect the tensions between social integration and system integration – between idealism and materialism – that Habermas used as a heuristic in *Between Facts and Norms*.[30]

---

24 Dyzenhaus, above n.14, at 9.

25 Ibid. 23.

26 Above n. 21.

27 Nor, as the case of Hayek illustrates, is it reducible to a division between normative and functional accounts of law. Cf. Paul Craig's review of *Public Law and Political Theory*, (1993) 13 *Legal Studies* 275–83. Craig persists in this misunderstanding: see Craig, above n.10, at 441: 'Nor do I believe that Loughlin's distinction between normative [sic] and functionalist theories is helpful for reasons I considered in detail elsewhere. It is, I think, regrettable that a generation of lawyers is emerging with the belief that there are political theories that are not normative'. The clumsy conjunction of these sentences makes the meaning unclear. Is he saying that I have influenced lawyers in a belief that political theories are not normative? I doubt whether many readers would conclude that *Public Law and Political Theory* conveys that message.

28 Rawls' *A Theory of Justice*, for example, promoted an egalitarian conception of social justice within a normativist frame of thought. We might also note Duncan Kennedy's comment that, although he remained highly critical of Ronald Dworkin's 'liberal legalist' project, his 'left liberal' values are such that 'I would certainly vote for Dworkin if he were running for the Senate and support his appointment to the bench, supposing in each case there was no radical alternative': Duncan Kennedy, *A Critique of Adjudication {fin de siècle}* (Cambridge, MA: Harvard University Press, 1997), 128.

29 Carl Schmitt, for example, deployed a variant of the functionalist style ('decisionism' and then later 'concrete order thought') as part of a rightist political project: see Carl Schmitt, *Les trois types de pensée juridique* [1933] Mira Köller and Dominique Séglard trans. (Paris: Presses Universitaires de France, 1995).

30 Jürgen Habermas, *Between Facts and Norms: Contributions to a Discourse Theory of Law and Democracy*, William Rehg trans. (Cambridge: Polity Press, 1996), esp. ch.2.

In seeking to locate my own writing within this frame, Dyzenhaus makes several errors. Firstly, despite my criticisms of it, he equates my position to functionalism.[31] Secondly, he then equates normativist and functionalist styles to right/left political positions. Thirdly, although he acknowledges that I have criticised the conception of law adopted by 'some of the most important figures in the legal left',[32] I am somehow taken to be its representative figure. Consequently, he implies that my approach is driven by a desire to promote specific political objectives, which is precisely the criticism I have been voicing about so much of contemporary British public law scholarship.

Commentaries

The seam between the book's critical reception and the commentaries in this volume is Dyzenhaus' claim that I 'avoid a theory which seeks to be serviceable *in any* way'.[33] This makes sense only if legal theory is conceived as an exercise in helping the judiciary justify the ways in which they carry out their tasks. If this is right, then it also proves useful in explaining why the misreadings regard an explanation as a political intervention, treat a theory that criticises a particular species of liberalism as anti-liberal, and deem an analysis inadequate if it fails to provide an answer to some specific jurisdictional puzzle. More generally it indicates how these critics treat the task of trying to make sense of public law as an adversarial contest: public law v. private law, politics v. morality, political constitution v. legal constitution, left v. right. As a group they seem wedded to the conviction that all explanations must be turned into arguments to be presented before some authoritative tribunal, whether court or court surrogate.

This understanding of the subject yields a rather impoverished notion of the scholarly enterprise. The court-centred conception of public law overlooks important aspects of legal practice, such as the world of regulatory law through which most of governmental activity is conducted, and tends to convert law-talk to rights-talk. It fails to address the relationship between legality and legitimacy other than dogmatically – that is, by refusing to consider the conditionality of legal normativity. One consequence is that it is unable to offer any sensible explanation of constitutional change. This overlooks a major aspect of public law as political right, which must touch on the question of how societies are integrated, and of the juristic dimensions to this process. These are difficult questions involving the relationship between system integration and social integration, the ways in which constitutional norms acquire social meaning, and of the symbolic and systemic functions of such

31 This was evident even in his review of Allan's, *Law, Liberty and Justice* in which he claims functionalism as my own position: 'It follows that there are no legal limits on what a legislature can do, and, driving *Loughlin's Theory* into absurdity, no limits on what administrative officials can do under legislation': (1996) 45 *University of Toronto Law Journal* 205–207 at 206 (emphasis supplied).

32 Dyzenhaus, above n.14, 13.

33 Ibid. 8 (emphasis supplied).

norms. This difficulty is not, however, a reason for excluding them from the remit of legal studies.

Ultimately, the division between the misreadings and the critical commentaries stems from a basic disagreement over the objectives of legal scholarship. In contrast to those misreadings the three chapters in this volume that engage with *The Idea of Public Law* accept the general nature of the exercise. Tierney examines the claim that sovereignty is the key concept of modern public law and questions whether my account can deal with the ways in which some of its underpinnings – singular central authority and freedom from external authority – are today being challenged. This is of central importance since sovereignty, I argue, is a representation of the autonomy of the political domain. Veitch takes this aspect of sovereignty as the starting point for his investigation. What, he asks, is the political sphere supposed to be autonomous from? Does the book adequately differentiate the material and private from the political and public, or is this exercise in itself ideological? Christodoulidis cuts deeper still. Focusing on the idea of *droit politique*, Christodoulidis directs his challenge to what he calls 'the problematic articulation of law with the political'. I will examine each of the three in turn.

Sovereignty in the contemporary world

Stephen Tierney recognises that the conception of public law I sketch seeks to circumvent the limitations of 'law as politics' (functionalism) on the one hand and 'pure theorists of positive law' (legal positivists and liberal normativists) on the other, and he accepts the value of the relational account of sovereignty. His comment highlights two trends in contemporary government that raise issues about the way sovereignty is now to be conceptualised: internal coherence and external independence.

In the book, I distinguished between legal and political conceptions of sovereignty mainly for the purpose of showing how a legal doctrine concerned with identifying an institution that has the 'last word', thereby acting as the guarantor of the regime, should not be confused with the more fundamental political conception of sovereignty, which signifies the autonomy of the political realm. This is the distinction between sovereign and sovereignty. Tierney questions the impact on the idea of sovereignty of a situation in which there is no longer any clear institutional figure of the sovereign. For Schmitt, the sovereign was the decisive governmental actor, he who decides on the state of the exception, and in the British system this sovereign has been conceptualised as the Crown-in-Parliament. But in the usual arrangements of states with formal constitutional structures that allocate and divide jurisdictional authority, that role of ultimate guardian can only be performed by an even more abstract representative figure – the idea of 'the people' or, as we see most clearly in French discourse, 'the Nation'. Taking our cue from these more usual arrangements, we might reformulate Tierney's two questions thus: can the Nation be divided? Can the Nation be superseded?

Tierney's questions can easily be answered. His main concern is the fragmentation of contemporary governmental structures that have arisen either from the assertion of the political claims of territorial communities within certain states (such as Catalonia in Spain, Quebec in Canada, Scotland in the United Kingdom) or from the growth of governmental arrangements at the supranational level (such as the European Union). These are practical political problems and while they might *in extremis* touch on the question of the sovereign, they generally do not affect sovereignty. The manner in which these problems are accommodated remain matters of political prudence, whose solutions will be reflected in the arrangements of positive public law. But pluralistic accommodations – whether through the special claim of a group to form a 'distinct political society' demanding asymmetric federal arrangements within the state or through the ambiguities and disputes about EU-member state relations – do not concern sovereignty.

Put another way: just as we must not confuse the sovereign with sovereignty, so too we must not confuse the actual people, with their multiple concerns and divided loyalties, with the idea of 'the Nation'. Much of Tierney's innovative work on these questions is directed towards the practical political issues – the silences, fudges and accommodations that have been made within constitutional arrangements to address these points of contention.[34] Almost all of his insights can be accommodated within a relational perspective on sovereignty. Our point of disagreement comes only when he draws philosophical conclusions from his sociological investigations. It can be accepted, as he claims, that the 'plurinational state can ... become a site of contestation in respect of the most fundamental constitutional tenet of all – the source and locus of ultimate sovereignty', but only if by 'ultimate sovereignty' we mean the figure who has the last word.[35] However, this cannot extend to an argument 'that sovereignty within a state is in fact divisible, or at least shared'.[36] This, it appears, is what Tierney seeks to do when he deploys relationality to challenge the contention about indivisibility.[37] Governmental authority can be divided or shared, but sovereignty cannot. Sovereignty is constitutive of public law; it is an authoritative expression of a particular way of being. We cannot move beyond sovereignty without destroying the idea of public law. That may of course be the destination that certain radical thinkers, using the language of post-sovereignty, are driving towards. If so, they must do something that has not yet been done: develop a conceptual vehicle through which to address the issues coherently.

The autonomy of the political realm

If sovereignty represents the autonomy of the political sphere, then Scott Veitch's questions about autonomy also affect sovereignty, and his comments underline the need to somehow transcend modern practices. From his opening remarks, however, it

34 See Stephen Tierney, *Constitutional Law and National Pluralism* (Oxford: Oxford University Press, 2004).

35 Stephen Tierney, '"We the Peoples": Constituent Power and Constitutionalism in Plurinational States', in Martin Loughlin and Neil Walker (eds.), *The Paradox of Constitutionalism: Constituent Power and Constitutional Form* (Oxford: Oxford University Press, 2007), 229–45, at 239.

36 Ibid. 238.

37 Ibid.

appears that we treat the issue of autonomy differently. By 'autonomy of the political sphere' I am not referring to some discrete area of social life where matters are contested politically (that is, concerned with voting, party competition, legislative assemblies, and so on) and which might, for example, be distinguished from the legal sphere of courts.[38] In *The Idea of Public Law*, the political sphere does not denote a sub-system of society which can be differentiated from other spheres, such as the family, markets, the institutions of civil society, and the courts. Rather, it stands as a representation – from a distinctive perspective – of the entire society. It is not, therefore, simply 'a political claim ... [which], like other political claims, ... has no intrinsic validity'.[39] It is a conceptual claim, founded on the attempt to elaborate the essential character of public law.

The claim of autonomy is, then, a corollary of the claim that we are seeking to identify a particular way of understanding, a specific mode of thinking and acting, a singular universe of discourse – a distinctive way of world-building.[40] Veitch comes closer to direct engagement with this position when he asks whether this is merely an ideological discourse which, although the product of modern European thought, has remained inextricably linked to European imperialist ventures. It is, he claims, a mode of rule that masks the realities of exploitation. And it does this in particular by drawing a distinction between private and public, between property ownership and rulership, and between the material and the ideal.

As a general observation, who would disagree? I do, however, want to question some of the implications of his argument. Although the book presents a positive theory, Veitch's criticisms come entirely from a normative perspective. Furthermore, all the normative work is affected by just one word: exploitation. This presumably is a motif for some theory of justice that Veitch maintains but does not explain. Are the practices of governing such that the powerful tend to triumph over the weak? We do not have to go to the other end of the world to an unusual case involving the relationship between government, law and the claims of indigenous populations in former colonies to have this demonstrated. What about the Norman conquest of England, the English subjugation of the Celtic populations of the British Isles, the use of governmental power to modernise the British economy by imposing huge burdens on the weakest groups through enclosures, land clearances, the imposition of cruel disciplinary regimes, and such like? The dynamic Veitch identifies is not confined to imperialism; it is inherent in the logic of rule.

Recognising this, we can highlight an important point about public law. Public law (the precepts of political right) emerged in modern European practice as the explanatory and justificatory language of a particular mode of ruling. This was

38 Veitch, *Authority, Exploitation and the Idea of Public Law* (supra). All references to Veitch are to his chapter in this volume.

39 Ibid.

40 Since Veitch approvingly quotes a political statement of Bourdieu in his comment, I should say that this is a mode of inquiry – the identification of a 'generative scheme objectively adjusted to the particular conditions in which it is constituted' – that Bourdieu the philosopher would recognise: Pierre Bourdieu, *Outline of a Theory of Practice* (Cambridge: Cambridge University Press, 1977), 95.

founded on basic ideas of sovereignty and citizenship and, later, on notions of democracy and rights. It is a mode of rule that claims to be law (*droit*)-governed. It therefore yields a conceptual language through which our practices of governing can – and have – evolved. To work effectively with this mode of governing we need to identify its conceptual structure. This is all that *The Idea of Public Law* was seeking to do. The achievement of a system of public law does not mean that exploitation is eliminated from the world. But it does mean that exploitation is eliminated *conceptually* from the world of public law.[41]

The point to be emphasised is that there is a significant difference between suzerainty (on which colonisation was justified) and sovereignty (rooted in the principle of equal citizenship), between dominion (disposition of power through property) and imperium (disposition of authority through rule), and between wants claims (claims enforced by wealth) and rights claims (claims enforced through law). Does this mean that any functioning system of governing has eliminated the power of property from its operations? Of course not. But the establishment of a public discourse that operates on the *principle* of formal political and legal equality and the deliberative procedures of open institutions does at least open up the possibility of achieving a distinctive type of governing arrangement.[42] After all, the *Mabo* judgement from which Veitch quotes approvingly would have been inconceivable without the establishment of this discourse of public law.[43]

The tensions that Veitch's comments highlight are driving factors of the discourse. There are various ways of expressing these: some refer to a political struggle to be included in 'we the people' and achieve full status within 'the [political] Nation',[44] others more generally to the playing out of tensions between formal equality and material inequality, between differing conceptions of liberty, between liberty and democracy, and so on. Veitch claims that my analysis 'misunderstands the material

41 Veitch asks: 'If the logic of rule and of exploitation are – or ought to be seen as – autonomous, does this mean that exploitation is therefore *non*-political?' The answer is that there are likely to be aspects of exploitation inherent in the ontological category of the political (the friend-enemy distinction), but that the objective of the (ontic) mode of rule as political right is to eliminate it from its (legitimating) discourse.

42 Consequently, the quotation that Veitch uses from Tawney is mostly right but seems to me to miss the most important point: 'Political authority is a genuine form of power … it is one form … To represent it as unique in kind and unrivalled in degree is to draw a picture which has little relation to the facts of life'.

43 Particular attention might be paid to the last sentence of the excerpt from Brennan C. J.'s judgement that Veitch quotes: 'it is appropriate to identify the events which resulted in the dispossession of the indigenous inhabitants of Australia, in order to dispel the misconception that it is *the common law* rather than *the actions of government* which made many of the indigenous people of this country trespassers on their own land' (emphasis supplied). Since Veitch quotes extensively from, and comments approvingly on, this decision, I am surprised that he remains puzzled about the situation in which 'the legal establishment has somehow managed to achieve the impression … that it is an engine of progressivism'.

44 See, for example, Judith Shklar, *American Citizenship: The Quest for Inclusion* (Cambridge, MA: Harvard University Press, 1991).

realm's constituent relation to the political',[45] but since this claim is not developed, I am unable to answer it. I am also puzzled by his comment that, with respect to present tensions between the political, economic and juridical spheres, 'while Loughlin rightly diagnoses the problem, he mistakes the prognosis'.[46] I am not aware of having made predictions. For Veitch 'the problem is that it is the wrong kind of political programmes that are currently succeeding'.[47] On this matter, the book can offer no assistance. My objective was to sketch the component elements of the discourse of public law not for the purpose of moralising about this development, but only to explain the basic ways in which it does its work.

Political jurisprudence

Emilios Christodoulidis's contribution focuses on two fundamental aspects of the book's claims. He firstly returns to the issue of autonomy: if public law is an autonomous discourse it must explain the objective meaning of the legal act, and he asks whether this issue has been adequately addressed. Secondly, he analyses what he calls 'a problematic articulation of law with the political', especially with respect to the distinction I draw between three orders: the political, politics and positive public law.[48] These two issues highlight some of the most basic and difficult aspects of the book's claims.

The issue of autonomy causes fewer difficulties. In relation to Veitch's comments, I have already mentioned that the political domain is not a sub-system of society but represents the entire society viewed from a distinctive perspective. The political sphere is not some limited engagement that can be separated from civil society or the market. Its claim to autonomy therefore does not derive from the type of exercise that seeks to distinguish between political action on the one hand and moral or economic action on the other. Since the political sphere is a comprehensive representation of society, its claim to autonomy comes from its ability to offer an authoritative expression of the world.

Christodoulidis highlights my characterisation of the exercise as that of sketching a 'pure theory' of public law. By presenting it in this way, I intended to highlight certain features of the exercise. Firstly, that this was a positive and not a normative account, seeking to explain how public law actually operated in the world rather than presenting a normative theory of how it should be conceived. Secondly, just as Kelsen presented a pure theory of positive law – an attempt as Christodoulidis expresses it 'to think the legal in terms that are properly its own'[49] – so this account sought to present 'political right' on its own terms. But Kelsen invoked the idea of the *Grundnorm* in order to eliminate from the legal any consideration of political questions, and while this might be defensible for the purpose of identifying positive law, it eliminates from consideration those issues concerning the constitution of

45 Veitch, supra.

46 Ibid.

47 Ibid.

48 Christodoulidis, *Public Law as Political Jurisprudence* (supra).

49 Ibid.

authority that are central to the identification of political right. If Kelsen claimed that 'in the beginning was the word' (or at least the objective meaning of the word), then in relation to public law 'in the beginning was the deed'. The deed is that act through which collective association is brought into existence, and it creates a 'we' only by differentiation from a 'they'.[50] This is the act of inclusion/exclusion – otherwise of friend/enemy – that lies at the root of the political world. This deed is the founding act of the claim to autonomy.

Christodoulidis suggests that I tie the claim of autonomy to a function – the activity of governing – and notes the difficulties of doing so. But this is not quite accurate. I tie the claim to the activity of governing the state, and it is the latter term that is of particular importance to the claim of autonomy, as contrasted to the claim of distinctiveness. The set of propositions that determine the unique character of public law is underpinned by the idea of the state. By 'the state' I do not mean the institutional apparatus of government. The state is the entity created by the foundational deed; the state is a collective representation of a people (a 'we'). This basic philosophical idea of the state (otherwise, 'the Nation') provides the founding assumption on which an elaboration of the precepts of political right becomes conceivable. This structure of political right generates a series of truths about the political world. Consequently, the claim to autonomy is ultimately an ontological claim: it expresses a particular way of seeing, and being in, the world.

It is right to note, as Christodoulidis does, that Luhmann's autopoietic theory 'queries a long tradition of political thought that inclines us to see only a unified political-legal system'.[51] In this respect, *The Idea of Public Law* distances itself from Luhmannian theory and presents a modern account of the discipline.[52] Whether the nature of the late-modern world is such that this modern account has now been overcome is not an issue I examine in any depth.[53] But I do suggest that if that claim has force, it requires a radical shift in thought about government, power, regulation and agency of the type that Luhmann has promoted, and whose implications for public law thought have not yet been fully worked through.

Christodoulidis' second line of analysis concerns the orders of the political, politics and positive law. He argues that 'continuity between the three levels is the book's organising thesis' and this involves 'the neat transition from register to

50 On this see Hans Lindahl's contribution to this volume: 'Democracy and Reflexive Identity: Reconsidering the Monism-Pluralism Debate'. Specifically, see also Lindahl, 'Constituent Power and Reflexive Identity: Towards an Ontology of Collective Selfhood' in Loughlin and Walker (eds.), above n.35, 9–24 (which critically analyses Kelsen and Schmitt's treatment of collective agency and offers a reflexive reading).

51 Christodoulidis, supra.

52 Christodoulidis, supra, also notes rightly that in *Public Law and Political Theory* (at 250–264) I had speculated on the degree to which Luhmann's systems theoretical approach could be of assistance in developing a neo-functionalist style of public law. IPL involves a re-orientation and the challenges that Luhmann's work presents have not yet been fully addressed.

53 See IPL, 95–98 (analysis of the radical challenge to the modern conception of sovereignty).

register' – an 'act of substitution' of one for the other.[54] This 'continuity thesis', as he calls it, 'too easily misses the dangers of a certain *internalisation of the constituent in the constituted* and with it of a significant loss of the political'.[55] This is a seductive argument, especially since he claims that 'the flipping over of the "partisan" framework [the political] into one conducive to the imperatives of the state is an *ideological* move in the most basic terms of social analysis, a move to distort and misrepresent, an act of symbolic simulation'.[56]

But the argument is overstated. The 'continuity thesis' belongs to Christodoulidis, not to me. He might criticise the book for failing adequately to explain relations between the three orders, especially since I note that the orders are only outlined and not fully fleshed out.[57] But he takes a step too far in thereby assuming that the relationship must be one of continuity. The evidence does not support this. I concluded the discussion of constituent power, for example, by stating that the concept 'cannot be entirely absorbed into norms', that 'it expresses a form of power that mediates between the three orders of the political', that it 'gives constitutions their open, provisional and dynamic qualities', and it reminds us that 'we must not idealize these political relationships by underestimating the power of domination expressed in constituted power'.[58] These statements stress tension and conflict as much as continuity.

Christodoulidis surely makes this assumption because he can then promote his own approach. His basic position is that 'we need to resist the collapse of the "constituent" into the pathways of the already instituted' and doing this 'is harder than one thinks' since 'democracy' and 'self-government' are 'irreducibly antinomic'.[59] He proclaims the 'irreducibility of the political to politics, of the constituent to the constituted' because only by doing so will we be able to retain 'our ability to break from, to imagine otherwise, and to renew beyond the modalities of what has already been instituted'.[60] Christodoulidis here is asserting the necessity of maintaining a space for revolutionary politics, a politics of emancipation. Does this challenge the thesis of *The Idea of Public Law*?

To the extent that his argument is a political analysis, it does not affect the book's argument. In order to explain this, I refer to the work of Jacques Rancière, a political philosopher whose arguments possess similarities to Christodoulidis'. For Rancière, politics begins with a 'major wrong': the gap between inequality and equality or a gap between 'empty freedom' and 'true freedom'.[61] Politics is thus 'a sphere of a common that can only ever be contentious'.[62] This conception of politics must not

---

54 Christodoulidis, supra.

55 Ibid. (emphasis in original).

56 Ibid. (emphasis in original).

57 IPL, 52.

58 IPL, 113.

59 Emilios Christodoulidis, 'Against Substitution: The Constitutional Thinking of Dissensus' in Loughlin and Walker (eds.), above n.35, 189–208, at 191.

60 Ibid. 195.

61 Jacques Rancière, *Disagreement: Politics and Philosophy*, Julie Rose trans. (Minneapolis: University of Minnesota Press, 1999), 18–19.

62 Ibid. 14.

be confused with 'the set of procedures whereby the aggregation and consent of collectivities is achieved, the organization of powers, the distribution of places and roles, and the systems for legitimating this distribution'.[63] That system – analogous to what I call the second order of the political or the practices of politics within an instituted system – is given the name 'the police'. For Rancière, the police is 'an order of bodies that defines the allocation of ways of doing, ways of being, and ways of seeing, and sees that those bodies are assigned by name to a particular place and task'.[64] This characterisation enables Rancière to argue that politics is an activity that is entirely antagonistic to the activity of policing or, as I would say, governing. Political activity is a term reserved for action that challenges the established regime, that 'makes visible what had no business being seen, and makes heard a discourse where once there was only a place for noise'.[65]

Does Rancière's radical reconfiguration of politics affect my argument? *The Idea of Public Law* makes no special claim that a regime of public law has established ideal conditions of justice, freedom or equality; rather it tries to explain the ways in which, through an instituted order, these terms are played out. Rancière seems to be arguing that such struggles follow a logic of police (or governing), and what he calls politics – Christodoulidis' idea of the political or the constituent – must operate beyond instituted order. (At least that is how I read it: Rancière also suggests that 'for politics to occur there must be a meeting between police logic and egalitarian logic'[66] and this opens up the possibility that it occurs more conventionally at the intersection of the first and second orders). For those who adhere to the possibility of a revolutionary politics being realised, the word 'politics' in the book can be replaced by the term 'the police' without any loss of cogency in its argument.

But Christodoulidis does not seem simply to be making a political argument; he appears instead to be making an ontological claim about the nature of political reality. This would bring him closer to another French political philosopher, one whose work he cites extensively and one who, in the course of criticising Rancière for inscribing himself 'within the French anarchist and utopian traditions of old', says, modestly, that 'I recognise myself in important parts of Rancière's work'.[67] Alain Badiou has a singular notion of politics: 'politics is a thought ... There is certainly a "doing" of politics, but it is immediately the pure and simple experience of a thought, its localisation'.[68] 'Politics', says Badiou, 'cannot be governed by the State'.[69] Politics is not concerned with governing, and it cannot have anything to do with opinion, even of common opinion as in democracy; invoking a Platonic distinction, Badiou argues that it is concerned with truth.[70] For Badiou, politics is specific, momentous and ephemeral. Whenever it emerges as event, the state

63 Ibid. 28.
64 Ibid. 29.
65 Ibid. 30.
66 Ibid. 34.
67 Alain Badiou, *Metapolitics*, Jason Barker trans. (London: Verso, 2005), 109, 116.
68 Ibid. 46.
69 Ibid. 87.
70 Ibid. ch. 1: 'Against "Political Philosophy"', 10–25.

inevitably reveals itself: 'It reveals its excess of power, its repressive dimension. ... The State is in fact the measureless enslavement of the parts of the situation'.[71] By contrast, 'politics is freedom'.[72]

For Badiou, politics is universal truth. He argues that in its true philosophical sense democracy 'is that which *presents equality*' and it therefore 'maintains politics in the realm of universality proper to its destination'.[73] This means 'that "immigrant", "French", "Arab" and "Jew" cannot be political words' since these 'necessarily relate politics to the State, and the State itself to its lowest and most essential of functions: the non-egalitarian inventory of human beings'.[74] There is, Badiou suggests, an old word that 'designates philosophically those instances of politics which emerge victorious from this ideal: it is the word "justice"'.[75]

Badiou's philosophy is puzzling: the event that characterises politics cannot be predicted, requires a leap of faith on the part of the subject, is spontaneous, never organised, and yet also is emancipatory. It is austere, ephemeral, universal and Platonic. Given these strictures, Badiou's 'politics' – other than through its absence – cannot tell us much about our present situation. Yet this is the philosophy that Christodoulidis invokes 'to think the constituent in its own terms and against its uncritical accommodation in the usual forms'.[76] If Christodoulidis accepts Badiou's philosophy – his ontological claim about 'politics' as a truth procedure – then there is little point in his spending time dealing with configurations of public law.[77]

But Christodoulidis then equivocates. Recognising such difficulties he argues that Badiou's notion of politics must be coupled with 'mass political activity'.[78] While he makes light of this difference – suggesting that this linkage is empirical rather than conceptual[79] – it seems to me to undermine the essence of Badiou's philosophical claim. Badiou believes that 'politics will only become thinkable once it is delivered from the tyranny of number, number of voters as well as numbers of demonstrators or strikers'.[80] This is a long way from Marx's materialism, dialectical method and notions of class struggle and Christodoulidis' attempt to bring these categories back into Badiou's philosophy destroys its character. Consequently, although we know that Christodoulidis wants to keep open the constituent space, it remains unclear

71 Ibid. 145.

72 Ibid.

73 Ibid. 94 (emphasis in original).

74 Ibid.

75 Ibid.

76 Christodoulidis, above n.59, 196.

77 On this matter I agree with Koselleck that 'political Utopianism is as much a contradiction in terms as is, for example, dogmatic scepticism': Victor Gourevitch, 'Foreword' to Reinhart Koselleck, *Critique and Crisis: Enlightenment and the Pathogenesis of Modern Society* (Cambridge, MA: MIT Press, 1988), viii.

78 Christodoulidis, above n.59, 197.

79 Ibid.

80 Badiou, *Peut-on penser la politque?*, (Paris: Seuil, 1985), 68; cited in Nick Hewlett, 'Politics as Thought? The Paradoxes of Alain Badiou's Theory of Politics', (2006) 5 *Contemporary Political Theory*, 371–404, at 393.

whether his argument embraces Badiou's ontology, Rancière's anarchism, or Negri's 'liberation of the *multitudo*'.[81]

Whichever way he goes, Christodoulidis' stance does not much affect the argument of *The Idea of Public Law*. Just as Kelsen claimed that even an anarchist could accept his pure theory of law,[82] so too does the pure theory of public law work irrespective of one's personal political convictions. In relation to the three orders, it maintains two critical positions. The first is that the legal framework of government (the third order) acquires its basic meaning from those political practices that sustain a governing regime (the second order). In relation to the British system, this point – *pace* Dicey[83] – seems self-evident. But it has equal force with respect to a regime with a formal, entrenched constitution. Political practices not only fill the silences and abeyances of constitutional documents, but also alter the meaning – often radically – of a fixed text.[84] The second is that constituent power operating at the ontological level of the political can retain its impetus, often in the ability of 'the people' to amend their constitutions but also in their power to bring about a fundamental break – through revolutionary action – in the nature of the governing regime.[85] Whether we call the second order the constitutional order, the governing order or 'the police', one of its basic functions is that of working so as 'to keep conflict inside a framework of order' (IPL, 36). And whether we think that political right eliminates exploitation as a conceptual category or whether, following these two French pupils of Althusser, we believe that the entire structure of political right forms part of an ideological state apparatus that masks exploitation makes little difference to its mode of operation.

Conclusion

The aim of *The Idea of Public Law* was not to explain the way we would wish the world to be. It was more ambitious than that. The objective was to outline the structure of beliefs that constitute the idea of public law. By this I mean that set of ideas which we are obliged to accept if we wish both to think coherently about the subject and to act effectively within the discipline. The objective was to expose for examination those basic concepts which are pre-supposed when we seek to speak and act in public law terms. It was certainly not intended to be a political intervention. Insofar

81 Antonio Negri, *Insurgencies: Constituent Power and the Modern State* (Minneapolis: University of Minnesota Press, 1999), 335.

82 Hans Kelsen, *The Pure Theory of Law*, M. Knight trans. (Berkeley: University of California Press, 1967), 218 (n.82): 'Even an anarchist, if he were a professor of law, could describe positive law as a system of valid norms, without having to approve of this law'.

83 See A. V. Dicey, *Introduction to the Study of the Law of the Constitution*, E. C. S. Wade ed. (London: Macmillan, 1959) 10th edn., 469–470. Hickman uses Dicey's text as the epigraph to his review: above n.12, 981.

84 Think, for example, of the ways in which the 14th Amendment of the US Constitution has altered its meaning over time as the judiciary have sought to re-determine what equal protection of the laws has come to mean for the contemporary American political nation.

85 For a cogent analysis of the reflexive character of these founding moments see Lindahl, 'Constituent Power and Reflexive Identity', above, n.50.

as it makes criticisms – as it does in relation to liberal legalism, transcendental rights claims and radical post-sovereignty arguments – this is not because I hold political objections to these positions. It is because I cannot understand how, in terms of public law, those advocating these positions are speaking coherently. I am grateful to reviewers for highlighting points of ambiguity and to the editors of this volume for this opportunity to clarify some of the points of contention.

PART 2
Public Law and Imperialism

Chapter 6

On Law, Democracy and Imperialism

James Tully

Introduction: The Field of Political Theory and Public Law

Since formal decolonisation in the mid-twentieth century most theories of public law and political formations begin from the presupposition that the field of law and politics is one of sovereign, constitutional states bound together by public international law.[1] Yet, over the last fifteen years this widely shared presupposition has been challenged as simply one way of characterising the field of constitutional law and political association among others, and this broader issue of how to characterise the field of law and politics has become a central question to which rival answers have been presented and debated.[2]

Over the last six or seven years, the oldest answer to this central question has been re-introduced into the mainstream debate: namely, that the world legal and political order is best characterised as an imperial order of some kind or another. There are a number of scholars since decolonisation who continued to study state and international law and politics as an imperial field, but their work remained on the margins of the mainstream debate. However, since 2000, and especially after 2001, imperialism has returned to the mainstream. There is now a large body of literature arguing that the field of public law and political organisation is characterised better as some form of 'new imperialism' or of 'empire' than as any of the other rival answers to the central question of the nature of the field we are trying to study.

Roughly speaking, the 'new imperialism' is said to be comprised of: the United States as the primary, but not necessarily exclusive or unilateral, imperial hegemon, working with or against an informal league of co-operating and competing sovereign

1 I follow Martin Loughlin in using 'public' law and 'constitutional' law as interchangeable. I also follow him in taking public law to be the basic laws that juridicalise or legalise the distribution, institutionalisation and exercise of the political powers of governing, including governing the economy, in any form of legal and political association. Like Loughlin, who follows Foucault on this, I call the basic legal and political institutions 'practices of governance' (Martin Loughlin, *The Idea of Public Law* (Oxford, 2003), 5–31, especially 29–31). Whether public law 'constitutes' the basic forms of political and economic power (liberalism), or is constituted by them (Marxism), or some more complicated relationship (my view) is not a question we need to answer for the analysis that follows (see the important discussion in Martin Loughlin, 'Constitutional Theory: A 25th Anniversary Essay', *Oxford Journal of Legal Studies*, 25, 2 (2005) 183–202).

2 See, for example, David Held and Andrew McGrew, eds., *The Global Transformations Reader*, 2nd edition (Cambridge, 2002).

constitutional, representative states or 'great powers' (the Great 8) and transnational corporations; operating through, or in tension with, the International Monetary Fund (MF), the World Bank (WB), the World Trade Organisations (WTO), unequal or manipulable international or transnational legal regimes such as the General Agreement on Tariffs and Trade (GATT); and backed up by the full spectrum global dominance of the US military and its coalition of willing and unwilling allies, proxies and dependencies. This imperial view of the field, in one variation or another, is advanced and praised by a large number of realists, neo-conservatives and neo-liberal and traditional liberal imperialists;[3] and it is advanced and condemned by a large number of anti-imperial scholars on the left and on the so-called 'isolationist' right.[4]

The introduction of imperialism into the mainstream debate over the central question was closely associated with the foreign policy of the United States under the George W. Bush administrations (2000–2008) and the expansion of the 'war on terror' that began earlier under Presidents Reagan and George Bush senior. As a result, 'imperialism' in general has tended to be equated with this specific form of 'new imperialism' in both theory and practice. Consequently, those who deny that the field is imperial, and those critics who agree that the field is imperial but criticise it and claim to advance a non-imperial alternative to work towards, both tend to take the new imperialism as the exemplar of imperialism in general. By focusing

---

3 See David Armstrong, 'Dick Cheney's Song of America: Drafting a Plan for Global Dominance', *Harper's Magazine* (October 2002), 76–83, William Finnegan, 'The Economics of Empire: Notes on the Washington Consensus', *Harper's Magazine* (May 2003), 41–54, and Nichols Guyatt, *Another American Century?* (London: Zed Books, 2003), for the rise of the neo-conservative Project for a New American Century since 1997. For the proponents of US empire, see Richard H. Haass, 'Imperial America', 11 November 2000, www.brookings.edu/dvbdocroot/articles/haass/2000imperial.htm, Sebastian Mallaby, 'The Reluctant Imperialist: Terrorism, Failed States, and the Case for American Empire', *Foreign Affairs*, 81, 2 (2002) 6–25, Robert Kagan, 'The Benevolent Empire', *Foreign Policy*, 111 (Summer 1998) 24–35, Robert D. Kaplan, *Warrior Politics* (New York: 2002) and *Imperial Grunts: The American Military on the Ground* (New York: Random House, 2006). For the new liberal imperialists, see Michael Ignatieff, *Empire Lite* (London: Vintage, 2003), Robert Cooper, 'The New Liberal Imperialism', *Observer Worldwide*, http://observer.guardian.co.uk/worldview/story/0,11581,680095,00.html, Robert Cooper, *The Post Modern State: Re-Ordering the World*, (2002), http://fpc.org.uk/hotnews/full?activied=169&tabeid=writes. Fareed Zakari, *The Future of Freedom: Illiberal Democracy at Home and Abroad* (New York: Norton, 2003), Niall Ferguson, *Colossus* (New York, 2003), Deepak Lal, *In Praise of Empires* (Palgrave, 2005). For a critical assessment of them, see Rahul Rao, 'The Empire Writes Back (to Michael Ignatieff)', *Millennium*, 33, 1 (2004), 145–66, Michael Cox, 'The Empire's Back in Town: Or America's Imperial Temptation – Again', *Millennium*, 32, 1 (2003), 1–27, Clyde Prestowitz, *Rogue Nation: American Unilateralism and the Failure of Good Intentions* (New York: Basic Books, 2003). For the continuity between the new liberal imperialists and the earlier liberal international law imperialists of the interwar period, see Jeanne Morefield, *Covenants Without Swords: Idealist Liberalism and the Spirit of Empire* (Princeton University Press, 2004).

4 I discuss the critics of contemporary imperialism, in its narrow and broad definitions, below. For a representative collection see John Bellamy Foster and Robert W. McChesney, (eds), *Pox Americana: Exposing the American Empire* (New York: Monthly Review Press, 2004).

on the specific definition of the new imperialism as the object of contrast, these presumptively or allegedly non-imperial theories of what the nature of the field is or should be, I will argue, tend not to notice the features of both the shared languages of description they employ and practices of governance (legal and political institutions) they refer to that are imperial in a broader sense of the term. The opportunity to subject our leading theories of public law and politics to a deeper self-examination of their persisting imperial features is thus bypassed.[5] Fortunately, these unexamined imperial features can be brought to light by referring to the broader history of imperialism and the work of anti-imperial scholars who have studied its persistence throughout the twentieth century, yet whose work has not been part of the recent mainstream debate over the character of the global field of law and politics.[6]

Accordingly, I proceed in the following manner. Each of the five sets of presumptively or allegedly anti-imperial theorists I examine in the following sections foregrounds and criticises a range of political and legal phenomena they take to be imperial. They then present an alternative based on languages and practices that they take to be non-imperial in contrast. However, in each case, I argue that the presumptively or allegedly non-imperial languages and practices on which their criticism and alternative are based are neither outside of contemporary imperialism nor the means of liberating us from imperialism. Rather, in each case, features of both the languages and practices they presume to be external to imperialism (non-imperial) turn out on closer examination to be internal to, or play a role in, contemporary imperialism.[7]

Another way of putting this point is that the range of phenomena that each set of writers foreground as 'imperial' is not the entire imperial field, but only specific aspects of it. So, what they present as an alternative is often another aspect of imperialism they did not foreground in their criticism but left unexamined in the background. So, what we see by the end of the examination is that certain features of many allegedly or presumptively non-imperial languages of description and practices are internally related to imperialism in some way or another. The conclusion is that we are entangled in a more complex web of imperial relationships than the defenders and critics of imperialism suggest.[8]

---

5 For a complementary examination see James Tully, 'The Imperialism of Modern Constitutional Democracy', Martin Loughlin and Neil Walker (eds) *The Paradox of Constitutionalism* (Oxford: Oxford University Press, 2007), 315–38.

6 There are exceptions to this generalisation. For example, Michael Hardt and Antonio Negri, *Empire* (Cambridge, MA, 2000), and Noam Chomsky, *Hegemony or Survival* (New York: Metropolitan, 2001), are discussed to some extent in the mainstream debates and they have broader conceptions of empire and imperialism respectively.

7 For a defence of this historical and critical approach, see James Tully, 'Political Philosophy as a Critical Activity', *What is Political Theory?*, (ed.) Donald Moon and Stephen White (London: Sage Publications, 2004), 80–102.

8 I do not mean by this that there is no 'outside' or that everything is empire (as Hardt and Negri claim). As we will see, imperialism is more complex than its defenders and critics presume, but it is only 'features' of the hegemonic political and legal languages and practices that are implicated in it, not the languages and practices simpliciter, and these features are contingent and changeable. Indeed, if my investigation is correct, imperialism is not as global

1. The first or traditional critics: overlooking the continuity of informal imperialism

Before I turn to the writers who explicitly reject or accept and criticise the hypothesis that legal and political power is organised to some extent imperially in the present, I would like to start with those writers who start from the presupposition that the legal and political field is non-imperial. This response is especially pronounced among traditional state-centred legal and political theorists. They argue, or more commonly presuppose, that there is not an imperial order today and carry on a traditional form of legal and political theory that takes for its horizon the system of sovereign constitutional states and public international law, or, secondly, the modification of this 'Westphalian' framework by the United Nations Charter and Declaration of Human Rights and new forms of global governance. This well-established framework gains strength from the widely-held assumption in the late twentieth century that a necessary criterion of imperialism is the possession of colonies. Since the world went through a period of decolonisation, independent state building and democratisation in the mid twentieth-century, and thus entered into a post-colonial period after the 1970s (or after 1989 in the case of the land-based Soviet empire), then the present post-colonial period of 1970–2005 must be, by definition, a post-imperial period.

The presumption that imperialism ends with decolonisation is reinforced by the fact that international law recognises formally equal and independent states, and this form of recognition seems to exclude the possibility of imperialism. Secondly, the global governance literature further entrenches the presumption by presenting global governance as the recent transformation of the pre-existing system of independent states, and thus two steps away from imperialism.[9] Moreover, the system of independent states is often projected back to 1648 by characterising it as a Westphalian system of states, thereby overlooking the last 400 years of European empires and colonies.[10]

However, the assumption that imperialism always entails colonies is false. One of the major forms of imperial rule in the West has been non-colonial: that is, the

---

and total is it appears, and alternative, non-imperial ways of living in the present are not only possible, as the *World Social Forum* puts it, but actual, in the lived experience of millions of people.

9 See, for example, David Held, Anthony McGrew, David Goldblatt, Jonathan Perration, *Global Transformations* (Cambridge: Polity Press, 1999), and David Held, *Models of Democracy*, 3rd Edition (Cambridge: Polity Press, 2006), final chapter.

10 Whereas the classic theories from Hobbes to Schmitt, on which the contemporary Westphalians construct their theories of national and international public law and representative government, always distinguish between the system of states within Europe and the system of imperial states and colonies between Europe and the rest of the world. That is, the European state was always considered to be an 'imperial state' or 'state empire' in competition with other imperial states over the resources of the non-European world until after the Second World War. See Kelly and Martha Kaplan, 'My Ambition is Much Higher than Independence', *Decolonization*, Prasenjut Duara (ed.) (London: Routledge, 2004), 131–57, Edward Keene, *Beyond the Anarchical Society* (Cambridge: Cambridge University Press, 2002), Antony Anghie, *Imperialism, Sovereignty and the Making of International Law* (Cambridge: Cambridge University Press, 2005), and below.

tradition of 'informal' imperial rule over another people or peoples by means of military threats and military intervention, the imposition of global markets dominated by the great powers, and a host of other informal techniques of indirect legal, political, educational and cultural rule, such as spheres of influence and protectorates, without or after the imposition of formal colonial rule. The rule of Britain over the Middle East in the early twentieth century and the informal rule of the United States over Latin America in the nineteenth and twentieth century are classical examples of informal imperialism prior to decolonisation.[11]

More importantly, when the US turned to overseas economic expansion in 1898–1903 (into Latin America, South America and China), the policy debate was between those who favoured colonial imperialism (as in the Philippines, Puerto Rico and the Virgin Islands) and those who favoured non-colonial, informal imperialism by means of military bases (as with the Guantanomo Bay military base of 1901), economic power and military intervention whenever necessary to protect and extend US economic interests. Charles A. Conant summed up the options and put the case for informal imperialism in 1898:[12]

> Whether the United States shall actually acquire territorial possessions, shall set up captain generalships and garrisons, [or] whether they shall adopt the middle ground of protecting sovereignties nominally independent, or whether they shall content themselves with naval stations and diplomatic representations as the basis for asserting their rights to the free commerce of the East, is a matter of detail.... The writer is not an advocate of "imperialism" from sentiment, but does not fear the name if it means only that the United States shall assert their right to free markets in all the old countries which are being opened up to the surplus resources of capitalistic countries and thereby given the benefits of modern civilization.

After the US war against the Philippine nationalists who had supported them in their war against colonial Spain, and the colonisation of the Philippines, the defenders

11 The classic text of informal or 'free trade' imperialism is Ronald Robinson and John Gallagher, 'The Imperialism of Free Trade', *Economic History Review*, 6, 1953. It is analysed by Wolfgang Mommsen, *Theories of Imperialism* (Chicago: Chicago University Press, 1979), 86–93, Michael Doyle, *Empires*, and Harry Magdoff, *Imperialism without Colonies* (New York: Monthly Review Press, 2003). Stephen Howe, *Empire* (Oxford, 2002), and 'American Empire: the History and Future of an Idea', 12 June 2003, www.openDemocracy.net, summarises how it applies to US imperialism throughout the twentieth century. Mommsen sees it as the most important development in the theory and practice of imperialism in the modern age and suggests that formal colonial rule is only the 'tip of the imperial iceberg'. All the following texts on US imperialism use the concept of informal imperialism.

12 Charles A. Conant, 'The Economic Basis of Imperialism', *The North American Review*, 167, 502 (September 1898), 339. www.mtholyoke.edu/acad/intrel/toa1914.htm. Like all the great theorists of imperialism in the late nineteenth century, from Marx and Lenin to Hobson and Kautsky, Conant sees the huge expansion of informal imperialism over the non-European world in the nineteenth century as driven by the transformation to 'corporation' capitalism in Europe and the United States.

of non-colonial imperialism won the debate.[13] They justified it in the terms Conant presented, the 'Open Door' policy of Secretary of State John Hay, and a series of 'corollaries' to the Monroe Doctrine of 1823 by which the US gave itself the right to intervene to open the doors of Latin American countries to 'free trade' dominated by US firms, against indigenous movements that tried to protect their own resources and economies from foreign control on the one hand, and against the European imperial powers' claim to exclusive control of their formal or informal colonies on the other. This doctrine and language of informal imperialism, 'freedom' as the opening of doors to free trade dominated by US and European corporations, and so to the spread of 'modern civilisation', was repeated by Theodore Roosevelt in the first decade of the twentieth century, Woodrow Wilson in the second, and Franklin Roosevelt in the 1940s. As Andrew Bacevich, Chalmers Johnson and Neil Smith have shown in detail (expanding the earlier scholarship of Charles Beard, William A. Williams and Robinson and Gallagher), this free trade 'imperialism without colonies' has been the acknowledged form of global rule exercised by the United States for over a century, and it is the form of informal imperialism that persisted through formal decolonisation and is exercised by the US today according to both the defenders and critics of the new imperialism.[14] Informal imperialism consists in, first, imposing a structure of domestic public law and political institutions, or 'structurally adjusting' an existing constitutional order, that opens the resources, labour and markets of the imperialised country to free trade dominated by the great powers; and, second, subjecting this legal and political order in turn to regimes of public and private international laws, again constructed and dominated by the great powers.[15] Yet, it is unnoticed by current legal and political theorists, who continue to write as if imperialism is a thing of the distant past.

In summary, the traditional or Westphalian legal and political theorists, who probably comprise a majority of mainstream legal and political theorists, presuppose

13 John B. Foster, H. Magdoff and Robert McCheney, 'Kipling, the 'White Man's Burden', and U.S. Imperialism', *Pox Americana*, Foster et al. (eds), 12–21.

14 Andrew Bacevich, *American Empire: Realities and Consequences of U.S. Diplomacy* (Cambridge: Harvard University Press, 2002), Chalmers Johnson, *Sorrows of Empire* (New York: Metropolitan, 2004), Neil Smith, *American Empire: Roosevelt's Geographer and the Prelude to Globalization* (Berkeley: University of California Press, 2004). The classic text of an earlier generation of US historians, is William A. Williams, *Empire as a Way of Life* (New York: Oxford University Press, 1980). For a brief description of their account of informal imperialism today, see the Introduction above, and see the analysis of it in the following sections. For the historical development of informal or 'free trade' imperialism in imperial Britain in the nineteenth century, see Bernard Semmel, *The Rise of Free Trade Imperialism* (Cambridge: Cambridge University Press, 1970).

15 For the history of these two main legal and political features of informal imperialism, see Anghie, *Imperialism*, and Koskenniemi, *The Gentle Civilizer*. For their operation today, see James Petras and Henry Veltmeyer, *Empires with Imperialism: The Globalizing Dynamics of Neo-liberal Capitalism* (New York: Palgrave, 2005).

that the present order is non-imperial, and thus overlook the persistence of informal imperialism.[16]

2. The second critics: overlooking the historical length and breadth of informal imperialism

The second critics of imperialism acknowledge the existence of informal imperialism but claim that it is restricted to the President Bush administrations, or at least no older than the Reagan administration. It thus could be ended by the election of a new administration. For example, Michael Mann, one of the leading theorists of modern forms of power, argues that a Democratic administration would signal the end of empire.[17] This is to greatly under-estimate the longevity and breadth of this form of imperialism. As we have seen, informal imperialism has been in operation, with varying degrees of success, since the nineteenth century and thus is not a recent phenomenon, as these critics assume.

Moreover, this strategy of informal imperial rule has always had two 'faces' or 'wings'. One is the more unilateral and overtly militaristic face of the European 'new imperialism' over the 'scramble for Africa' in the 1880s, of the Theodore Roosevelt Administration in early twentieth century United States, and the George W. Bush administrations today. The other is the more multilateral and covertly militaristic approach of Woodrow Wilson, John F. Kennedy and William Clinton. The latter wing is more inclined to work with allies, especially the great imperial powers (G8); through the League of Nations, United Nations and the Bretton Woods institutions set up after the Second World War; in accordance with international law where possible; employ economic pressure and sanctions; and turn to military intervention only as a last resort, to (as Conant put it above), 'open doors' to the 'surplus resources of the capitalistic countries'.[18] Hence, these current critics do not notice the longevity and breadth of informal imperialism because they identify imperialism with only one of its wings; the unilateral, and thus see the multilateral wing as non-imperial in contrast.[19]

---

16 While Martin Loughlin presents what is in many respects a classic Westphalian theory of public law and political theory, he does explicitly respond to the imperial hypothesis, but only in the specific form presented by Hardt and Negri in *Empire*, and only with respect to their challenge to the traditional state-centred account of sovereignty, which is very different from the histories of imperialism I am drawing on here. See Loughlin, *Pure Theory*, 96–98.

17 Michael Mann, *Incoherent Empire* (London: Verso, 2001). For similar narrow (critical) interpretations of contemporary imperialism, see Stefan Harper and Jonathan Clarke, *America Alone: The Neo-Conservatives and the Global Order* (New York, 2004), John Newhouse, *Imperial America: the Bush Assault on the World Order* (New York, 2004), George Soros, *The Bubble of American Supremacy* (New York, 2004).

18 Conant at note 12 above. See William K. Tabb, 'The Two Wings of the Eagle', *Pox Americana*, 95–103, is a short introduction. The two wings are discussed in detail by Bacevich, *American Empire*, and Johnson, *Sorrows of Empire*.

19 The debate over the 'new imperialism' of the late nineteenth century is strikingly similar. The critics of imperialism focused on the unilateral and militaristic imperialism of Cecil Rhodes and tended to construe what Hobson and Kautsky called the 'hyper-imperialism'

Moreover, the differences between these two wings within the broad, overall imperial strategy are often over-emphasised by these narrow critics. For example, Woodrow Wilson invaded China, Haiti, Mexico and the Dominican Republic to protect American economic interests from local democratic control while he was proclaiming the right of self-determination of the same countries and saw no contradiction between them.[20] The defenders of the distinction often cannot agree on whether a particular administration, such as the Clinton administration, should be seen under one wing or the other.[21] Similarly, while the George W. Bush administration justified the invasion of Afghanistan and the second Iraq war in terms of an aggressively unilateral pre-emptive strike doctrine in the United States Security Strategy of September of 2002, they went on to justify both in terms of UN resolutions and international law and to build a multilateral 'coalition of the willing'. Neither was presented as an 'exception to the norm', as Agamben suggests, nor as a 'moralised' non-juridical policy, as Habermas interprets it in order to draw a categorical distinction between the Wilsonian and (Theodore) Rooseveltian faces of US policy.[22] The ease with which international laws and UN resolutions can be manipulated to legitimate the invasion and occupation, and used, conversely, to try to de-legitimate it by the opponents of the war, suggests that the analysis of Martti Koskenniemi is correct in general terms. He argues that public international law is not a formal public law autonomous from geo-political forces but, rather, an informal set of laws open to effective manipulation by the imperial western powers of the day: to justify imperialism in terms of 'civilising' the non-European peoples in the nineteenth century, military intervention against 'communists' during the Cold War, and 'terrorists' and 'rogue states' during the present Anti-Terror War.[23]

---

of the great powers co-operating informally over the exploitation of the non-European world as non-imperial.

20 See Bacevich, *American Empire*, 115–16 and below.

21 See the debate in *Foreign Affairs* between Robert Tucker and David Hendrickson, defenders of the multilateral wing as non-imperial, and Robert Kagan, defender of the unilateral wing as imperial (December 2004 and January 2005).

22 For the use of international law and UN resolutions, see Stephen Toope and Jutta Brunee, 'Slouching Towards New Just Wars: The Hegemon after September 11th', (forthcoming). The unilateral *National Security Strategy of the United States of America* is available at www.whitehouse.gov/nsc/nss.pdf. The new Security Strategy of May 2006 repeats the same argument. Some rights were partially extended to prisoners at Guantanomo Bay by *Rasul et al. v. Bush, President of the United States et al.* 24 April, 2004, Supreme Court of the United States (available on website). See the discussion in relation to Agamben in Martin Puchner, 'Guantanamo Bay', *London Review of Books* 26, 24 (16 December 2004), 7. For Jurgen Habermas' interpretation of US foreign policy as moralisation rather than juridification, see Jurgen Habermas, 'The Kantian Project of the Constitutionalization of International Law: Does it still have a chance?', Omid A. Payrow Shabani, ed. *Multiculturalism and Law: A Critical Debate* (Cardiff: University of Wales Press, 2007), 205–18.

23 Koskenniemi, *The Gentle Civilizer*, 480–509. Koskenniemi does not discuss that the subaltern subjects of international law are also able to make public international law arguments in countering the claims of the hegemonic powers, and sometimes even win the debates, as in the Landmines Convention, as legal constructivists have shown. See below, section 7: The fifth critics.

As Gerry Simpson concludes, international law can function as a form of 'legal hegemony' of the 'great powers' or, as he calls them after decolonisation, the 'unequal sovereigns'.[24]

Finally, both wings of this shared imperial strategy accept the presence and continuing expansion of the US global military empire of 'bases' or 'garrisons', which, according to the Pentagon, exercises 'full spectrum dominance' over the planet. Since the building of overseas garrisons and fuelling stations during the first imperial expansion of 1898–1917, itself based on the earlier military model of fortresses along the western 'frontier' of wars against the Native Americans from 1620 to 1890, there are now over 725 military bases outside of the United States. These military bases are literally the bases of informal imperialism. Built on the model of the earlier naval bases of the British empire, they enable an imperial power to intervene, or simply threaten to intervene, in any formally free and independent state at a moment's notice if their economic and geo-political interests, or those of their allies, are threatened by demands for local control of resources and markets. The military bases are also supported by the continuous surveillance of the planet by the navy, air force, satellites and the recent plans for the weaponisation of space. The US military command divides the world into four zones or 'provinces' governed by four US Commanders in Chief (CINC) or 'pro-consuls'. This global system of full spectrum dominance is ready for military intervention, or the effective threat of military intervention, anywhere on the planet at a moment's notice, as the military's Joint Vision 2020 explains.[25]

In summary, these critics of the narrow interpretation of the 'new imperialism' overlook the long and broad background of informal imperial rule, the co-operative imperialism of the multilateral wing, and the global system of US military imperialism that protects and extends the persisting imperial order of domestic and international public laws and institutions.

3. The third critics: overlooking the imperial features of the state system, development, and institutions of global governance

The third critical response is to recognise the length and breadth of informal imperialism, but not the global military empire, and then to argue that there is a European tradition of multilateralism, the rule of international law, respect for the

24 Gerry Simpson, *Great Powers and Outlaw States* (Cambridge: Cambridge University Press), 2003.

25 *An Evolving Joint Perspective: US Joint Warfare and Crisis Resolution in the 21st Century*, 28 January 2003, www.dtic.mil/jointvision/. This rise of this global military empire is analyzed by Johnson, *Sorrows of Empire*, and Bacevich, *American Empire*, both of whom served in the military. See also the endorsement of it by new imperialists such as Max Boot, *The Savage Wars of Peace: Small Wars and the Rise of American Power* (New York: Basic Books, 2003), and Kagan, *Imperial Grunts*. For the effects on sovereignty and public law of the extension of global military dominance by means of the weaponisation of space see Jonathan Havercroft and Rod Duvall, 'Sovereignty and the Weaponization of Space', paper delivered at the annual International Political Science Association annual meeting, San Diego, 25 March 2006.

United Nations and the post-Bretton Woods international regulatory regimes of global governance, now best exemplified by the European Union. This alternative, they argue, is a genuinely non-imperial alternative to both wings of the US global strategy. This response comes in a number of different forms. David Held argues that his 'cosmopolitan democracy' offers a 'social democratic alternative' to the 'Washington Consensus'.[26] Jurgen Habermas, following Bardo Fassbender, suggests that the constitutionalisation of the UN Charter, as the public law of the existing 'international community', and the empowerment of the UN to enforce compliance offer a clear alternative.[27] Even some authors on the left, who have written important works on the history and presence of western imperialism, such as Samir Amin and David Harvey, suggest that a social democratic European Union offers the best hope, although both concede that it would still be a kind of imperialism, albeit a less-bad type.[28]

While the European and cosmopolitan critics arguably present an alternative to US informal imperialism, at least in its neo-liberal and neo-conservative forms, it is difficult to see how it is non-imperial. It fails to call into the space of questions the historically layered character of European and American imperialism over the last half millennium. Firstly, as we have seen, they seem to present an alternative to the unilateral and neo-liberal wing of US imperialism while embracing a version of the multilateral and more social democratic wing. Secondly, like the earlier deniers and critics they take the existing system of independent, constitutional states, public international law, global markets and corporations, and processes of development for granted as the basis of their proposals (to constitutionalise, modify or transform it). While they acknowledge that the system of states is 'stratified', they do not enquire into the colonial origins of the system of stratified states to see if it is a persisting imperial system.[29] Similarly, because these critics disregard the depth and breadth of informal imperialism they do not ask if the post-Second World War institutions on which their proposals for global governance and cosmopolitan democracy are built are not themselves institutions of continuing informal imperialism. I think that if we enquire into these two questions we will see that there is a yet deeper layer of imperial features of our legal and political institutions that these critics leave unexamined and so presume to be the foundation of a non-imperial future.

---

26 David Held, *Global Covenant: The Social Democratic Alternative to the Washington Consensus* (Cambridge: Polity, 2004).

27 Habermas, 'The Kantian Project', and Bardo Fassbender, 'The United Nations Charter as Constitution of the International Community', *Columbia Journal of Transnational Law*, 36 (1998), 531–618.

28 David Harvey, *The New Imperialism* (Oxford: Oxford University Press, 2003), Samir Amin, *Liberal Virus: Permanent War and the Americanization of the World* (New York: Monthly Review Press, 2004).

29 Habermas, 'The Kantian Project', and John Rawls, *The Law of Peoples* (New York, 2001). See Simpson, *Great Powers and Outlaw States* for a criticism of both on these grounds. For a rejoinder to Habermas, see Frank Deppe, 'Habermas' Manifesto for a European Renaissance: A Critique', *Socialist Register* (2005), 313–23, and Neil Walker, 'Making a World of Difference?' Rayrow Shabani, (ed.) *Multiculturalism and Law*, 219–34.

Firstly, the nominally sovereign and independent non-European states recognised by international law are in fact the former colonies, whose legal and political structures were constructed by the European powers to serve their interests over two periods of colonial imperialism: 1500–1776 and the second period of hyper-colonisation 1800–1905, when 85 per cent of the non-European world was under formal or informal imperial rule.[30] Under the 'standard of civilisation' of nineteenth-century international law, these 'uncivilised' colonies were opened to free trade and structured accordingly by the imperial powers under the Mandate System of the League of Nations and the Trustee System of the United Nations.[31] During the period of decolonisation, state building, and the Cold War competition between the US and the USSR, the indigenous, westernised elites wrested formal political power from their former masters, but, this involved a 'transfer of power' and the 'continuation' of existing 'informal' imperial relationships.[32]

To survive in the imperial world system in which they found themselves, the national elites were both constrained and induced to modernise their ethnically diverse peoples and their hinterland, often with great violence to traditional legal and political formations; to define sharp boundaries of territory and unified nationhood where none existed; to strengthen the western-style legal, political and military institutions of the colonial period over indigenous legal and political pluralism; to open their doors to a highly structured capitalist world economy over which they had no control (or to the socialist economy until 1989) at the expense of local control of their economic affairs; to subordinate their own legal and political sovereignty over their resources to international law, and to learn to call this imperial subalternisation 'freedom'; to take on enormous debt to survive in the developmental race; to enter into the escalating dependency and debt of the arms race; and, as a result of these relations of dependency, to submit to the waves of modernisation programmes imposed by the new institutions of post-colonial, informal imperialism.[33] The assault on the multiplicity of local forms of economics, politics, 'customary' law and ethnicity that informal imperialism and dependency entail tends to turn the people against their westernising elites, and this causes the elites to become even more dependent on military rule and repression of local democracy.[34] This entire

30 For this legal and political history, see note 15 above.

31 Anghie, *Imperialism, Sovereignty*, 32–196. For the expansion and intensification of western imperialism to 85 per cent of the planet in the latter half of the nineteenth century, See Doyle, *Empires*, 141–352.

32 Wolfgang Mommsen, 'The End of Empire and the Continuity of Imperialism', 50.

33 For a recent overview of the research on Decolonisation and informal imperialism, see Duara, ed. *Decolonization*. For a restatement of this thesis for Latin America and neo-liberal imperialism, see Duncan Green, *Silent Revolution: The Rise and Crisis of Market Economies in Latin America* (New York: Monthly Review Press, 2003). For the resulting unequal sovereignty of the former colonies under international law, 'global governance' and the war on terror, see Anghie, *Imperialism*, 196–310, and, for Africa, Siba N'Zatioula Grovogui, *Sovereigns, Quasi-sovereigns and Africans: Race and Self-determination in International Law* (Minneapolis: University of Minnesota Press, 1996).

34 The classic area study of this phenomenon is B. Gills, J. Rocamora and R. Wilson, 'Low Intensity Democracy', in B. Gills et al., ed. *Low Intensity Democracy: Political Power*

process is what Frantz Fanon called, late in life, 'the apotheosis of independence … transformed into the curse of independence'.[35]

As Alexander Wendt and Michael Barnet have shown, the consequence is highly unstable and unrooted 'states' whose levels of inequality, dependency and foreign control have increased rather than decreased since decolonization.[36] These subaltern states are now often called 'failed states' and this status justifies further informal military intervention and economic adjustment to the global economy. Very few neo-liberal imperialists mention that the 'failed state' is itself the product of waves of formal and informal imperial 'replication' nation-state building on one side, and the struggles of resistance by the peoples who dream of creating their own forms of political association and governing themselves in their own ways on the other.[37]

Thus, it is difficult to see how the existing state system and public international law can be taken as the unexamined constitutional basis for constructing a non-imperial alternative to contemporary imperialism.[38] The so-called 'Westphalian' system is actually an imperial system of hegemonic and subaltern states constructed in the course of 'interactions' between imperial actors and imperialised collaborators and resistors. It is the foundation of contemporary imperialism, laid in the colonial period and strengthened during decolonisation. Informal imperialism would scarcely work at all if these colonial foundations did not provide a historically-sedimented background structure of institutions and relations of domination within which the more flexible relations of informal imperialism are exercised in the foreground.[39]

Secondly, the global governance critics place their hopes for the global rule of law and democracy on the international institutions and laws established after the Second World War to govern a post-colonial and post-sovereign world. However, it is difficult to see how these institutions and deformalised international laws of humanitarian and human rights intervention can be seen as an unproblematic basis

---

in the New World Order (London: Pluto Press, 1993).

35 Frantz Fanon, *The Wretched of the Earth* (New York: Groove Press, 1968), 97–8.

36 Alexander Wendt and Michael Barnett, 'Dependent State Formation and Third World Militarization', *Review of International Studies*, 19 (1993), 321–47. For a forceful restatement, see Noam Chomsky, *Failed States* (New York, 2006).

37 For this oversight among recent liberal imperialists, see Rao, 'The Empire Writes Back'. For the classic statement of the aspiration to draw on their own traditions and creativity rather than being forced into the western state form, see Fanon, *Wretched of the Earth*, 312–3, and more recently, Dipesh Chakrabarty, *Provincializing Europe: Postcolonial Thought and Historical Difference* (Princeton: Princeton University Press, 2001).

38 This point was raised of course by the former colonies as soon as they entered the United Nations, in their demand for a New International Economic Order and for permanent sovereignty over their resources. It was also raised by the Fourth World of Indigenous Peoples who still have no representation in international law. But, these challenges were overridden by the great powers and the structured inequality of the United Nations constitution. It was raised within international law scholarship by Gerald Gong, *The Standard of Civilization in International Society* in 1984, before Koskenniemi, Simpson and Anghie in the early 2000s.

39 Mommsen, 'End of Empire', Op. cit., and, from the World Systems' perspective, Steven Sherman and Ganesh K. Trichur, 'Empire and the Multitude: a Review Essay', *Journal of World Systems Research*, 10, 3 (Fall 2004) 819–45.

for reforms that would lead to a non-imperial future. As I have suggested, these legal and political institutions were created by the European imperial powers and the United States at the end of the Second World War to end the destructive wars of imperial competition (the First and Second World Wars), to submit themselves to an international system of laws rather than separate systems of imperial law and military competition, and to continue opening the resources, labour and markets of the former colonies to free trade competition in the expanding global market dominated by them.[40]

In *American Empire*, Neil Smith gives one of the best recent histories of the rise to hegemony of the United States in this global field of public law and political institutions. For him, the resurgence of US global influence after 1945 is the second moment of the expansion of US informal imperialism (the first was the expansion from 1898 to the failure of the League of Nations). This second moment failed to become global because it was blocked by the socialist Second World and the defeat of the US in Vietnam. The third moment began with the collapse of the Soviet Union in 1989, the resurgence of US 'global' power in the 1990s, and the successful extension of informal neo-liberal imperialism around the globe, precisely by means of these global institutions:[41]

> To the extent that the geography of the American century remains obscure, the origins, outlines, possibilities, and limits of what today is called globalization will remain obscure. There is no way to understand where the global shifts of the last twenty years came from or where they will lead without understanding how, throughout the twentieth century, U.S. corporate, political, and military power mapped an emerging empire.

The imperial character of the World Bank and the IMF can be seen in the unequal power of the G8 states and transnational corporations; the policies of 'structural adjustment' they impose on subaltern states; the scandalous increase in inequalities, debt and dependency of subaltern peoples in the post-colonial period; and the continual direct and indirect military intervention to prop up repressive regimes and topple those who support local democracy – all in the name of freedom. [42]

---

40 Antje, *Imperialism, Sovereignty*, 196–235, and Harvey, *The New Imperialism*.

41 Smith, *American Empire*, 4–25. This is also roughly the chronology of Bacevich, *American Empire*, which was published a little earlier, from a conservative perspective.

42 For a short introduction to these enduring features of the present world order, see Jeremy Seabrook, *The No-Nonsense Guide to World Poverty,* Toronto: New Internationalist, 2003, James Petras and Henry Veltmeyer, *Globalization Unmasked: Imperialism in the 21st Century* (London, 2001), and, from the inside, Joseph Stiglitz, *Globalization and its Discontents* (London: Allen Lane, 2002). For the paramountcy of the great imperial powers in the World Trade Organization, which was introduced in 1995 as a form of 'global governance', see Amrita Narlikar, *The World Trade Organization*, (Oxford, 2005). Robert Fisk, in *The Great War for Civilization* (New York, 2005), and Derek Gregory, *The Colonial Present* (Oxford, 2005), show the seamless continuity between formal colonial imperialism over the Middle East in the first half of the twentieth century and informal imperialism in the second half, including the present Iraq and Afghanistan wars.

Alex Callinicos concludes from another perspective that it is 'naïve' to think that these global institutions could be the basis of a non-imperial alternative.[43] My point is somewhat similar. Several features of the legal and political institutions of the international system of states and the newer institutions of global governance are part of contemporary imperialism, not in any fleeting way, but, rather, the carefully designed instruments of the exercise of informal hegemony over subaltern actors. The public law and low intensity democratic institutions of the non-European states were imposed by the former colonial powers and modified and continued by local, dependent elites during decolonisation and post colonialism, and thus 'imperial' in the traditional sense of imposed on the people who are subject to them rather than under their shared, democratic authority of self-rule. The various regimes of public international law and the corresponding 'global' institutions that now govern the access of post colonial peoples to their own resources, as well as their subalternised forms of political and economic arrangements, are also imperial in that they have been developed without the former colonial peoples who are subject to them (and subjectified by them) having an authoritative and effective democratic say over them. These imperial features of existing public law and practices of governance should not be the accepted ground of criticism of imperialism, but the objects of sustained, democratic criticism by those who are oppressed and exploited by them.[44]

4. Kantian Imperialism

I want to address the question of why the critics of the new imperialism do not bring the system of states and global institutions into question and examine them as constitutive features of contemporary imperialism. My answer is that the basic language of description of the global order they employ makes it very difficult to see these imperial features. Any language of disclosure of an object domain reveals certain aspects of the phenomena it brings to language at the expense of concealing other aspects. All languages are aspectival in this sense. The language they use tends to conceal, and to represent in non-imperial terms, precisely the imperial aspects of the present that I have been trying to uncover and call into question. This would not be so important if this language were just one among many used to discuss the world order and its historical trajectory. But this is not the case. It is a hegemonic language, not only of mainstream academic reflection on the world order, but also of much of the public discussion, whether the public work for or against the present world order, and whether their acceptance of it is normative, pragmatic, or habitual.

---

43 Alex Callinicos, *Against the Third Way* (Cambridge: Polity, 2002). See also the reply to David Held's recent formulation of cosmopolitan democracy, *Global Covenant*, by Patrick Bond, 'Top Down or Bottom Up? A Reply', and Held's response, in Held, (ed.), *Debating Globalization* (Cambridge: Polity, 2005).

44 In their recent introduction to globalisation, Jurgen Osterhammel and Niels Peterson, *Globalization: A Short History*, (London, 2005), go a considerable distance in bringing the imperial features of globalisation back into the central debate. I discuss this section in more detail in 'The Imperialism of Modern Constitutional Democracy', in Loughlin and Walker, eds., *The Paradox of Constitutionalism*, 315–338.

This hegemonic language comprises three very general sub-languages and their various iterations over the long imperial age. The first two are: a normative and juridical language of an international system of constitutional states and a social scientific language (and philosophy of history) of the system's world historical progress through stages of development from savagery to civilisation, or through stages of 'modernisation'. The third sub-language (which I discuss in section 6), is the language of self-determination of peoples. Although the first two languages have a variety of articulations in different traditions of European and North American theory and policy, and, in the twentieth century, non-European-American theory and policy, one of the most influential and presumptively universal accounts of this normative ideal and set of processes is given by Immanuel Kant in *Idea for a Universal History with a Cosmopolitan Purpose* (1784) and *Perpetual Peace: A Philosophical Sketch* (1795). I would like to use it as an exemplar of the general kind of meta-narrative these two languages in their various iterations narrate in different ways. Kant's formulation gives particularly clear and uncompromising expression to many of the central features of the classic modern imperial meta-narrative (except for the third part of it, self-determination, which is grafted on to it during the decolonisation struggles of the nineteenth and twentieth centuries).[45]

In these two short texts in practical philosophy, Kant combined two of the most influential products of the European Enlightenment: a social theory consisting of the stages of universal historical development of all peoples and societies, with Europeans at the highest and most developed stage; and, a normative or juridical theory of the just and final ordering of all people and societies that would come about at the end of the historical development. It pictures a just and universal post-colonial world of identical, free and independent constitutional states under public international law, opened to capitalism and free trade, and governed informally by a 'league' of the advanced states, that is nonetheless the particular historical product of European colonial imperialism.

The normative theory is laid out in three definitive articles of *Perpetual Peace.* Firstly, the only right ordering of all of humanity globally is the gradual establishment

45 I have discussed the various historical and contemporary formulations of this kind of story of modernisation from Locke through the eighteenth century to the present in various works. For a recent summary of the central imperial features of these ways of thinking about the world order as the development of global modernity see Mark Salter, *Barbarians and Civilization in International Law* (London: Pluto Press, 2002), and, from a post-colonial perspective, Bill Aschcroft, *Post-Colonial Transformation* (London: Routledge, 2001), 82–104. Kant locates his own imperial narrative relative to the structure of other early modern and Enlightenment narratives at *Universal History* 51–53. For a more detailed analysis, see Tully, 'The Kantian Idea of Europe: Cosmopolitan and Critical Perspective', *The Idea of Europe* A. Pagden (ed.) (Cambridge: Cambridge University Press, 2003), 331–58, and *Strange Multiplicity* (Cambridge: Cambridge University Press, 1995). The theories of Hegel, Marx and Mill could be used to illustrate a similar narrative structure of the two languages, with, or course, specific internal variations, as Salter and others have shown, but I choose Kant's because it his particular fusion of developmental and juridical universalism that have become so influential since 1945 in our field. All references to Kant, *Political Writings*, Reiss, (ed.) (Cambridge: Cambridge University Press, 1991).

of European-style, identical republican or constitutional states that legally recognise individuals as negatively free, formally equal and substantively unequal, and dependent on a single system of laws and representative government. Secondly, these 'republican' constitutional states are formally equal and sovereign, and they form a world system of states subject to a set of universal international laws. The system of laws is enforced by a 'league' or 'federation' of the most advanced European-style states that use primarily 'financial power', and military power if needed, to protect their members and bring other, less-developed and formerly colonised states into the federation over time. Thirdly, each state has a duty of cosmopolitan hospitality to open its borders to the cosmopolitan right of voluntary 'commerce' and free trade of other nations, even if the imperial powers initially abuse this right, as Kant acknowledges they do. This duty is enforceable by the league.[46] Finally, although constitutional states cannot intervene in other *constitutional states* unless they break down or close their doors to free trade, Kant emphasises in no uncertain terms that the league, or any single constitutional state, has the right to intervene militarily into any society that has not reached the state of a 'civil constitution' of European states, which is thus by definition posited as in a 'lawless state of nature', and impose a western-style constitutional order on it.[47]

The social theory of universal historical development in the earlier *Universal History* explains how this normative order gradually comes into being over the centuries. Development is guaranteed by 'nature', who works through the unintended consequences of competition of individuals and states; what Kant calls 'asocial sociability'. The main form of asocial sociability used by nature to develop the capacities of the human species towards a world system of states and perpetual peace is 'warfare':[48]

> Wars, tense and unremitting military preparations, and the resultant distress which every state must eventually feel within itself, even in the midst of peace – these are the means by which nature drives nations to make initially imperfect attempts, but finally, after many devastations, upheavals and even complete inner exhaustion of their powers, to take the step which reason could have suggested to them without so many sad experiences – that of abandoning the lawless state of savagery and entering a federation of peoples, even the smallest, could expect to derive its security.

As he explains in systematic detail in the First Supplement to *Perpetual Peace*, nature works especially through the wars of European competitive expansion and colonisation in order to, firstly, spread people around the planet, moving the lower and savage peoples to more inhospitable climates as they move them off their traditional territories; secondly, Europeans spread and impose European law by

46 Kant, *Perpetual Peace: A Philosophical Sketch*, 99–108. There is a fair degree of indeterminacy in all three universal articles in Kant's various formulations in different texts and so in the interpretation of them over the last two hundred years in different circumstances. I suspect that this indeterminacy and ambiguity is part of the explanation of its continuing hold on the modern imagination that it shaped so profoundly.

47 *Perpetual Peace*, 98, introductory note to the three definitive articles.

48 *Universal History*, 47.

means of colonisation; and, thirdly, they spread commerce, an ethos of competitive individualism, and the pacifying relations of free trade and economic interdependency to the rest of the world.[49]

These three features then lead to more wars of competition and development, but they gradually lead to the formation of the league to resolve wars among states, first among European states. These processes lead to the gradual replacement of military competition among states by economic competition, which is spread by 'cosmopolitan right' and 'mutual self-interest', so that 'the spirit of commerce sooner or later takes hold of every people'.[50] These three 'natural' globalising processes work along with the right of the league to intervene militarily in pre-constitutional states, or in constitutional states that break down into 'anarchy', violate contract law, or close their doors to foreign commerce, and impose a civil constitution on them. But the preferred instrument of the league is the use of economic sanctions once states are subject to global economic interdependency.[51] These processes move the world progressively towards the normative ideal of identical constitutional states, bound together by commerce and universal public international laws, and governed by the league of united states. That is, the natural mechanism described in the developmental social theory 'guarantees' the 'progress' towards the normative telos:[52]

> In this way, nature guarantees perpetual peace by the actual mechanism of human inclinations [asocial sociability]. And while the likelihood of its being attained is not sufficient to enable us to prophesy the future theoretically, it is enough for practical purposes. It makes it our duty to work our way towards this goal, which is more than an empty chimera.

As we can see from this remarkably influential picture of world historical development and normative universalism, the period of European colonial imperialism is an absolutely *necessary* stage in the development of the human species towards the end state of a world system of European-style states bound together by global economic relations and international law and governed by a league of states exercising post-colonial informal imperial rule. Although European colonial imperialism is necessary, its actual, excessively violent wars cannot be justified in terms of Kant's three universal principles. As we have seen, Europeans are perfectly justified in coercively imposing western law on non-Europeans if they fail to submit voluntarily

---

49 *Perpetual Peace* 108–14. This is repeated from *Universal History*, where he explains that Europeans 'will probably legislate for all other continents', 52.

50 *Perpetual Peace*, 114.

51 *Perpetual Peace*, 96, 98. For the league's (or a single state's) defence of contracts against 'unjust enemies' who violate them, see *Metaphysics of Morals*, section 60 (6: 349), in Immanuel Kant, *Practical Philosophy* (Cambridge: Cambridge University Press, 1999), 486–487.

52 *Perpetual Peace*, 114. This duty to work towards the Europeanisation of the globe is performed by exchanging public reasons about public policy in accordance with this normative and developmental framework (*Perpetual Peace* 114–5, further explained in *What is Enlightenment*?)

to western colonial law or to move off their traditional territories when the colonisers arrive, but Kant roundly condemns the excessive violence of European expansion as unjust and inhospitable.[53] Even though it is unjust, it is *necessary*: it is means by which nature herself raises humans up the stages of historical development. Unlike utilitarian defenders of imperialism, the ends never *justify* the excessively violent means for the deontological Kant.[54] Nature does what is necessary through humans' unjust actions.[55]

Next, although the excessive violence of European imperial expansion is unjust, it cannot be resisted. According to Kant, there is an absolute duty to obey the law, no matter how unjust it may be or how unjust its original imposition. It is even a duty not to look into the origins of a colonial state, let alone resist it. The unjust foundations of any state, colonial or not, or of the imperial world order itself, cannot be enquired into with a view to challenging either, or revolting against them, no matter how violently they are imposed or how intolerably unjust they may be in the present.[56] The question of whether the people agreed to the fundamental constitution and sovereign authority 'are completely futile arguments' and 'a menace to the state'.[57] The absolute acceptance of the foundations of the European-imposed world order and the absolute duty not to resist this order, by a group within a state or a state within the system, constitute an 'idea expressed as a practical principle of reason, requiring men to obey the legislative authority now in power, irrespective of its origin'.[58] Each state has the right to crush a rebellion within a state and the league to intervene if the rebellion gets out of control.[59] The reason for this conclusion is that unsociable humans must have the law coercively imposed upon them by a master in order to establish the basis for the development of a lawful and rightful order in the first place.[60] Just resistance to the law or the sovereign authority, even against the 'most intolerable misuse of supreme power', is thus 'self-contradictory'.[61] Resistance to the coercive imposition of the law just shows that the resistors are exercising their asocial 'lawless freedom': that is, their antagonistic dispositions

---

53 *Perpetual Peace*, 106–8.

54 *Metaphysics of Morals in Political Writings*, 173. For Kant, humans can be expected to exercise coercion within the bounds of morality once they have reached the higher end of the stages of development. They are 'civilized' but not yet 'moral', so they will in fact act unjustly in conquering the non-European world and constructing it in accord with his legal and political plan. *Universal History*, 49.

55 Marx presents a somewhat similar argument that the wars of imperial expansion are unjust but necessary in his writings on India. More recently, Max Boot has presented a similar argument in the *The Savage Wars of Peace*. This influential liberal defence of US imperialism is a history of US wars of intervention since 1890 and an exhortation to see them as savage yet necessary to economic freedom, progress and eventual peace among all liberal democratic states.

56 *Metaphysics of Morals*, 143–5, 162, 173, 175.

57 *Metaphysic of Morals*, 143.

58 Ibid., 143.

59 Ibid., 143–5, *Perpetual Peace*, 105, 114.

60 *Universal History*, 45–6.

61 *Metaphysics of Morals*, 145.

have not yet been sufficiently socialised and moralised into commercial and other forms of individualistic competitiveness within the imposed legal structure of the three definitive articles.[62]

In summary, Kant combined two very powerful imperial stories: a presumptively universal and Eurocentric narrative of historical development or modernisation and an equally universal and Eurocentric juridical theory of global justice. The Kantian theory or meta-narrative is imperial in the classically modern sense. Firstly, while it does not justify the excessive violence and pillage of European colonial imperialism and of the ongoing remaking of the world in the political, legal and economic image of European state formation (even one particular image of it), it is presented as the universally necessary and irresistible path of development and modernisation. Secondly, it presents the post-colonial phase of development as a universal system of formally identical European state forms, abstracted from their continuing colonial relations of historical construction, deepening dependency and substantive inequality, *and* a system of informal imperial rule through the league, in a completely non-imperial vocabulary. It redescribes and occludes in these formal and abstract terms precisely the imperial features of the present that I have tried to recover in the previous sections. Thirdly, this particular story of progress and its goal are not only presented as universal and necessary, but also as obligatory; as something all rational human beings have a 'duty' to work towards.[63]

Fourthly, precisely because it is presented as universal, necessary and obligatory (that is, as a *meta*-narrative), it cannot recognise and respect any other of the plurality of narratives, traditions, or civilisations as equal yet different, and enter into a dialogue with them on equal footing. Rather, it always already captures other peoples in its own presumptively universal categories: as identical to European constitutional states, and so friends of peace and freedom, or 'lower peoples' somewhere down the developmental ladder (from 'barbarism' to 'culture' and 'morality'), and thus subject to imperial rule in some form or another. The 'lower peoples'' moral and rational capacities are less developed than the universalising rationalists and moralists at the higher stage.[64] The person who adopts this meta-narrative, as Kant's pupil Johann

62 *Idea for a Universal History*, 46, and *Perpetual Peace*, 113 where he explains that moral behaviour follows after an established constitutional order. See his remarks on the so-called 'lawless freedom' of Indigenous peoples as the exemplar of unjust and regressive resistance to the external imposition of law by individuals and lower states at: *PP* 102–103; and Tully, *Strange Multiplicity*, 79–82.

63 In 'Political Philosophy as a Critical Activity' (note 7 above) the tradition of critical history set out by Foucault in his last lecture, *What is Enlightenment?* He saw the central aim of this critical tradition to be, in direct reference to Kant, to challenge what is given to us as 'universal, necessary, and obligatory' by showing in it what is 'single, contingent and the product of arbitrary constraints'. For similar interpretations of Kantian imperialism, see Brett Bowden, 'In the Name of Progress and Peace, the standard of civilization and the universalizing project', *Alternatives*, 29, 1 (2004), 43–69, Thomas McCarthy, 'On the way to a world Republic: Kant on race and development', *Festschrift Zum 65: Geburststag von Karl Graf Ballestrem*, Verlag, forthcoming.

64 Kant depicts hunting and gathering indigenous peoples ('lawless savages') and the pastoral peoples (their existence 'scarcely … more valuable than that of their animals') at

Herder put it in response, cannot approach another people's way of life as an alternative horizon, thereby throwing their own into question, and experiencing human finitude and plurality, the beginning of insight and cross-cultural understanding. Rather, the exchange of public reasons takes place within this allegedly universal, necessary and obligatory worldview.[65]

5. Neo-Kantian imperialism

We are all familiar with how this dual language of universal norms and historical processes has been adopted and adapted in the Liberal and Marxist traditions, the social sciences, developmental studies, the policy communities of developed and developing states, international law, the League of Nations and the United Nations, and, as I have suggested, the description and exercise of US informal imperialism over the twentieth century.[66] One of the most influential post-Cold War reformulations of it, drawing explicitly on Kant, was presented by Francis Fukuyama in 1992.[67] By early 2005 it had clearly attained hegemonic status.[68]

The neo-Kantians today argue that they have made three major changes to the original Kantian story while retaining it universal, necessary and obligatory character. Firstly, they now see the so-called processes of historical development and modernisation as 'dialectical' rather than linear, yet still leading in a general

---

the 'lawless' lowest stage and his contemporary Europeans as barely half way up the ladder: civilized but not yet moral (*Universal History*: 45, 47–9).

65 Johann Herder, Kant's pupil, presented scathing criticisms of Kant's imperialism: See F. M. Barnard, *Herder on Nationality, Humanity and History* (Montreal: McGill Queens, 2003). For Burke's criticisms, see Uday Singh Mehta, *Liberalism and Empire: A Study in 19th Century British Liberal Thought* (Chicago: University of Chicago Press, 1999). For Hans-Georg Gadamer's classic criticism of Kantian universalism as monological and closed to the other, see *Truth and Method* (New York: Continuum, 1999), 346–62. There is now a vast literature on Kant's imperialism and racism. See Brett Bowden, 'In the Name of Progress and Peace, the Standard of Civilization and the Universalizing Project', *Alternatives*, 29, 1 (2004), 43–69, Robert Bernasconi, 'Kant as an unfamiliar source of racism', *Philosophers on Race: Critical essays*, Julie Ward (ed.) (Oxford: Basil Blackwell, 2002), 145–66, Thomas McCarthy, 'On the Way to a World Republic: Kant on Race and Development', *Festschrift Zum 65: Geburststag von Karl Graf Ballestrem* (Verlag, forthcoming), Barry Hindess, 'The Very Idea of Universal History', (forthcoming), and Michael Murphy, 'Civilization', Paper presented at the *First Nations Second Thoughts* Conference, forthcoming.

66 For the global spread of these two languages over the last two centuries, see Vincent Tucker, 'The Myth of Development: A Critique of a Eurocentric Discourse', *Critical Development Theory*, ed. Ronaldo Munck and Denis O'Hearn (London: Zed Books, 1999), 1–26, Ronaldo Munck, 'Deconstructing Development Discourses: of Impasses, Alternatives, and Politics', Ibid., 196–210, Salter, *Barbarians*, and Gilbert Rist, *The History of Development from Western Origins to Global Faith* (London: Zed Books, 1997).

67 Francis Fukuyama, *The End of History and the Last Man* (New York: 1992).

68 For a graphic illustration of its broad and enthusiastic endorsement, see 'Fukuyama was right: We've come a long way', *The Globe and Mail*, 1 January 2005, A14.

way to a similar general universal normative endpoint.[69] The processes continue to promote the conditions of peace yet they also make its attainment more difficult. Furthermore, modernisation is not imposed 'unilaterally' onto a receptive non-European world, but is 'dialectical' in the sense that non-European peoples interact with these processes and modify them somewhat, making the overall direction less linear. A somewhat similar change has occurred in imperialism studies since the Second World War; from unilateral accounts of imperial rule to more interactive and agonistic accounts of hegemon-subaltern relationships, yet without the neo-Kantian faith that is leading to peace.[70]

Secondly, Kant's account of sovereignty has been modified to some extent by globalisation and multilayered global governance through the Bretton Woods institutions, changes in international law, the rise of powerful multinational corporations, and the role of soft-norm creation by non-governmental organisations.[71] This has given rise to a more 'differential and polycentric' form of global rule. However, they do not describe this as informal imperialism as I have done. As I mentioned in the Introduction, they present this form of rule as 'non-imperial' by contrasting it with a centralised world empire, as if this is the only form of imperialism, just exactly as Kant does, in contrasting his 'league' with a world state-empire.[72]

Thirdly, they argue that neo-Kantian universalism is more open to pluralism and democratic deliberation over the norms of association than Kant's view that all states must be identical in constitutional form. However, all other civilisations and traditions are characterised as 'particulars' within the 'general' or 'universal' framework of Kant's three definitive articles (the foundational cosmopolitan public law). In so far as their members can democratically negotiate some form of 'minority' recognition within this global empire (and this varies among the authors), they must do so within a presumptively universal framework for the exchange of public reasons over the norms of association (discourse ethics).[73]

---

69 James Bohman and Matthias Lutz-Bachman, 'Introduction', *Perpetual Peace: Essays on Kant's Cosmopolitan Ideal* (Cambridge MA: MIT Press, 1997), 1–25. The Introduction is a summary of the main themes presented in the chapters of the volume.

70 Ibid. 9–12. For the change in imperialism studies, see Mommsen, *Theories of Imperialism* 70–141. For a critical survey and refutation of the neo-Kantian thesis of progress to 'democratic peace', see Andrew Lawrence. 'Paradigm Wars and the "Democratic Peace", *Political Knowledge and Social Inquiry*, R. Lebow and M. Lichbach (eds) (Detroit: University of Michigan Press, 2006).

71 Ibid. 12–15. This modification is deeply indebted to the scholarship of David Held (see 'Cosmopolitan Democracy and Global Order', Ibid. 235–52).

72 Ibid. 14, *Perpetual Peace*, 102–3. Kant changed his mind on this, seeing the league as a kind of negative surrogate for a world government that he seemed to have endorsed earlier. Habermas is one of the few neo-Kantians in the volume to argue for a kind of world republic at the UN to enforce international human rights: 'Kant's Idea of Perpetual Peace with the benefit of two hundred years of hindsight', Ibid, 113–54.

73 Ibid. 15–18. In his recent writing, David Held, *Global Covenant* (2003) is particularly concerned to draw a sharp boundary around cultural rights, drawing more than before on Brian Barry's liberalism. And, Axel Honneth, in his exchange with Nancy Fraser, has argued against the recognition of cultural or legal diversity and for the 'integration' and 'individuation' of

In summary, these three modifications change the internal composition of the Kantian language to bring it in line with post-colonial informal imperialism and its dispersed institutions, international laws and particularities, while retaining its overall imperial character for the four reasons given above.[74] In addition, the Kantian and neo-Kantian languages both have a tendency to serve to justify imperialism in practice when they are adopted as the language of foreign policy in the context of deformalised international law. During the Cold War Hans Morgenthau argued that it could not but lead to 'a pax Americana or American Imperium in which the political interests and legal values of the United States are identified with universal values'.[75] Koskenniemi argues that the neo-Kantian project today has the same consequence in practice, leading either to a 'rational imperialism', where the decision-maker identifies his or her preferences with the abstract, universal values of the meta-narrative (moral and just) and others' with 'mere preferences' (the ethics of a particular community), or to 'cynical imperialism', where the decision-maker does not identify his preferences with universal values, but, having no alternative for justifying his or her actions, acts as if they are.[76]

6. The fourth critics: self-determination, democratisation and imperialism

The fourth set of critics see the length and breadth of informal imperialism and often the layers of imperial relationships laid down during the age of colonial imperialism. In response, they argue that the language and practice of popular sovereignty or the self-determination of peoples and democracy offer a genuinely non-imperial and anti-imperial alternative. If subaltern peoples and indigenous peoples could only exercise their right of self-determination, through international law and reform

---

humanity into his formulation of the neo-Kantian universal framework: Honneth and Fraser, *Recognition or Redistribution* (London: Verso, 2003), 160–89.

74 Both Habermas and Honneth attempt to respond to objections that the neo-Kantian global project is imperial in their chapters in the volume. They do not address the four reasons presented here. For a recent statement of my fourth reason, see Bruno Latour, 'Whose Cosmos, Which Cosmopolitics?', *Common Knowledge*, 10, 3 (Fall 2004), 450–63. For the failure of this general approach to recognise and accommodate democratic pluralism within states, let alone among different political societies, see Stephen Tierney, *Constitutional Law and National Pluralism* (Oxford, 2004). For the argument that this kind of approach fails to take into account a democratically grounded legal and political pluralism beyond the state, see Neil Walker, 'The Idea of Constitutional Pluralism', *Modern Law Review*, 65, 3 (2002), and Vito Breda, 'A European Constitution in a Multinational Europe or a Multinational Constitution for Europe?', *European Law Journal*, 12, 3 (2006), 330–344. For objections to Habermas' formulation of the constitutionalisation of international law, see Walker, 'Making a World of Difference?' Payrwo Shabani, (ed.) *Multiculturalism and Law*, 219–34.

75 In Koskenniemi, *The Gentle Civilizer*, 482.

76 Ibid. 483–93. He argues that the theories of both Habermas and Rawls are imperial in this pragmatic sense. For the view that Rawls' *The Law of Peoples* is a justification of US imperial foreign policy, see Jeffrey Paris, 'After Rawls', *Social Theory and Practice*, 28, 4 (October 2002), 679–700. For similar objections , see Bond, 'Top Down or Bottom Up', Deppe, 'Habermas's Manifesto', and Benjamin Barber, 'Global Governance from Below', in Held, (ed.), *Debating Globalization.*

of the UN or through revolution and liberation, they would free themselves from European and American imperialism. This view is widely expressed in the South and the Third World. It is also advanced in a modified way by critical international law theorists, who rightly see the new 'democratic norm' of international law (and the 'right to democracy') as the extension of the right of self-determination. On this view, a state would be recognised under international law only if it were democratic, or democratising, and if it recognised the right of self-determination for any peoples within its territory. To be able to exercise the powers of self-determination or to be able to organise as a democracy is to be free of imperialism on this view.[77]

Unfortunately, these two theses do not stand up to scrutiny. The protection of self-determination and democratic government under international law and the exercise of powers of self-determination and democratic self-rule are internal to informal post-colonial imperialism, at least in their present form. They are literally the two main ways by which the conduct of subaltern actors is governed by informal imperial rule: that is, through supporting, chanelling and constraining their self-determining and democratic freedoms.

During the early years of decolonisation, one of the first leaders to see the internal relation between informal imperial rule, self-determination and democratisation was Woodrow Wilson. He argued that most colonised peoples should be able to exercise the right of self-determination and democratic self-rule, but that the more advanced democratic states had the responsibility to educate the elites, train the military and intervene militarily from time to time to guide the self-determination of former colonial peoples along its proper stages of development to openness to free trade and western-style democratisation.[78] The United States was the world leader in this form of enlightened rule because of its long experience of this kind of rule by means of the Monroe Doctrine over the former colonies of Central and South America. The US also had the responsibility to intervene militarily to protect the decolonising peoples from their two main foes: the old European colonial powers who claimed the colonies as their closed spheres of influence and the reactionary internal leaders and movements who tried to close their economies to foreign domination and build up economic and democratic self-reliance through controlled trade (as the US has always done in its own case).[79] In this way, Wilson was able to respond to the demands for self-determination of colonised peoples, except for the indigenous peoples of the fourth world,[80] yet to channel informally their exercise of self-determination into state building and economic development within the existing imperial system. Of

77 This is the third sub-language that I mentioned in section 4. The language of self-rule and self-determination has a long and complex history in Europe and the Third World prior to and in relation to the developmental and normative languages that Kant combined.

78 This responsibility of the more advanced states to guide the former colonies in their exercise of self-determination was a continuation of the nineteenth century 'duty to civilise' and its application in the Mandate System of the League of Nations (Antje, *Imperialism, Sovereignty*, 245–68).

79 Woodrow Wilson, 'An Address to the Senate', January 27, 1917. See Bacevich, *American Empire*, 114–115.

80 Tully, 'The Struggles of Indigenous peoples for and of freedom', *Political Theory and the Rights of Indigenous Peoples*, ed. Paul Patton, D. Ivison and D. Sanders (Cambridge

course, the granting of the right of self-determination to colonised peoples was a repudiation of Kant's non-resistance theory, However, it provided a normative justification and explanation from another western tradition – popular sovereignty and self-determination – for the transition from colonialism to post colonialism, something Kant's theory did not provide, while retaining the constitutive features of Kant's two normative-juridical and developmental-historical languages. Moreover, Wilson expressed the right of self-determination and the responsibility of informal imperial guidance in terms of the distinctive US tradition of the Monroe Doctrine, its corollaries, the doctrine of opening doors to free trade and democracy, and the ever expanding frontiers.[81] In Chalmers Johnson's words:[82]

> Wilson … provided an idealistic grounding for American imperialism, what in our own time would become a 'global mission' to 'democratize' the world. More than any other figure, he provided the intellectual foundations for an interventionist foreign policy, expressed in humanitarian and democratic rhetoric. Wilson remains the godfather of those contemporary ideologists who justify American power in terms of exporting democracy.

Major-General Smedley Butler, the famous Marine in charge of implementing the Wilsonian doctrine of military intervention and self-determination, called it by its more familiar name, 'gangster capitalism':[83]

> I spent 33 years and four months in active service … I served in all commissioned ranks from Second Lieutenant to Major-General. And during that time, I spent most of my time being a high-class muscle man for Big Business, for Wall Street and the Bankers. In short, I was a racketeer, a gangster for capitalism … I helped make Mexico, especially Tampico, safe for American oil interests in 1914. I helped make Haiti and Cuba a decent place for the National City Bank boys to collect revenues in. I helped in the raping of half a dozen Central American republics for the benefit of Wall Street … I helped to purify Nicaragua for the international banking house of Brown Brothers in 1909–1912. I brought light to

University Press, 2000) and J. Anthony Hall, *The Fourth World and the American Empire,* (McGill Queens, 2004).

81 As I mentioned earlier, Wilson saw no contradiction in combining self-determination and democratisation with continual informal imperial intervention (military, economic and educational). William A. Williams presented this as the great contradiction in the Wilson doctrine a generation ago, but the present generation of US historians converge on the concordance of Wilson's writings and later US policy: that is, in what Andrew Bacevich calls a grand strategy of freedom as openness to free trade dominated by US economic and military power (*American Empire* 46–51, 115–6). For the nineteenth-century development of this tradition on which Wilson drew, see the classic study of Albert K. Weinburg, *Manifest Destiny: A Study of Nationalist Expansion in American History* (Johns Hopkins University Press, 1935). For the role of wars against Native Americans (Kant's lawless savages) in the development of this tradition and military intervention up to Wilson and to the war in Vietnam, see Richard Drinon, *Facing West: The Metaphysics of Indian Hating and Empire Building* (University of Minnesota Press, 1979), 2005.

82 Johnson, *Sorrows of Empire*, 51. As Weinberg shows, the policy of democratising the world and acting as a global policeman predates Wilson.

83 Smedley Butler, 'On Interventionism', www.fas.org/man/smedley.htm. Accessed 15 March 2006.

> the Dominican Republic for American sugar interests in 1916. In China I helped to see that Standard Oil went its way unmolested.

At the same time, decolonising elites *and* radicals in the former colonies adopted the language of self-determination to justify decoloniation and polity-building, but they were constrained – by the plenitude of overt and covert means of informal imperialism and the deeper dependency relations that continued through decoloniation – to exercise their political, legal and economic powers in accord with the latest versions of the developmental and normative sub-languages of the shared narrative of modernisation.[84]

> Far from [Benedict] Anderson's image of peoples whose inchoate dreams finally found form in nationalism, the social and political movements of the decolonized nation-states have been highly various in their dreams, and have been repeatedly forced to attempt to fit their dreams and goals into the limits of the nation-state form, to become nations or parts of a nation, content with local sovereignty and the project of national development.

Throughout the Cold War this way of governing the former colonies through the 'guided' exercise of self-determination was extended to the fight against communist and socialist movements from Franklin Roosevelt and Truman to Kennedy and Johnson. Today, a very similar tripartite language is employed. The league or 'coalition' of the US and its allies are said to bring free trade and democratisation, to support the self-determination of peoples subject to tyranny and 'closed societies' by military intervention and economic sanctions against 'failed', 'rogue' or 'outlaw' states.[85]

The kind of imposed or constrained democracy that is developed in these relationships of self-determination and dependency are not only 'unstable' (as we saw in section 3), but also 'low intensity democracy'. This is a form of elite

---

84 John Kelly and Martha Kaplan, 'My Ambition is much higher than independence: US power, the UN world, the nation-state, and their critics', in Duara, ed. *Decolonization*, 131–51, 142. See also William R. Louis and R. Robinson, 'Empire Preverv'd: How the Americans put anti-communism before anti-imperialism', Ibid. 152–61, and Michael Adas, 'Contested Hegemony: the great war and the Afro-Asian assault on the civilizing mission', Ibid., 64–78 for the spread of the languages of developmental and self-determination throughout the Third World. This collection contains an excellent set of case studies on the co-constitution of self-determination, democratisation and informal imperialism. For the military, economic and educational means employed to exercise informal imperial power, see William Blum, *Killing Hope* (Monroe ME: Common Courage Press, 2004).

85 This is the main thesis of Simpson, *Great Powers and Outlaw States*. President Bush, 'The National Security Strategy of the United States of America' (September 2002 www.whitehouse.gov/nsc/nss.pdf) is a now classic formulation of this US global strategy of military intervention and the extension of bases around the world all for the sake of market freedom, openness, and imposed democratisation throughout the world and against its latest enemies. Although the document failed to mention the support and guidance of self-determination, this was quickly remedied in the President's 2003 address on the support the war in Iraq was giving to Iraqi self-determination: 'Iraqi Democracy will succeed', www.nytimes.com/2003/politics/06Text-Bush.html. These longstanding imperial themes were repeated in his second acceptance speech in 2004.

representative democracy dependent on foreign economic and military relations, and in tension with the more participatory democratic aspirations of the majority of the population. As the authors who introduced this term state: 'By invoking the American counterinsurgency catch-phrase 'Low Intensity Conflict', it is our intention to show that perhaps more than in any time in the recent past, it is now that the struggle to define 'democracy' has become a major ideological battle'.[86] As area scholars of recent global governance, democratisation and the creation of civil societies by the World Bank, IMF, transnational corporations and many aid agencies have shown, the imperial civilising project of opening the former colonies to free trade, labour discipline and market-oriented individual behaviour from indirect colonial rule to the beginnings of controlled self-rule under the Mandate System continues apace today.[87]

A related trend appears to exist in international law. A norm of democratic governance was introduced by Thomas Franck and Anne-Marie Slaughter towards the end of the Cold War enjoining that a state should be recognised only if its internal constitution is liberal-democratic and based on popular sovereignty. Frank, somewhat like Fukuyama, argues that this international norm is emerging out of self-determination, decolonisation, human rights and the criterion that elections lend legitimacy, and is almost universally celebrated. In addition, it is a norm that expressly 'opens the stagnant political economies of states to economic, social and cultural, as well as political, development'.[88] In short, it is a neo-Kantian reformulation of Kant's three definitive articles and developmental theory, with the addition of the constrained right of self-determination and the Wilsonian language of freedom as openness to global markets. Anne Marie Slaughter explicitly draws the connection to Kant and states the universal norm of legitimacy in the following imperial way:[89]

> [Liberal democratic states] are defined broadly as states with juridical equality, constitutional protection of individual rights, representative republican governments, and market economies based on private property rights. 'Non-liberal states', by contrast, are defined as those states lacking these characteristics.

In her fascinating study of the emergence of this norm of informal neo-liberal imperialism, Susan Marks goes on to show how 'social democratic' neo-Kantians, discussed above, develop their theories out of the same tradition but 'deepen' the narrow commitment to 'low intensity democracy' of neo-liberal imperialism.[90] If I

---

86 Gills, et al. 'Low Intensity Democracy', 52. Their general thesis is based on studies of Guatemala, Argentina, the Philippines, Korea, Chile, Nicaragua and Haiti.

87 Alison Ayer, 'Demystifying Democratization: the Global Constitution of Neo-liberal Polities in Africa', *Third World Quarterly* 27(2) (2006), 321–38, for a detailed study of informal imperialism in a number of African states today.

88 Thomas Franck, 'The Emerging Right to Democratic Governance', *American Journal of International Law*, 86, 1992, 46–95.

89 Anne-Marie Slaughter, 'Law among Liberal States: Liberal Internationalism and the Act of State Doctrine', *Columbia Law Review*, 92 (1992), 1909.

90 Susan Marks, *The Riddle of All Constitutions* (Oxford: Oxford University Press, 1999). While she is critical of the cosmopolitan democrats, she does not call their form of neo-

may put it this way, these two wings of liberal democratic international law replicate the two wings of informal US imperialism.

After criticising the cosmopolitan democrats for a self-limiting definition of global democratisation, Marks argues for extending the norm of democratisation further by deepening the commitment to 'democratic inclusiveness'. However, this critical response would have to take into account the underlying imperial features of the state and international system into which peoples would be included if it were to avoid assimilation and subordination. It cannot be by simply extending the paramount forms of neo-liberal or social-democratic representative democracy further that imperialism will be challenged, for they are imposed forms of law and democracy, controlled indirectly by the techniques of informal imperialism. Rather, it would be by promoting diverse 'high intensity' forms of local and global democracy, self-determination and legal pluralism that world leaders would enable the people subject to these low intensity structures of law and politics to bring them under their shared democratic authority, without impoverishing and disempowering forms of dependency and threats of intervention.[91]

In summary, the dominant forms of representative democracy, self-determination and democratisation promoted through international law are not alternatives to imperialism, but, rather, the means through which informal imperialism operates against the wishes of the majority of the population of the post-colonial world.[92] The genuine non-imperial alternatives are more participatory democratic forms of democracy and self-determination that either draw on persisting *non*-imperial legal and political practices and traditions or create new ones.

7. The fifth critics: post-colonialism, legal constructivism and interactive imperialism

The final critics I wish to discuss are the post-colonial critics of imperialism. Drawing on and extending the later work of Edward Said in *Culture and Imperialism* and the later work of Michel Foucault in 'The Subject and Power', they share much of the critical analysis I have presented above. They start from the premise that humans are 'field beings', always already in relationships of meaning, power and modes of relational subjectivity; and they see themselves as writing and acting *within and*

---

kantian 'imperial' even though it has the imperial characteristics of neo-liberal imperialism. She sees the emergence of the democratic norm as something new, in contrast to the norm that a state should be recognised independently of its constitution. But, the Kantian tradition has always had a 'civic constitution' criterion and has defined 'non-states', open to intervention, in contrast, as Kant does. In fact, the liberal imperialists of the interwar years anticipated this norm of liberal democratic orthodoxy in many respects (Jeanne Morefield, *Covenant Without Swords*, above).

91 For a similar criticism of the norm of liberal democracy in international law, see Jose E. Alvarez, 'Do Liberal States behave better? A critique of Slaughter's liberal theory', *European Journal of International Law*, 12, 2 (2001), 183–246.

92 Gills et al., *Low Intensity Democracy*, Introduction, and Seabrook, *The Guide to World Poverty*.

against the specific fields of informal imperial relationships of meaning, power and subjectification among hegemonic and subaltern actors.[93]

They argue that imperial relationships are not unilaterally and monologically imposed on passive subjects who submit to the logic of capitalist development and western juridification, as the Kantian narrative prescribes. Rather, like the theorists of 'interactive' and 'excentric' imperialism, they see imperial relationships as agonistic and, to a large extent, mutually constitutive. That is, hegemonic imperial actors and their legal and political institutions and instruments of informal rule, and the corresponding subaltern actors are mutually constituted by the historical interactions among them; from the initial rise of the West and the subalternisation of the colonial world out of the dispossession and exploitation of their resources and the resistances internal to these processes, down to the complex field of interaction today.[94]

Post-colonial critics are also critical of the theories of self-determination and liberation of the decolonising period in much the same way as I have been above. They argue that these narratives of decolonisation and 'liberation' occlude the emergence of informal imperialism and, secondly, reproduce the great script of subject/sovereign 'doubles' of the western tradition, rending post-colonial subjects 'conscripts' of modernity.[95] Further, they suggest that there is no unified 'self', either hegemon or subaltern, who could stand outside the fields of linguistic, legal, political, economic, military and cultural relations in which we find ourselves and 'determine' the relations that bear us, as the self-determination narrative presupposes. 'Hegemon' and 'subaltern' are multiplex: dispersed across complex, criss-crossing and overlapping fields of unequal and mutually constitutive relationships of interplay.

93 For a general survey of post-colonial writing on imperialism, see Bill Ashcroft, *Post-Colonial Transformation* (London: Routledge, 2001). For a succinct statement of the post-colonial approach to international relations and international law, see Taraki Barkawi and Mark Laffey, 'Retrieving the Imperial: Empire and International Relations', *Millennium*, 31, 1 (2002), 109–27. I also take the legal constructivists, represented by Stephen Toope, Martha Finnermore, Jutta Brunée and Antje Wiener in international law, and Neil Walker, Emilios Christodoulidis, Jo Shaw and Stephen Tierney in European public law, to share many of the features of postcolonial analysis, even though they have not addressed the question of whether the field of study is 'imperial'. That is, they understand domestic, transnational and international law to be a network of relationships among unequally situated subjects of law (hegemons and subalterns of various kinds) who are able (to unequal extents) to negotiate and modify the laws to which they are subject *en passant*. Stephen Toope and Martha Finnermore, 'Alternatives to Legalization: Richer views of law and politics', *International Organization*, 55, 3 (Summer 2001), 743–58, Antje Wiener, 'The Dual Quality of Norms: Stability and Flexibility', *CRISPP*, forthcoming, Neil Walker, 'Legal Pluralism', Emilios Christodoulidis, 'Constitutional Irresolution: law and the faming of civil society', *European Law Journal*, 9, 4 (2003), 401–32, Jo Shaw, 'Postnational Constitutionalism in the European Union', *Journal of European Public Policy*, 1999, 579–97, Tierney, *Constitutional Law*.

94 Eric Wolf, *Europe and the People without History* (University of California Press, 1982) was one of the first to put world history in this way, although he drew heavily on earlier interactive accounts, such as Rosa Luxembourg and Eric Williams.

95 David Scott, *Conscripts of Modernity: the Tragedy of Colonial Enlightenment* (forthcoming). See also Said's development of these two criticisms in *Culture and Imperialism*. For a brief summary see Ashcroft, *Post-Colonial Transformation*, 1–18.

They are not conveniently located in the West and the Non-West or the North and South, but within and across these binary categories of colonial geography,[96] dividing subaltern (and hegemonic) societies into complex hegemonic-subaltern classes and ethnicities, and often mobilising local pre-colonization relationships of imperialism, quasi-imperialism and resistance.[97]

For post-colonial critics, the central feature of these multiple relationships of informal imperialism is the interaction or agonism between hegemons and subalterns. One of the discoveries of twentieth century theorists and policy-makers of both rule and resistance is that the subject (individuals and groups) is more effectively and economically governed *through* his or her own freedom – his or her own participation in relations of governance of production, consumption, militarisation, securitisation, leisure and so on – by incorporating degrees of subaltern legality (customary law), democracy, and self-determination into informal and indirect modes of governance of political and economic life. As we have seen in the previous section, this invention in the realm of governance developed out of indirect colonial rule and decolonisation and then spread to neo-liberal modes of governance domestically and globally.[98]

The implication of this for post-colonial writers is that there is always a limited range of possible ways of exercising one's freedom in accordance with the rules of any practice of governance – following the rules as closely as possible, acting differently, trying to modify them to some extent overtly or covertly, seeking to call them into question and negotiate them with the powers-that-be in the corresponding legal and political institutions, and, at the limit, confronting them directly in the recourse to non-violent or violent revolt. (From this perspective, the great theories of self-determination and independence focused on one type of revolt to the exclusion of all the other possible practices of freedom available to subaltern actors.)[99]

Thus, instead of being seen as the passive constructs of imperial processes of 'interpellation', as in Louis Althusser's account, subaltern subjects are seen, extending Said and Foucault, as 'interpolators', writing and acting back in a multiplicity of ways within fields of discursive and non-discursive relationships.[100]

96 Stephen Flusty, *De Coca-Colonization: Making the World from the Inside Out* (London: Routledge, 2003), Tully, *Strange Multiplicity*.

97 Taraki Barkawi and Mark Laffey argue that this thesis is a constitutive feature of Chomsky's analysis of imperialism as well (note 88 above).

98 For its employment within advanced liberal societies see Nikolas Rose, *Powers of Freedom* (Cambridge: 1999). Loughlin integrates governmentality into his account of public law in *Pure Theory* and Antje, *Imperialism*, treats its development with the international law and the civilizing project. For an overview of research in colonial and imperial history on these techniques of colonial governmentality, see Peter Pels, 'The Anthropology of Colonialism: Culture, History and the Emergence of Western Governmentality', *Annual Review of Anthropology*, 26 (1997), 163–83.

99 The classic sketch of this way of thinking about law and government is Michel Foucault, 'The Subject and Power' in *Michel Foucault: Power, The Essential Foucault, I,* New York, 1997, 326–49. The section on writing back in Edward Said's *Culture and Imperialism* (New York: Vintage, 1994), 191–281 is quite similar.

100 Ashcroft, *Post-Colonial Transformation*, Sarah Mills, *Discourse* (London: Routledge, 2001), chapter 5.

While subalterns are constrained to act 'tactically' in these ways, because of their unequal and subordinate position, hegemons act 'strategically'. Hegemons try to structure the field of possible responses, to induce, train, encourage, fund, bribe, persuade, channel, threaten and constrain the conduct of subalterns at a distance, or infrastructurally, to maximise results, by employing all the indirect means available, and to deploy military intervention if all else fails. Hegemons and subalterns are thus mutually constituted to a considerable degree by their strategic-tactical interaction over time.[101]

Accordingly, any imperial relationship of knowledge, power, rules and modes of subjectification is not a command-obedience imperative, as in Kant, but a complex site or field of contestation over it and over the instruments and institutions that hold it in place. These sites can be as various as a contest over the language or literature of the imperial countries, a meeting of the World Bank, the United Nations forum, the norm of democratic inclusion in international law, rights in a sweatshop, brand marketing, local struggles over dispossession, and so on. The aim is not to engage in these contests for their own sake, as critics often allege. It is to criticise and expose the dominant discourses and practices in such a way as to effect not only a modification but also a possible 'transformation' of them from the inside.[102] The master's house and tools are not something that one stands back from and tries to overthrow from the outside, as in Audra Lourdes' classic metaphor of the decolonisation and nation-building era. Rather, the master's house and tools are the ongoing indeterminate construction of the strategic and tactical interactions of the hegemons and subalterns within. It is not only that the shape of the imperial houses change over time as a result of the contests, but that the relationships that constitute them are always in principle open to a possible transformation.

For all its considerable virtues, the problem with this response to contemporary imperialism is that it is not so much an alternative to contemporary imperialism but a move within the strategic-tactical logic of informal imperialism. It exploits the 'play' or 'indeterminacy' of relations of meaning and power in order to extend and modify them *en passant*. It appears as an alternative to imperialism because it is standardly presented in contrast to the boundaries and binary logic of the colonial and decolonisation periods. It is certainly an alternative to both. But, if the tactical forms of resistance recommended by post-colonial writers are viewed alongside the corresponding transformation in the way imperial power is exercised informally – as now governing former colonials through their constrained freedom of self-determination and low intensity representation – then they appear to be the ways subalterns are already 'conscripted' to conduct themselves in post-colonial imperial relationships, and, in so doing, play a role in developing them in new ways.[103]

---

101 John Scott, *Power* (Cambridge: Polity, 2001) has developed a complex theory of types of power on this basic model that covers power relations in informal imperialism. The idea of strategic-tactical interplay in everyday practices has also been developed by post-colonial writers from the work of Michel de Certeau (Ashcroft, *Transformations*, 53).

102 Ashcroft, Ibid. 45–56.

103 Hardt and Negri make a somewhat similar point in *Empire* from a different perspective.

If, for example, post-colonial actors try to modify and transform the international law norm of democracy beyond 'low intensity democracy', they find that there are international fora in which they *can* enter into contestation. They find that an international norm is often open to democratic deliberation and modification, as the liberal-democratic theory of the equiprimordiality of the rule of law and democracy requires. However, the deformalised international law norm does not become the subject of the exchange of public reasons among free and equal actors, but, rather, the exchange of strategic and tactical acts among hegemonic and subaltern actors positioned in a vastly unequal field of institutions of informal imperialism. In these circumstances, it is the hegemon who is usually able to prevail and reconfigure hegemony in the course of modifying the deformalised norm, as we have seen in the section on the evolution of this democratic norm. The reason for this is not only the enormous substantive inequalities of the partners in these types of contest over the somewhat flexible norms of informal imperial rule, but the underlying, inflexible, relations of dependency laid down over the last 500 years that structure the field itself.[104]

In summary, post-colonial and legal constructivist critics of imperialism, like the earlier theorists of informal and interactive imperialism, have transformed the way we think about imperial relationships in the manner I have summarised. They have also gone on to suggest how it is possible for individual and groups to act within and against the relationships that constitute the imperial field of law and politics today. This is an important advance on the other critics. However, they (myself included) have not yet been able to distinguish between a form of contestation that 'modifies' an imperial relationship, which leaves the underlying imperial features in place and to which the powers-that-be can respond and co-opt, and a form of contestation that 'transforms' an imperial relationship, whereby it comes under the shared democratic authority of those subject to it (and thus is de-imperialised). The traditional struggle of liberation and self-determination against colonisation was the classic model for transformation throughout the twentieth century, but we now know, as Fanon first pointed out above, that even this form of contestation did not overcome imperialism but only led to its modification into informal imperialism. So, we do not know if post-colonial forms of individual and collective anti-imperial contestation will lead to modifications that only reproduce the hegemony of the informal imperial features I have enumerated, or if they might lead to its transformation. This is not so much a criticism as a question for future research.[105]

---

104 This is of course Koskenniemi's worry as well at the end of *The Gentle Civilizer of Nations,* 494–509. I have discussed this dilemma of inclusion and subordination in more detail with respect to the law in 'Exclusion and Assimilation: Two forms of domination in relation to freedom', in *Domination and Exclusion*, M. Williams and S. Macedo, (eds) (New York, 2005), and more generally in 'Communication and Imperialism', *1000 Days of Theory Ctheory,* 2006, www.pactac.net/ctheory. The role of 'structures of domination' in setting the stage of unequal agonistics contests over flexible norms of action coordination in Foucault's influential formulation in 'The Subject and Power' is occasionally overlooked in post-colonial writings.

105 See Emilios Christodoulidis, 'Constitutional Irresolution: Law and the Framing of Civil Society', *European Law Journal*, 9, 4 (2003), 401–32, and 'Against Substitution:

Conclusion

I want to suggest that we can gain a clearer understanding of the imperial features of the present field of public law and political theory by means of the kind of historical and critical approach I have employed above. The result is that a number of discursive and non-discursive features of public law and political practices that critics have assumed to be alternatives to imperialism, turn out to be implicated in a very complex imperial ensemble. The old and new features I summarised at the end of each section, whether we like it or not, play imperial roles in what Martin Loughlin calls the 'governance' of contemporary legal and political associations. We are not 'entrapped' in these fields of imperial relationships, but, to use Wittgenstein's alternative phrase, we are 'entangled' in them, and not so sure of our way out as the critics of imperialism lead us to believe.[106]

I would like to end on a slightly less gloomy note. The critics I have examined overlook not only many imperial features of the present, but also, as strange as this sounds, many non-imperial features as well. That is, their criticisms tend to be made within the broad horizons of the hegemonic languages of western imperialism and their many modifications over the last two hundred years, from Kant and Marx, through to the critics and defenders of imperialism today. These languages of historical development, the global spread of western legal and political institutions, and of self-determination and democratisation, and of post-colonial contestation from within make it appear that the world is actually made over accordingly by imperial expansion and subaltern resistance.

As a result, the critics tend not to see the alterity beyond their horizon: the legal, political and economic pluralism that has not been re-constituted by western imperialism, but continues to exist in the day-to-day lives of millions of people, even when they are constrained to work within the fields of imperial relationships. These old and new alternative ways of living in the present survive and continue to develop in their own complex and creative ways, in relation to their own traditions, because imperialism has always depended for its very existence on indirect and informal rule, leaving local alternative worlds in operation to some constrained extent, and building its relationships of control and exploitation on them. These continuing non-imperial forms of life are the living basis underlying western imperialism. Without these networks of local economic self-reliance, gift relationships, mutual aid, fair trade,

---

the constitutional thinking of dissensus', in Loughlin and Walker, eds. *Paradox of Constitutionalism*, 189–210, for the most sustained critical reflection on this central dilemma. I do not mean to suggest that 'modifications' are not important (quite the opposite). But I do mean to suggest that research needs to be done on the type of modifications that are possible in this complex field of post-colonial imperialism and if there are ways to make minor modifications add up to something more transfiguring and lasting.

106 For a survey of the themes of entrapment, emancipation and immanent critique that run through the theories I have discussed, see Eyal Chowers, *The Modern Self in the Labyrinth* (Cambridge: Harvard University Press, 2004), Ludwig Wittgenstein, *Philosophical Investigations* (Oxford: Basil Blackwell, 2003), section 125.

networks and legal-political pluralism imperialism would not survive.[107] Imperialism has not made the world over to the extent the promoters and critics presuppose.[108] The world of lived experience is actually different from the world portrayed in the texts we have considered. For the most part, this 'strange multiplicity' is overlooked because it is recognised and categorised within inherited imperial languages as being 'less developed', 'pre-modern' or 'particular'. We in the West have yet to enter into the difficult kind of dialogue with the others of the world that brings this horizon of persisting languages and practices into the space of questions and opens the interlocutors to a non-imperial relationship of dialogue and mutual understanding.[109] This would be the beginning of an alternative to imperialism.[110]

107 See, for example, Lauren Benton, *Law and Colonial Cultures: Legal Regimes in World History 1400-1900* (Cambridge University Press, 2002) 1–31, 253–66; and J. Seabrook, *World Poverty*, 117–25.

108 My point is somewhat similar to the 'alternative modernities' movement associated with Dipesh Chakrabarty and Charles Taylor and the 'living democracy' movement of Vandana Shiva. The classic example is the indigenous peoples of the world, who have been colonised and post-colonised more than any other peoples of the world, yet they have been able to preserve, live and develop their forms of live in the face of genocide, dispossession and assimilation. But, non-imperial ways of life are also elsewhere: *Notes from Nowhere, We are Everywhere* (London: Verso, 2002), The International Forum on Globalization, *Alternatives to Economic Globalization* (San Francisco: Berrett Koehler, 2003).

109 For this non-imperial type of dialogue, see *Strange Multiplicity*, 99–139. Boaventura de Sousa Santos suggests, somewhat optimistically, that the World Social Forum could act as a forum for this kind of dialogue, in 'The World Social Forum: Towards a Counter-hegemonic Globalization I and II', *Challenges to Empire*, Jal Sen et al. (ed.) (2004), www.choike.org/nuevo_eng/informes/1557.html.

110 I would like to thank all the generous scholars who participated in the discussion of an earlier version of this chapter when I gave it as a lecture at the University of Edinburgh in 2005: Gavin Anderson, Zenon Bankowski, Emilios Christodoulidis, Hans Lindahl, Martin Loughlin, Sir Neil MacCormick, Paul Patton, Stephen Tierney, Neil Walker. Their questions and criticisms have been immensely helpful in rewriting the lecture for publication, even though I am sure I have failed to answer them to their satisfaction.

Chapter 7

Democracy, Political Reflexivity and Bounded Dialogues: Reconsidering the Monism-Pluralism Debate

Hans Lindahl[1]

I

Instead of directly addressing Tully's unstinting critique of and his alternative to informal imperialism, my aim in this chapter is to scrutinise the fundamental opposition that governs his Edinburgh lecture, namely the opposition between monism and pluralism. It is perhaps not exaggerated to say that, for Tully, empire *is* monism. In general, monism is not merely a specific way of organising polities, but also, and perhaps most fundamentally, a specific way of thinking about political community. Tully leaves no room for doubt, both in his Edinburgh lecture and in an earlier piece,[2] that Kantian and neo-Kantian theories of democracy have played an important role in consolidating monism in modern philosophical thinking. The task of the politics of cultural recognition defended by Tully is, therefore, to recover a pluralistic understanding of law and politics, a pluralism, he holds, which is constitutive for the notion of democracy itself. While I share Tully's concerns about neo-Kantian theories of democracy, I will largely bracket his critique thereof, focusing, instead, on what I take to be the conceptual core of the opposition he sets up between monism and pluralism: the problem of identity. Indeed, to the extent that democracy is defined as *self*-rule or *self*-legislation, the debate between monism and pluralism centres on the conception of identity appropriate to political self-rule. Accordingly, the question to be addressed in this chapter is the following: is the concept of identity germane to political self-rule at all compatible, as Tully argues, with the notion of *legal* pluralism? If not, and I will argue that it is not, then in what way is plurality the indispensable condition of politics? The chapter concludes by very tentatively drawing out the implications of my argument for the problem of the

1 A research grant by the Netherlands Organisation for Scientific Research (NWO) provided the financial support which enabled me to write this chapter.

2 See James Tully, 'The Kantian Idea of Europe: Critical and Cosmopolitan Perspectives', in Anthony Pagden (ed.), *The Idea of Europe: From Antiquity to the European Union* (Cambridge: Cambridge University Press, 2002), 331–58.

spatial boundaries of political community, an issue that goes to the heart of empire and imperial thinking.

II

The central claim of Tully's lecture is perhaps best captured in a passage that I quote in full:

> it cannot be by simply extending the paramount forms of neo-liberal or social-democratic representative democracy further in existing states that imperialism will be challenged, for they are imposed forms of law and democracy, controlled indirectly by the techniques of informal imperialism. Rather, it would be by promoting diverse "high intensity" forms of local and global democracy, self-determination and legal pluralism that would enable the people subject to these low intensity structures of law and politics to bring them under their shared democratic authority by the exercise of their constituent powers ...[3]

This passage neatly sums up the series of oppositions that organise Tully's critique of imperialism and his alternative thereto. Whereas representation, constituted powers, heteronomy and legal monism hold sway in informal imperialism, non-imperial rule promotes participation, constituent power, autonomy and legal pluralism. Notice, however, that the principle of self-determination eludes neat classification within these oppositional pairs. Although Tully explicitly places it in the set of concepts apposite to non-imperial rule, representative democracy is also a manifestation of the principle of self-determination, albeit in a 'low-intensity' form. The problem is, of course, that if representative democracy is a form of self-determination, it becomes difficult, if not impossible, to hold on to the simple oppositions between heteronomy/autonomy, constituted/constituent power, and representation/participation. I will return to this point shortly. But let us first scrutinise the opposition between legal monism and pluralism, as depicted by Tully.

Tully's discussion of the contrast between ancient and modern constitutions reveals the general thrust of his argument. Whereas ancient constitutions are 'multiform', modern constitutions are 'uniform'. Legal monism takes for granted that 'the sovereign people in modern societies ... establish a constitution that is legally and politically uniform: a constitution of equal citizens who are treated identically rather than equitably, of one national system of institutionalised legal and political authority rather than many ...'[4] Modern history shows that 'the requirements of one sovereign people (in one of three forms), one nation and one uniform order of modern legal and political institutions make the recognition and accommodation of diversity impossible'.[5] At the heart of legal pluralism is an understanding of constitutionalism that is sensitive to competing demands for cultural recognition. The privileged manifestation thereof is 'diverse federalism', namely 'federations of

3 James Tully, 'On Law, Democracy and Imperialism', in this volume.

4 Tully, *Strange Multiplicity: Constitutionalism in an Age of Diversity* (Cambridge: Cambridge University Press, 1995), 66.

5 Ibid. 140.

more or less self-governing and overlapping political associations with somewhat dissimilar legal and political ways'.[6]

Dialogue, in Tully's view, is the appropriate vehicle for legal pluralism and a politics of cultural recognition. To put it another way, legal pluralism acquires concrete institutional form through a constitutional dialogue between the different groups vying for cultural recognition. Tully contrasts the dialogue of legal pluralism to the monologue of legal monism, as illustrated, amongst others, by Habermas' theory of communicative action. The universalism of Habermas' model of practical discourse reduces demands for cultural recognition to forms of contingent particularity that threaten the unity of a constitutional association. '[P]recisely because [Kantianism] is presented as universal, necessary and obligatory (that is, as a meta-narrative), it cannot recognize any other of the plurality of narratives, traditions, or civilizations as equal yet different, and enter into a dialogue with them on equal footing'.[7] In contrast to the monologue to which universalism ultimately falls prey, Tully appeals to the Gadamerian notion of dialogue. The experience of finitude and plurality so powerfully portrayed in Gadamer's philosophical hermeneutics clearly resonates in the closing sentences of Tully's lecture: 'We in the West have yet to enter into the difficult kind of dialogue with the others of the world that brings this horizon of persisting languages and practices into the space of questions and opens the interlocutors to non-imperial relationship of dialogue and mutual understanding'.[8]

III

I will return in the following section to consider the Gadamerian notion of dialogue. Firstly, however, I want to examine more closely the notion of democratic identity at the basis of Tully's opposition between legal monism and pluralism. In other words, we need to scrutinise the 'self' of self-rule or self-legislation. The problem turns on the people as the source of the authority of a democratic legal order. At first glance, Tully wants to avoid any reading of popular sovereignty that would collapse its plurality into an alleged unity. The question, however, is whether any sense can be made of self-legislation as such in the absence of a claim to collective unity. Having recognised, at the outset of *Strange Multiplicity*, that 'demands for cultural recognition are aspirations for appropriate forms of self government', Tully goes ahead to say that the apposite minorities share 'a longing for self rule: to rule themselves in accord with their customs and ways'.[9] Notice that this passage refers to minorities as a manifold of individuals that aspire to or engage in self-rule – as a group. While the minority does not exist independently of its members, these members raise a joint claim to self-rule, and precisely in virtue of having, or claiming to have, a joint interest in government in accordance with their shared customs and ways. But a couple of paragraphs further on, Tully reformulates the democratic principle in a way that seems to take up the perspective of an individual:

6 Ibid. 164.

7 Tully, 'On Law, Democracy and Imperialism'.

8 Ibid.

9 Tully, *Strange Multiplicity*, note 4 above, 4.

'self rule in accord with one's own customs and ways'. This shift may seem to be a minor point, but it in fact concerns an issue of the greatest importance for Tully's critique of legal monism: can one at all make sense of a claim to self-rule by a minority unless a manifold of individuals, in the plural, view themselves as a people, in the singular? If not, doesn't this entail recognising that monism is inscribed in the democratic principle of self-rule, to the extent that political self-rule, whatever its specific legal form, is unthinkable in the absence of a claim to unity?

These considerations highlight an ambiguity in the notion of identity implied in self-government. The overwhelming majority of political theorists take for granted what might be called a 'co-referential' reading of democratic identity: the 'self' of 'self-rule' means that the ruled are the same as – and in this sense identical to – the rulers. This is precisely the notion of democratic identity which Habermas endorses, when referring to popular sovereignty: 'The idea of self-legislation by citizens ... requires that those subject to law as its addressees can at the same time understand themselves as authors of law'.[10] Despite his vigorous critique of Habermas, Tully often seems to embrace this conception of identity as well. This co-referential reading of democratic identity is, however, reductive: legislation is enacted from the first-person plural perspective of a 'we'.[11] To put it another way, the 'self' of self-legislation entails the reflexive stance of a collective, the stance whereby individuals refer to themselves as the members of a group that creates norms in its own interest. Borrowing a distinction introduced by Ricœur, this stance is the plural form of reflexive or *ipse*-identity, in contrast with *idem*-identity, that is, identity as sameness.[12]

When viewed in this way, political self-rule amounts to the reflexive act of a collective. I will successively highlight four features of this thumbnail sketch of political self-rule. *The reflexive act of a collective*: (i) As Christopher Kutz points out, contemporary theories of social action generally take their cue from the model of 'an individual agent acting alone in the pursuit of his or her own goals'. This reductive model is incapable of explaining social action as shared action, in particular as the act of a collective subject. 'The self of self-government', he asserts, 'is a "we", not an "I"'.[13] The reductive movement whereby we-intentions are levelled down to an aggregation of I-intentions is precisely what renders Habermas' reading of identity co-referential rather than reflexive. By contrast, the collective character of legislation

10 Jürgen Habermas, *Between Facts and Norms*, trans. by William Rehg (Cambridge, MA: MIT Press, 1996), 120.

11 Bert van Roermund develops this insight at length in his powerful article, 'First-Person Plural Legislature: Political Reflexivity and Representation', *Philosophical Explorations* (2003) 6, 236.

12 Paul Ricœur, *Oneself as Another*, trans. by Kathleen Blamley (Chicago, IL: Chicago University Press, 1992 [1990]), 1–3; 115–25.

13 Christopher Kutz, 'The Collective Work of Citizenship', in *Legal Theory* (2002) 8, 472. For studies on collective intentionality, see, amongst others, Michael Bratman, *Faces of Intention* (Cambridge: Cambridge University Press, 1999); Philip Pettit, *A Theory of Freedom* (Oxford: Polity, 2001); John Searle, *The Construction of Social Reality* (New York, NY: Free Press, 1995); Raimo Tuomela, *The Importance of Us* (Stanford: Stanford University Press, 1995).

comes to the fore in Tully's references to minorities as groups that demand cultural recognition. For, to participate as a member of a minority is to take on the first-person plural perspective of a collective: 'we have decided to regulate our relations in this or that way'. (ii) The preposition 'of' indicates that an act is the collective's own act. Terms such as 'own', 'my', 'our' and 'together' are related to the first-person indexicals 'I' and 'we'. To act, a self must be able to ascribe acts to itself as 'its' – as 'my' or 'our' – acts, and to take on responsibility for these acts. Collective selfhood, taking on the first-person plural perspective of a 'we', and identifying acts as 'our' acts are interrelated terms. (iii) Bratman characterises collective action as (minimally) 'shared intentional activity'.[14] The core of collective action is reciprocity. On the one hand, collective action involves the reciprocity of intentions: my intention to act is co-determined by your intention to act and vice versa, and we know this of each other. On the other hand, collective action involves reciprocity in the 'meshing' of our individual plans and actions, with a view to bringing about the envisaged collective act. Importantly, Bratman notes that shared intentional activity need not be shared cooperative activity; an additional condition for the latter is that participants do not act under duress.[15] (iv) Collective acts are reflexive in a twofold manner. There is, firstly, the reflexivity proper to the reciprocity of intentions: a manifold of individuals view themselves (are, therefore, the object of an intention) as acting jointly (as, therefore, the subject of an act). There is, secondly, the reflexivity whereby a collective legislates for its own sake. A collective is not only the subject of legislation, but also its object, namely the group of individuals that have a shared interest in the enacted legislation. Self-legislation does not only imply that 'we enact norms'; a fuller formulation is: 'we enact norms in our own interest'.[16]

Although highly abridged, these considerations confirm that two distinct but related kinds of identity are at stake in self-government. On the one hand, the reflexive structure of collective acts points to ipseity, to collective selfhood, which stands in contrast to the other and, more radically, to the strange. On the other, a collective remains the same over time, or becomes different, in terms of interests that are deemed to be common, and which not only guide joint action but are also renegotiated in the ongoing process of acting collectively. My claim is, then, that although Tully often seems to take for granted a co-referential reading of identity, references to 'the local struggles of resistance by the people who dream of governing themselves in their own ways ...' and the like can best be read as manifestations of political reflexivity.[17] Political self-rule, whatever its concrete institutional form, entails the first-person plural perspective of a collective as a unity in action, that is, as a unity that posits norms in its own interest.

14 Bratman, *Faces of Intention*, note 13 above, 100, 118, 133, 142.

15 Ibid. 142.

16 See Van Roermund, 'First-Person Plural Legislature', note 11 above, for a full-blown characterisation of the different roles played by the indexical 'we' in collective self-legislation.

17 Tully, 'On Law, Democracy and Imperialism', note 3 above.

IV

This insight casts new light on Tully's defence of legal pluralism. As noted, Tully opposes any attempt to view the people that engage in self-rule in terms of 'one nation' or the like. Indeed, legal monism takes for granted that 'the unity of constitutional association consists in a centralised and uniform system of legal and political authority, or clear subordination of authorities, to which all citizens are subject in the same way, and from which all authority derives'.[18] The institutional response to the empire of uniformity in legal monism is 'diverse federalism', which, to quote Tully anew, consists in 'federations of more or less self-governing and overlapping political associations with somewhat dissimilar legal and political ways'.

Despite the apparently stark opposition between monism and pluralism, the foregoing analysis of political reflexivity shows that Tully's defence of pluralism is not incompatible with what he calls the 'unity of constitutional association'. To the contrary, the notion of a constitutional association that enacts a legal order in its own interest implies the first-person plural perspective of a 'we' as a unity in action. This perspective does not preclude plurality, for, obviously, any reference to a constitutional association not only presupposes shared interests but also the means for settling differences concerning what interests are shared. But, if they are at all to engage in a constitutional association, then the political associations that come together in 'diverse federalism' are not simply diverse; there has to be an interest or a set of interests that is deemed to be common, in the absence of which a constitution and a legal order would be pointless. Accordingly, it makes no sense to simply play off plurality against unity. To be intelligible as a defence of political self-rule, legal pluralism is not simply an argument against the unity of a legal order, as one might be led to believe, but rather a thesis about how legal order is to be constituted as a unity.[19] And this is, indeed, the crucial question: how does a political association constitute itself as a legal unity? In particular, what sense are we to make of political self-determination as the act by which a plurality of individuals – and a fortiori of political associations – constitute themselves as a legal collective?

The contrast between (collective) selfhood and the other to which I alluded at the end of the foregoing section provides the key to Tully's approach to this question. In effect, this contrast is of the greatest importance for Tully's political philosophy, for if selfhood evokes the problem of subjectivity, the other and the strange introduce the problem of intersubjectivity into political theory. Tully's basic philosophical move is, if I am not mistaken, to refuse a simple opposition between unity and plurality, by viewing the unity implied in political self-rule as the outcome of an *intersubjective process*. Crucially, Tully views this intersubjective process as dialogical, in the Gadamerian sense of the term. To get a sense of the nature of this process, a process that Tully qualifies as agonistic, we need to look more carefully at the dialogical mediation between self and other, as depicted by Gadamer.

---

18 Tully, *Strange Multiplicity*, note 4 above, 83.

19 I make a similar point about Gavin Anderson's defence of legal pluralism in his recent book, *Constitutional Rights After Globalization* (Oxford: Hart, 2005), in a review forthcoming in *Social and Legal Studies* (2007), 149–152.

As is well known, Gadamer's analysis of dialogue is governed by the distinction between the familiar and the strange. According to Gadamer, dialogue is sparked by misunderstanding, by the experience of what is strange, of what resists integration into the horizon of our expectations. Dialogue, as an exemplary manifestation of the hermeneutic endeavour, plays itself out in the polarity between 'strangeness and familiarity'.[20] And, Gadamer adds, 'the true locus of hermeneutics is this in-between' (ibid.). The hermeneutic 'in-between' (*Zwischen*) is, of course, none other than the 'dia' of 'dialogue'. Drawing on Heidegger, Gadamer eschews a derivative reading of the in-between: 'the primacy that language and understanding have in Heidegger's thought indicates the priority of the "relation" over against its relational members – the I who understands and that which is understood'.[21] Gadamer develops the primacy of the relation between self and other through a phenomenology of the game (*Spiel*). 'Whatever is brought into play or comes into play no longer depends on itself but is dominated by the relation that we call the game'.[22] This back and forth movement, which is constitutive for a game, determines intersubjectivity as the dialectical mediation of the familiar and the strange:

> The common agreement that takes place in speaking with others is itself a game. Whenever two persons speak with each other they speak the same language. They themselves, however, in no way know that in speaking it they are playing this language further. But each person also speaks his own language. Common agreement takes place by virtue of the fact that speech confronts speech but does not remain immobile. In speaking with each other we constantly pass over into the thought world of the other person; we engage him, and he engages us'.[23]

The outcome of a dialogue between self and other, in this strong sense of the term 'dialogue', is a higher-order unity, that is, a unity that encompasses both self and other in a situation of mutual understanding.

This conception of dialogue, of the symmetrical movement in which the engagement of the other by the self is correlative to the engagement of the self by the other, governs Tully's notion of a constitutional dialogue. Political self-rule, on this reading, marks the reciprocating forays of the self into the other, and the other into the self, in such a way that the ensuing constitutional association unites self and other in a higher-order 'we', a collective subject the members of which have overcome the experience of strangeness that separate them. As Tully puts it, 'if a contemporary constitution is to be culturally neutral, it should not promote one culture at the expense of others, but mutually recognise and accommodate the cultures of all the citizens in an agreeable manner'.[24] This passage confirms a point

---

20 Hans-Georg Gadamer, *Truth and Method*, 2nd edition, trans. revised by Joel Weinsheimer and Donald G. Marshall (London: Sheed & Ward, 1993), 295.

21 Gadamer, 'On the Problem of Self-Understanding', in Hans-Georg Gadamer, *Philosophical Hermeneutics*, translated and edited by David Linge (Berkeley, CA: University of California Press, 1976), 50.

22 Ibid. 53.

23 Ibid. 56–7.

24 Tully, *Strange Multiplicity*, note 4 above, 191.

I made at the beginning of this section. Tully's concern is not merely to conserve plurality, but to achieve a form of unity in which a plurality of perspectives can recognise themselves as being parts of a whole. The task of a politics of cultural recognition is to *overcome* plurality, albeit provisionally, in a constitution that is culturally – and politically – 'neutral', as Tully puts it. This approach to politics and law is faithful to the movement of dialogue, as depicted in Gadamer's account of the hermeneutic endeavour. For, paradoxically, the Gadamerian dialogue realises its most intimate finality if it effaces itself as a dia-logue. In other words, and despite Gadamer's insistence on the primacy of the relation over its two poles, the 'in-between' separating self and other is provisional, even if the self is ever vulnerable to novel experiences of strangeness that call for renewed dialogue.

One cannot help noting that, whatever their differences, Habermas, on the one hand, and Gadamer and Tully, on the other, agree on the essential. The *telos* driving political self-rule, whether deployed in a 'practical discourse' or in a 'dialogue', is the 'inclusion of the other'. This is, of course, the English translation of the title of a collection of essays written by Habermas. It is not without interest that the pivotal essay of Habermas' book is his essay on Kant's *Perpetual Peace*, and that Tully castigates both pieces in his Edinburgh lecture as illustrations of the political theory that informs western imperialism. At any rate, the translation of the title misses the essential point Habermas makes in his book. This point turns on an ambiguity of the German term *Inklusion*, which means both inclusion (*Einschließung*) and integration or involvement (*Einbeziehung*). Whereas Habermas opposes the first term to exclusion (*Ausschließung*), he introduces no oppositional term for the second.[25] The idea behind this conceptual distinction is to sketch out an alternative to forms of democracy that include by excluding. Popular self-rule, in the strong sense of the term endorsed by Habermas, consists in the *Einbeziehung des Anderen*. This is the German-language title of the book. Although Habermas no doubt chose this title to highlight the political import of his concept of practical discourse, I can think of no better or more concise characterisation of Gadamer's notion of a dialogue. Accordingly, it is of derivative importance whether one approaches political self-rule through the prisms of social contract or of a dialogue. Both positions take for granted that popular self-rule not only denotes a principle of collective unity, but also, and above all, a unity in which an initial experience of plurality gives way to an inclusiveness without exclusion.

In short, to the extent that it depends on Gadamer's notion of dialogue, Tully's defence of legal pluralism is thoroughly monistic. By the same token, although Tully argues that politics is agonistic, I don't think he endorses a strong sense of agonism.[26] For the experience of plurality which fuels agonistic politics is, in the light of his Gadamerian reading of dialogue, provisional. I would argue, to the contrary, that what makes politics agonistic is the experience of *irreducible* plurality, a plurality

25 Jürgen Habermas, *The Inclusion of the Other* (Cambridge, MA: The MIT Press, 1998), 139.

26 See James Tully, 'The Unfreedom of the Moderns in Comparison to Their Ideals of Constitutional Democracy', *Modern Law Review*, 65 (2002) 2. For a discussion of political agonism see my article, 'The Opening: Alegality and Political Agonism', forthcoming in Andy Schaap (ed), *Law and Political Agonism* (Ashgate, forthcoming).

that cannot be overcome by way of a dialectical mediation of the particular and the general, the many and the one. The strange, in a radical sense of the term, is what resists integration into the dialectic of the self and the other. On this strong reading of plurality, Tully cannot have it both ways: he must choose between an agonistic and a dialogical conception of politics.

V

Why, however, need plurality be irreducible? Why, in other words, might the Gademerian notion of dialogue not be adequate to the task of conceptualising political self-rule? Finding answers to these questions requires that we raise and consider anew the question formulated at the outset of the foregoing section: what sense are we to make of political self-rule as the act by which a plurality of individuals – and a fortiori of political associations – constitute themselves as a legal collective?

Closer consideration of Tully's definition of popular sovereignty – of political self-rule – points to a problem that remains beyond the pale of Gadamerian dialogue. Evoking a traditional distinction in modern political theory, Tully asserts that 'popular sovereignty takes two forms: either the people exercise political power themselves or they delegate political power to their representatives'.[27] At issue here are the oppositions between participation and representation, autonomy and heteronomy, constituent and constituted power, which, as noted earlier, structure Tully's critique of imperialism and his alternative thereto. If we look at the first opposition, there are certainly good normative reasons for institutionalising robust and effective forms of citizen participation. But a simple opposition between representative and participative democracy conceals the essential political problem concerning the genesis of political community: the preliminary questions (i) *who* may participate in citizen deliberation and decision-making, and (ii) what interests are *shared* interests, worthy of deliberation and decision-making between citizens, are not themselves the outcome of deliberation and decision-making between citizens.

Accordingly, Tully's definition of popular sovereignty occludes the condition governing the genesis of political community: someone must seize the initiative and, claiming to act on behalf of – to represent – the collective, indicate who belongs to the 'we' that join together into a political community, and what are the interests the pursuit of which makes political community a meaningful venture. Participation presupposes – and is itself a specific institutionalisation of – political representation. In other words, political power requires taking on the first-person plural perspective, but this perspective can only be elicited by acts that claim a representational status for themselves. By the same token, to the extent that someone must seize the initiative to get political community going, heteronomy is inscribed in popular sovereignty, not merely in fact but also in principle. Indeed, popular sovereignty is first and foremost the constitution *of* a collective self, rather than the constitution of a legal order *by* a collective self. Only retrospectively, to the extent that individuals are prepared to view and continue viewing themselves as the members of a collective, does the act

27 Tully, *Strange Multiplicity*, note 4 above, 194.

appear as their joint act, as the constitution of a legal order by a collective self. Only retrospectively, then, are the people the constituent power, yet in such a way that their constituted character never entirely disappears. A simple dichotomy between representation and participation, between heteronomy and autonomy, and between constituted and constituent power, fundamentally misconstrues the complex nature of acts of political self-determination.[28]

This insight exposes a problem in Tully's appeal to a constitutional dialogue as the means of mediating plurality and unity. Indeed, one of the remarkable features of his political philosophy is the paucity of reflections on political power. This is consistent with Tully's assumption that political power and dialogue are more or less interchangeable terms, at least normatively speaking. Yet a crucial passage in *Strange Multiplicity* shows why this assumption is problematic. Indeed, having rejected the idea that there must be a comprehensive form of constitutional dialogue, a presumption that remains 'an unexamined convention left over from the imperial age', Tully argues that 'only a dialogue in which different ways of participating in the dialogue are mutually recognised would be just (even if the first piece of business is to agree on which forms of dialogue are admissible)'.[29] Everything turns on how the 'first piece of business' is to be settled. In the same way that who is a party to the social contract, and what is the object thereof, are issues that cannot be resolved through a social contract, the prior decision concerning which forms of dialogue are admissible in a constitutional dialogue cannot be settled dialogically. Succinctly, non-dialogical acts get dialogues going. In other words, political reciprocity depends on non-reciprocal acts. Political power manifests itself most starkly precisely in such non-dialogical, non-reciprocal acts, which is another way of saying that political power is certainly related – but cannot be reduced – to dialogue.[30]

Moreover, it would be a grave distortion of the political significance of such manifestations of power to qualify them, as dialogical models of democracy are bound to do, merely as a deficient form of political action. In effect, the non-dialogical, non-reciprocal aspect of political power has an *enabling* function for dialogue. Yet there is more to political power than this: it not only gets dialogue going but also brings it to a *halt*. In this sense also, political power is non-dialogical, non-reciprocal. To complicate matters normatively, political power brings a dialogue to a halt in the same way it gets it going: by claiming to act on behalf of the very collective it contributes to creating. Thus, not only is a constitutional dialogue not dialogically established, but political power can invoke the constitution to shut down a dialogue that is deemed to be constitutionally out of bounds. This shows why Gadamer's phenomenology of a game is inadequate in view of securing an understanding of the nature of political power. The problem is not so much that the exercise of political power belies the 'levity' of a game, for, as Gadamer points out, games can be played

28 This idea is developed at greater length in my article, 'Constituent Power and Reflexive Identity: Towards an Ontology of Collective Selfhood', in Martin Loughlin and Neil Walker (eds), *The Paradox of Constitutionalism* (Oxford: Oxford University Press, 2007), 9–24.

29 Tully, *Strange Multiplicity*, note 4 above, 53.

30 See my article 'Dialectic and Revolution: Confronting Kelsen and Gadamer on Legal Interpretation', in *Cardozo Law Review*, 24 (2003) 2, 769–798.

with extraordinary seriousness.[31] The problem is, rather, that games and dialogues presuppose a *symmetric* relation between the parties thereto. Individuals engage in a dialogue to the extent that its internal lawfulness determines their own participation therein, rather than vice versa:

> The back and forth movement that takes place within a field of play does not derive from the human game and from playing as a subjective attitude. Quite the contrary, even for human subjectivity the real experience of the game consists in the fact that something that obeys its own set of laws gains ascendancy in the game.[32]

There is no such symmetry in the power relations whereby a collective self engages with its other. The (re)negotiation of constitutional rules, in response to demands of cultural recognition, presupposes that political power claims for itself the right to ultimately determine the bounds within which constitutional transformations are permissible, and precisely because what is at stake is maintaining the unity of a collective, that is, assuring political *self*-rule. In short, the relation to the other deployed by political power is essentially *asymmetrical*. In his debate with Derrida, Gadamer asks 'What, in the final analysis, is linguisticality? Is it a bridge or a barrier?' And he immediately adds:

> Is it a bridge built of things that are the same for each self over which one communicates with the other over the flowing stream of otherness? Or is it a barrier that limits our self-abandonment and that cuts us off from the possibility of ever completely expressing ourselves and communicating with others?[33]

The point I would like to make is that the form of dialogue in which political power can engage involves neither 'self-abandonment' nor 'completeness', but rather a *limited* capacity to listen and to respond to what calls into question the claim to unity raised on behalf of a collective. Constitutional politics is, in this strong sense of the expression, *finite*. Tully's invocation of the principle, 'listen to the other side because it is always possible to speak on either side of a case' (*audi alteram partem in utramque partem*), as the guiding principle of a constitutional dialogue, overlooks the decisive point that political reciprocity is always a limited reciprocity.[34] To lose sight of this is to deprive politics of its specificity, and to transform political philosophy into a theory of applied morality.

We touch here on what I take to be the fundamental shortcoming of Tully's political philosophy: his interpretation of political self-rule does not bear in mind that while political power can, up to a point, take on a dialogical form, it is also – and necessarily – the limit of a dialogue between self and other, by virtue of both enabling and disabling it. If the political relation between a collective self and its others is at all dialogical, then certainly not in the form of Gadamer's 'infinite dialogue'.

---

31 Gadamer, *Truth and Method*, note 20 above, 101ff.

32 Gadamer, 'On the Problem of Self-Understanding', note 21 above, 53.

33 Hans-Georg Gadamer, 'Text and Interpretation', in Diane P. Michelfelder & Richard E. Palmer, *Dialogue & Deconstruction: The Gadamer-Derrida Encounter* (Albany, NY: SUNY Press, 1989), 27.

34 Tully, *Strange Multiplicity*, note 4 above, 115.

Constitutional dialogues are perforce *limited dialogues*, in this twofold sense of the term 'limit'. The legal monism without which no sense can be made of collective self-legislation entails that political plurality is irreducible. My interest in defending legal monism against calls for legal pluralism is not, therefore, to undercut political pluralism but precisely the contrary, namely to show that *calls for legal pluralism are, at bottom, pleas for political monism.*

VI

While it is certainly not a sufficient condition thereof, I wonder whether acknowledging the irreducibility of political plurality is not a necessary condition for a non-imperial form of politics. To the extent that imperialism as a form of political, no less than economic, expansionism is linked to a specific way of thinking about boundaries, this acknowledgement would require reconsidering in what sense political communities are spatially bounded. Recalling Hegel's polemic with Kant concerning the 'thing-in-itself', Gadamer notes that 'what makes a limit a limit always also includes knowledge of what is on both sides of it. It is the dialectic of the limit to exist only by being superseded'.[35] Although Gadamer draws on Hegel's thesis as a thesis about the limits of thinking, I believe this passage neatly captures a certain understanding of the meaning and functions of spatial boundaries as well. Indeed, spatial boundaries are remarkable in that they both join together and separate. But everything turns on how one interprets these two functions of boundaries. If the relation of political power to boundaries is dialectical, then boundaries cannot separate places unless, more fundamentally, they *join* them. In a word, boundaries cannot exclude without including. And there is a certain truth in this, for it is only to the extent that boundaries join places that each of these can appear as being part of a whole, of a unity. Both Habermas' practical discourse and Gadamer's dialogue involve a specific hierarchy of these two functions of boundaries, whereby the separation introduced by boundaries is *subordinated* to the unification they bring about. This subordination is the guiding presupposition of the politics of boundaries intimated by their shared maxim: the *Einbeziehung des Anderen.* It would be foolish to assert that this subordination is the sufficient condition of the specific politics of boundaries we call imperialism; but it is certainly a necessary condition thereof. By contrast, my claim that political plurality is irreducible suggests that there is no political inclusion, spatial and conceptual, that is not also exclusive: an *Ein- und Ausschließung des Anderen.* A non-imperial politics deals with boundaries in a way that recognises that boundaries cannot include without excluding.

This is, admittedly, no more than a preliminary and abstract formulation of an alternative to Tully's critique of imperialism. But if we are to follow him in the call for a way of thinking about politics and law that acknowledges the central importance of plurality, then we should begin by recognising that boundaries not only join when separating, but also separate when joining. When characterised in

35 Gadamer, *Truth and Method*, note 20 above, p. 343.

this way, boundaries are a manifestation – perhaps the primordial manifestation – of the ‘in-between’ that makes plurality possible.

Chapter 8

The Reframing of Law's Imperial Frame: A Comment on Tully

Neil Walker

1. Introduction

Taking as his point of departure the recent renewal of interest in 'empire' as a code through which to understand the contemporary global legal and political configuration, Jim Tully offers an arresting analysis of the limitations inherent in the majority of theoretical expressions of this new wave. For many in the mainstream of public law, international law or the burgeoning field of 'law and globalization' studies, talk of empire in the same breath as contemporary law may seem anachronistic, distorting, even gratuitously provocative. But Tully's critique comes from the opposite direction. His basic thesis is that, far from making exaggerated claims about law's imperial character, most understandings of the contemporary relevance of empire, and of empire's law, are euphemistic. They neglect one or more of empire's key dimensions, and in so doing understate its scope and depth and underestimate what a successful strategy and process of de-imperialisation would require. His message, then, is offered not just as a critique of those positions that would celebrate the present global structure. It also poses a challenge to those many who would consider themselves to be keen critics of the *status quo*, but who, on our author's analysis, do not go far enough.

So ambitious and far-reaching is the offensive mounted by Jim Tully, indeed, that it would not be surprising if the first reaction of many across the broad spectrum of those challenged would be to look for holes in his argument rather than to question their own. Crudely, we can imagine two possible lines of objection. In the first place, there is the charge of *nominalism*. According to this argument, the price of a redefinition as radical as that offered by Tully is the loss of precisely that common sense of the zone of plausible contestation around the concept of empire which would make any such redefinition potentially persuasive and so worth making in the first place. On this view, the criticism is that Tully, armed with a stipulative definition that few share, may end up talking only to these converted few. In the second place, there is the charge of *structural fatalism*. According to this argument, the new definition of empire and of empire's law offered by Tully may be so encompassing that it becomes difficult if not impossible to imagine how law is to ever to escape the clutches of empire and operate in the service of an alternative geopolitical vision.

Of course, if the charges of nominalism is found proven, the second charge will be of little consequence, and indeed it might seem redundant even to pursue a verdict.

If one has no sympathy with how the box is constructed, one will care little or not at all if its builder subsequently finds himself 'boxed in'. Alternatively, if the charge of nominalism does not stick and the redefinition is found to be broadly engaging rather than narrowly idiosyncratic, then structural fatalism becomes a much more palpable concern. If we can be convinced that the expansive definition of imperialism offered by Tully is at least a reckonable one – one that *does* fall within the zone of plausible contestation, then we had better take seriously whatever threat of structural fatalism issues from such an expanded definition.

In what follows, I want to pursue two points. I want to argue, firstly, that the charge of nominalism is indeed ill-founded, and that those who are profoundly challenged by Tully's work should resist the temptation to dismiss that challenge as nothing more than conceptual overreach. I want to argue, secondly, that if the spectre of structural fatalism does hover over Tully's feast, then only a wishful form of thinking would equate this with a rebuttal of his argument. Even if we could demonstrate that his conclusions were deeply pessimistic about an alternative anti-imperial role for law, we would not be entitled to treat that demonstration as some kind of argumentative *coup de grâce*. Rather, it is our common task – ours as much as his – to try to find the most sharply constructive edge to the definition and critique of imperialism, and to show how what may be characterised as law's imperial dimension need not be treated as incorrigible.

2. In the Name of Empire

The main part of Tully's essay is taken up with the systematic peeling away of the various layers of what he claims to be deficient analysis of the contemporary global configuration in order to reveal a better and fuller understanding of empire's law. The top layer of analysis is for Tully the most flaky, and so easily brushed off. This consists of the complacent view that empire is a matter of colonies, and that with the great twentieth century waves of decolonisation, empire has simply disappeared into history. But, Tully argues, even where, in reaction against this narrow formalism, it is acknowledged that whatever it is in the structure of relations between political forms that makes such relations imperial may well obtain even in the absence of colonies, and so that empire is as likely to be informally as formally configured, such acknowledgment is often of limited consequence. For, at a second level of analysis, what is conceded as the domain of informal empire tends for many to be treated as a marginal and occasional aberration from the post-imperial norm. On this view, when (or if?) the American people come to their sometimes neglected senses and vote against the imperial throwbacks they occasionally let amongst them – most recently the Bush presidential dynasty, equipped with their strategies of overt militarism and unilateralism – they will also be voting Empire itself out of office. Yet, Tully contends, this is to take too narrow a view of informal imperialism, and to neglect the ways in which notionally multilateral institutions, including international law, can be and often are interpreted in the service of hegemonic economic and political interests under the silent but powerful shadow of accumulated military and cultural advantage.

However, even an expanded informalism does not satisfy Tully, if, at a third level of analysis, it holds that within the presently configured state system it is still possible, with the help of regional organisations such as the EU and other post-Bretton Woods institutions of global governance, to construct effective alternatives to imperialism. For Tully, this level of analysis, which he associates with the contemporary wave of neo-Kantian or cosmopolitan analysis and prescription, ignores just how deeply the form and content of the state system and its attendant complex of global regulation, aided and abetted by a universal meta-narrative of legal and cultural development, is implicated in the pattern of western political and economic hegemony. A fourth level of analysis, one which looks for progress through the adoption by the subaltern states themselves of the discourse and strategies of self-determination and democratisation, fares no better, and for similar reasons. The deep rules of the game have been set elsewhere, and so the price of playing the game tends to be either failure or Pyrrhic victory – success at the cost of conformity to imperial discipline and the suppression of those voices and forms of indigenous social relations which are out of kilter with imperial logic.

This brings us to a fifth and final level of analysis, one that concedes that the deep rules of the game are indeed skewed in favour of empire, but which argues that the disadvantages this visits upon the imperial subjects are by no means cast in tablets of stone. Rather, this post-colonial body of writing, as exemplified in the later work of Said and Foucault, would insist upon the capacity of the subalterns to challenge imperial relations from within in a manner which attacks their very imperial logic and form. Here, too, however, Tully remains sceptical. He wonders how any position that accepts the deep logic and form of imperialism can imagine forms of contestation within that logic and form which can be simultaneously transformative of that logic and form, and he suggests that the burden of proof rests squarely with those who would make such a bold claim.

What makes Tully's thesis, for all its sweeping and uncompromising internal critique of the field, nevertheless a plausible reworking of imperialism? This rests, in my view, on two factors. Firstly, Tully suggests a significant *causal* relationship between old and new – between colonial and post-colonial imperialism. Secondly, at the level of the structures identified and described there is also posited a close *analogy* between classical and contemporary imperialism, such that they might persuasively be seen as species of the same genus. What is more, the argument from causality and the argument from analogy are closely linked.

Take first the causal argument. For Tully, post-colonial imperialism is an outgrowth of colonial imperialism rather than simply its echo. The purpose of his emphasis upon the political writings of Immanuel Kant,[1] and upon the founding of the modern international order with which Kant is so closely associated, is precisely to demonstrate the deep embedding and continuing significance of the building blocks put in place in the founding phase. According to Tully, the sheer familiarity and venerability of the state system, as well as its claims to universality

1 Pursued at greater length in J. Tully, 'The Kantian Idea of Europe: Critical and Cosmopolitan Perspectives' in A. Pagden (ed.) *The Idea of Europe: From Antiquity to the European Union* (Cambridge: Cambridge University Press, 2000).

and formal equality, are such that it tends to be taken for granted as a neutral frame for thinking about global law rather than treated as itself an object of critical inquiry. Yet if we appreciate that the system of states began as a system contrived by some imperial states *inter se* and imposed by them on other communities, and that all later developments, including formal decolonisation and the ascent of the norm of self-determination, the slow development of a right to democracy, and even the last half- century's exponential sector-specific and region-specific diversification of the global regulatory structure, have all been grafted onto these same building-blocks, a rather different picture emerges; namely, one of an original bias that has loaded the form, and, it follows, progressively the content of international law in favour of an inherited power configuration. What is more, path-dependency is not just about structural inertia – about the objective difficulty of unsettling such an embedded framework, but is also a function of the very taken-for-grantedness, or reification, which, as we have noted, comes with such a lengthy pedigree, and which continues to provides a powerful ideological shield against claims of partiality.

Yet the causal argument does not persuade simply by pointing to the continuity of certain discrete structures of governance across the colonial and post-colonial periods. We must also be able to point to an overall similarity – a comparable asymmetry – of geopolitical relations as between the age of high imperialism and the contemporary period. Here, Tully's method, at least implicitly, is one of abstraction. In the course of his argument he points to a number of general features which all phases of global legal and political history since the onset of imperialism have had in common. Four in particular appear to stand out.

In the first place, with regard to the basic relations between imperial and subaltern powers, both colonial and post-colonial phases are characterised by what may be termed cumulative inequality. That is to say, inequality operates in a mutually reinforcing fashion over various sectors or fields. In particular, it is about the constitution of global markets with terms of trade heavily favourable to the great powers, which economic ascendancy is supported, on the one hand, by military threat or intervention, and on the other, by the 'softer' mechanism of political, educational, cultural and legal control and persuasion.

In the second place, the motivational underpinnings remain similar. While Tully readily concedes that informal imperialism, at least in its non-military variant, is less overtly exploitative in its design, he wants to argue not only that there remains a structural disposition towards inequality, but also that when the system that supports the great powers is deemed to be under threat, whether the key forum be the UN Security Council or the WTO or the Rio Convention on Biological Diversity, these great powers and their allies are not squeamish about willing the means to re-assert their preferred ends. That is to say, for all its internal complexity and structural depth, informal imperialism is not a machine that reliably runs by itself. At critical junctures it will require, and invariably receive, knowing intervention in one or more of various aggressive forms – political, legal, economic and , in the last resort, military.

In the third place, there is something deeply pervasive about the logic of imperialism. This is emphatically not to claim that no alternative forms of social relations can subsist alongside imperial relations, a point to which we return below.

Rather, it is to argue that the imperial framework purports to embrace everything within its own horizon. The imperial system understands itself 'imperially' so to speak – as a system whose operation is optimised to the extent that all social relations are subsumed within its logic and is threatened to the extent that certain social relations may escape its logic. This does not mean that the imperial system is narrowly dogmatic. Quite the opposite in fact. The imperial mind-set is prepared to adapt and to be flexible in its own terms to the extent necessary to maintain its hegemony rather than founder on its own rigidity. International law, transnational institutions, the collective security system, the free movement of the factors of production; all of these are amenable to modification as required to retain the authority-in-the-last-instance of the imperial system.

Fourth and finally, imperialism exhibits a high degree of resilience. This is not just a restatement of its deeply-layered historical continuity, but also a predictive inference from its other abstract properties. Its cumulative and mutually reinforcing prosecution of inequality, its motivated character and its adaptability all speak to a form of ordering that raises and meets expectations of high durability, of indefinite extension.

In summary, the combination of causal and analogous registers of argument in Tully's thesis is a potent one. An argument driven purely by causal dynamics would tend to undue concentration on the historical legacy of formal empire. Alternatively, an argument drive purely by analogy would tend to neglect the complex geology of imperialism, and to miss the profound sense in which many of our contemporary transnational relations of inequality do indeed possess a cumulative and continuous dimension, however intricate and uneven the historical trail might be. An argument such as Tully's that combines both, however, understand that, while they are closely related, neither pole of empire – neither its deep legacy not its persistent and recurrent character – is reducible to the other.[2]

Of course, some will be sceptical about the robustness of Tully's causal chain and the generous inclusiveness of his method of abstraction, and will remain unconvinced that he is not pitching his conceptual tent too far from the main camp. After all, the fact that global constellations in various phases of the modern age have in common cumulative inequality, the self-interested motivation and intervention of the powerful, pervasiveness of reach and high resilience, still leaves a lot of room for them to differ. Yet the point of this first stage of debate is not whether Tully's definition of imperialism commands or deserves widespread agreement. Rather, it is whether he has done enough to answer the charge of nominalism – of whether his definition provides a basis for critical engagement with the existing terms of debate rather than simply opening up an idiosyncratic furrow. And, in my view, this is precisely where his method of abstraction succeeds. For, even if it does not provide definitive answers, by providing an abstract frame of continuity and commonality, his thesis does at least succeed in posing in a challenging fashion the vital question

---

2 For example, Tully wants to stress the imperial characteristics of the twentieth century Soviet Empire, which rest much more easily on the argument from analogy than on the argument from causality. See *On Law, Democracy and Imperialism* (present volume) 5.

of the key areas of convergence and divergence and overall balance of similarity and difference between early imperialism and contemporary global relations.

3. Empire and Transformation: overcoming three oppositions

If we turn, then, to the charge of structural fatalism, this might come in two variants. In the first place, there is the full frontal assault which, while endorsing Tully's definition of the present conjuncture as imperial, argues that actually existing imperialism, if not procuring an ideal world, nevertheless represents the best of all *possible* worlds. The apologists for empire's latest brand, as Tully notes in his Introduction, cover a remarkably wide range – 'realist, neo-conservative and neo-liberal and traditional liberal'.[3] For them, moreover, the resilience of the current American-led imperial configuration, such as it may be, is not viewed as a matter of regret still less of despair, but as something to be vigilantly maintained. The difference here is clearly not a conceptual one, nor even fundamentally one of empirical assessment or strategic judgement. Rather, it is one of basic moral evaluation. For Tully, the cumulative harm of a configuration that produces not only deeply skewed distributive outcomes, but which in its reliance on the more or less enlightened self-interest of a single hegemon, or coalition of the willing, also countenances and encourages widespread forms of misrecognition and misrepresentation within the political process itself, can never be accepted as the best, or even as the least bad, solution.[4] To put it in other terms, insofar as we are able to agree a common, if abstract, understanding of key features of the present global configuration as imperial, this for Tully can never be a matter of acquiescence, still less celebration. And if the defining frame or structure of that configuration is as resistant to change as some hope and others fear, then, if one is in the latter camp, that is bound to raise the spectre of fatalism.

Many, myself included, would readily side with Tully that the current global configuration would be intolerable if and to the extent that its imperial characteristics reveal themselves as stubbornly resistant to change. The more difficult question, however, and the basis for the second variant of the charge of structural fatalism, concerns just how resistant to change the current global configuration is. For what Tully's redefinitional efforts succeed in placing in sharp relief is the relatively sanguine view of the transformability of the present structure held by both the neo-Kantians and the post-colonial school. From the perspective of the neo-Kantians, indeed, the scope for internal transformation of the new and increasingly differentiated form of global rule is such that they would hesitate before using the label imperial at all in the present tense. And while the post-colonial writers believe, in contrast, that the imperial legacy currently remains strong, they are nevertheless relatively confident as to its amenability to ongoing strategies of resistance and transformation. Accordingly, in conceptualising the resilience of the present structure as he does, Tully, as already intimated, seeks to shift the burden of proof back onto all those – neo-Kantians and post-colonials alike – who would acknowledge the durability

3 Ibid. at 2.

4 See for example, J. Tully, 'Struggles Over Recognition and Redistribution' (2001), 7 *Constellations* 469–82.

of structures long associated with imperialism, but would maintain that they can nevertheless be transformed from within.

In an argument, such as this, about the conditions of social and political *praxis*, it is not difficult to see why the burden of proof becomes so important. Not only is any discussion about the prospects and consequences of future change inherently speculative, but in that speculation there is always an unstable dialectic of optimism/pessimism at work. Some will accuse others of being too slow to recognise the ways and means of transformation, of setting the bar of plausible transformability so high that all viable options are foreclosed, and the shadows of fatalism descend. The others, in turn, will accuse the first group of being too quick to imagine transformative possibilities, of seeing open highways where there are in fact only hidden traps or dead ends, and thus of avoiding the hard but necessary work of exploring as critically and remorselessly as possible what stands in the way of genuine transformative possibilities. In both cases the accusation is, or at its most acute can be, a strong one – either defeatism or wishful thinking.

How well, if at all, then, does Tully succeed in avoiding the charge of fatalism and instead succeed in exposing as naïve and undertheorised those positions who would not share his scepticism about existing possibilities of changes and join his search for new possibilities? To answer this question, it is helpful to examine Tully's position in relation to three inter-related oppositions that are pertinent to much critical social and political theory but which seem particularly relevant to his own work. The first is the classic opposition between revolution and reform. The second is the opposition between inside and outside – between working within the system and operating outside it. The third is the opposition between what we may call 'top-down' and 'bottom-up' mechanisms of transformation.

Tully has always been consistent in his rejection of revolution and reform alike. Indeed, his reputation, certainly in the decade since the publication of *Strange Multiplicity*,[5] has been largely and justifiably built on the basis of his powerful cumulative efforts to think through a 'third way,' (lower case!) and, indeed, to do so in an essentially affirmative vein. On the one hand, he is no friend of revolution – of the overthrow of a government by those who are governed – not only for the obvious pragmatic reason that they tend not to succeed, but also on two other grounds. In the first place, as his citation of Franz Fanon's discussion of the 'curse of independence'[6] makes clear, merely cutting off the head of the King may change little if the new rulers inhabit the same structures and experience the same constraints. Revolution as usurpation, in other words, can be and often is highly conservative. In the second place, revolution can be *over*inclusive as well as *under*inclusive – it can cause indiscriminate and unjustified harm and can destroy the healthy tissue of social and political relations as much as it may dismantle the structures of oppression. In elaborating his three conventions of 'constitutionalism' *qua* intercultural dialogue in *Strange Multiplicity*, namely 'mutual recognition, consent and cultural continuity'.[7]

---

5 *Strange Multiplicity: Constitutionalism in an Age of Diversity* (Cambridge: Cambridge University Press, 1995).

6 Above n2, at 16.

7 Above n5, at 30.

Tully sets his stall firmly against this kind of forced evacuation of the past. The idea that there is and remains much to be valued beyond the imperial horizon, and that transformation is as much about recovery as innovation, are repeated themes of his work, and indeed are much emphasised in the present essay. Revolution, clearly, is too crude an instrument for these purposes.

On the other hand, Tully is equally alert to the dangers of reformism. For Tully, democratic freedom does not imply a particular institutional design, but is a principle of necessarily open-ended significance. In an important earlier formulation of his position, he put it this way:

> if citizens are to be free, then the procedures by which they deliberate, the reasons they accept as public reasons, and the practices they are permitted to test by those democratic means must ... themselves be open to deliberation and amendment *en passant* (not all at once) – in the course of the exchange of reasons – as the principle of democracy requires. The entire exercise of democratic freedom in relation to the existing rule of law must be intersubjective and open-ended practical reasoning.[8]

Democratic constitutionalism, therefore, requires 'acceptance of reasonable disagreement all the way down … not only over different conceptions of the good within a framework of fundamental principles of justice, procedures of deliberation or constitutional essentials, but over any such framework as well'.[9] In other words, if, as appears undeniable on all available evidence, disagreement and dissent are as inevitable and irreducible as regards the very rules of the political game as they are as regards its playing, and if the rules as always/already constituted are never neutral between different interests, identities, values and aspirations but always/already express a structural bias, then the relentlessly agonistic[10] conditions of democratic possibility demand that we are always as attentive to the frame within which we negotiate as we are to the quotidian substance of that negotiation. And insofar as the agenda of reform becomes one of bracketing off these framing questions and concentrating only on what is possible within the rules of the games, then it is by definition a truncated and democratically compromised agenda.

But, of course, if the twin dangers of revolution and reform are portrayed so fully and candidly, there will be no easy route for the third way to follow. The scale and depth of Tully's struggle here becomes apparent when he turns to discuss the second opposition – between inside and outside. Apparently more emphatically than ever before, in the present essay Tully wants to insist that the quality of social and political relations possible within the dominant imperial frame are quite distinct from and discontinuous with what is possible outside these relations. Opposition from within, he claims, is essentially 'tactical' and defensive rather than 'strategic' and offensive. Its capacity to exploit 'the "play" or "indeterminacy" of relations of meaning and

---

8 'The Unfreedom of the Moderns in Comparison to Their Ideals of Constitutional Democracy' (2002) 65 *Modern Law Review*, 204–28, at 217.

9 Ibid. 218.

10 On Tully's engagement with agonistic theory, see, for example, 'The Agonistic Freedom of Citizens', (1999) 28 *Economy and Society*, 161–82.

power in order to extend and modify them *en passant*'[11] – previously seen as the basic modality through which democratic freedom is simultaneously claimed and expressed[12] – is now seen, in a move that is crucial in distinguishing him from other post-colonial writers, as presumptively incapable of occasioning a change of sufficient profundity to do other than leave the basic imperial features intact. It is not that in principle Tully has given up on the idea of a form of democratic freedom that moves between different operational levels and is not constrained by the distinction between form and substance, but rather that on empirical grounds he finds it very difficult to imagine how such root-and-branch democratic interrogation is possible in the context of the 'vastly unequal field of institutions of informal imperialism'.[13] That is to say, his fear is that the deep structure of informal imperialism, with its promotion of low-intensity elite-led democracy in former colonial territories and its network of international institutions shaped through the unequal influence of a few old sovereigns, is just *too* deep to be amenable to this kind of challenge from within.

If, by contrast, we turn to relations situated beyond the imperial horizon – to 'the legal, political and economic pluralism that has not been reconstituted by western imperialism, but continues to exist in the day-to-day lives of millions of people',[14] then Tully remains much more optimistic. Recovery from the margins and cultural continuity, as we have seen, has always been a central theme of his work, and this remains the case. The problem, however, lies in the mutual articulation of inside and outside. If the inside is compromised, what is the outside to act upon other than itself, and if it can only act upon itself, how are imperial relations ever to be disturbed? That is to say, when Tully charges post-colonial writers with ultimately not yet being 'able to distinguish between a form of contestation that "modifies" an imperial relationship, which leaves the underlying imperial features in place … and a form of contestation that 'transforms' an imperial relationship … whereby it comes under the shared democratic authority of those subject to it',[15] he must also ask himself the same question. Just as the internal 'contestations' of his protagonists may be co-opted by their internality, so his own external 'contestations' may be marginalised by their externality.

Tully is clearly aware of this problem – hence his concluding admission that the complexity of our entanglement in imperial relations is such that *no-one* can be 'so sure of our way out as the [post-colonial] critics of imperialism lead us to believe'.[16] Hence, too, my final conviction that it would it be unfair to level the charge of structural fatalism against him. His only crime seems to be to have succeeded in formulating new theoretical and practical challenges for those committed to an idea of global justice, or at least to insist upon the continuing relevance of questions that no-one has satisfactorily answered. Moreover, he properly sees the posing of these questions as a common challenge in our understanding and development of

11 Above n2.

12 See above n8.

13 Above n2.

14 Ibid.

15 Ibid.

16 Ibid.

the theory and practice of social, political and legal *praxis* rather than a theoretical trump-card to flourish before his interlocutors.

But, in conclusion, and in the spirit of that common challenge, I would like to offer a way of developing the argument further – one that turns on the third opposition between 'top-down' and 'bottom-up' mechanism of change. Tully does not address this opposition directly, and three reasons might be offered, in ascending order of seriousness, why he might be resistant to such a move. Firstly, it may be tempting to conflate the 'top-down'/'bottom-up' division with the inside/outside distinction. That is to say, on one view, only external and imperially untainted democratic practices are properly 'bottom-up' – grounded in the grassroots of civil society – and, equally, all practices internal to the imperial structure are by the nature of their privileged domicile 'top-down'. But to insist upon this as the only relevant axis of variation within the anti-imperial field would be to gloss over potentially important differences. For alongside the basic inside/outside distinction, can we not think of a further set of sub-divisions within each domain between different operative levels?

Perhaps, however – and this would be a second and more serious objection – precisely because of his longstanding insistence on democratic interrogation 'all the way down', Tully would not want to allow too rigid a distinction of levels between 'bottom-up' everyday contestation over the meaning of a norm and more rarefied 'top-down' discussion of the procedures for its authorisation, or even of the meta-procedures for legitimating these procedures. But, of course, however wide the interpretive space for the ongoing adaptation of the substantive 'bottom-up' normative rules and guidelines, however amenable to democratic voice and participation the system of institutional design, and however flexibly the higher order rules of normative change might be constructed, a basic logical distinction remains between the first-order rules at the operational base of the legal-constitutional order, and the jurisgenerative framework rules at the apex of the pyramid.

The 'top-down'/'bottom-up' distinction, therefore, begins to suggest ways to rehabilitate insider strategies, and also to reconnect them to external strategies.[17] For whereas it may not be possible to view external agitation and insider tactics at the level of 'bottom-up' normative rules as a domain of practice which in isolation can do anything other than modify and mitigate the hegemonic system, the position may look rather different if we bring into the same strategic picture the 'top-down' framing legal and political structures of the global order. At least in theory, it is at the level of redesign of the deep regulatory structure – the basic 'Keynesian-Westphalian frame'[18] – of informal imperialism, and through the invocation of the principle of 'participatory parity'[19] in its more abstract contexts of 'meta-political

17 For an earlier formulation of this argument, see G. de Burca and N. Walker, 'Law and Transnational Civil Society: Upsetting the Agenda?' (2003) 9 *European Law Journal* 387–400.

18 See N. Fraser, 'Reframing Justice in a Globalizing World' (2005) 36 *New Left Review*, 69–88.

19 Ibid. at 87.

democratization',[20] that we imagine transformations of the informal imperial system as opposed to modifications that are in the final analysis system-endorsing.

Yet this is surely the cue for a third and key objection. For whatever the merits of such an approach *in theory*, is it not the case that in practice it is precisely the 'top-down' framing rules that are the most difficult to change? If informal empire remains a motivated achievement and one that is pervasive in its reach and resilient in its dominance, then is it not in these very framing contexts – the constitutional high-ground of the post-national constellation – that the agents of empire will be its most jealous guardians and be most highly motivated to retain the pervasiveness and guarantee the resilience of the prevailing order?

While no-one who has spent any time examining the contexts of original and ongoing negotiation of the basic postnational regulatory frame – whether in the context of the UN and its Security Council or the WTO or the EU or NAFTA – can have any illusions over the strong representation and sustained prevalence of the interests of dominant economic and political groupings, their continuing success is by no means inevitable. For, crucially, the very informalism or 'loose coupling' of the current structure of dominance that allows it to be so pervasive and so resilient, may also provide the key to its transformation. Informal empire is poly-centred and hydra-headed empire. It is not a centralised or even a federalised or consociationalised and in any rate 'singular' world system, but a more 'plural' constellation of overlapping functional and territorial national and postnational institutional forms.[21] Indeed, as we have seen, it is a key part of Tully's thesis that such plurality is one of empire's key strengths. It permits it more easily to assume an ideologically non-imperial guise, and it also allows it to present itself as a more diverse target – a series of strongholds rather than a single citadel to be toppled.

Yet plurality also offers transformative possibilities. The absence of a single citadel also means the lack of a monolithic power with the capacity and co-ordination to design and defend 'formally' what alternatively may evolve 'informally'. It means the relative autonomy, and sometimes mutual contestation, of the plural parts.[22] It means that although the democratic transformation of no one particular site of power will lead to the demise of all asymmetrical orders, there will nevertheless be a cumulative effect if there are simultaneous changes across sites. And it means that the odds are not so formidably stacked against any such particular transformations as they would be against the removal of a single monolithic structure – something of which we have current cause to remind ourselves as we see in the early years of the new century increasingly intense democratic challenges to the constitutional legitimacy of the Security Council, the WTO and, most acutely of all at present, the

20 Ibid. at 86.

21 See, for example, N. Walker, 'The Idea of Constitutional Pluralism', (2002) 65 *Modern Law Review* 317–59. And in the context of 'global administrative law', see N. Krisch, 'The Pluralism of Global Administrative Law' (2006) 17 *European Journal of International Law*, 247–78.

22 Krisch, above n21.

EU.[23] It is only if we are prepared to follow this flow and re-focus on the various commanding legal and political heights of our still significantly unbalanced global order, as well as on the detailed regulatory and practical depths and the 'alterity beyond'[24] that Jim Tully has done so much to address and highlight, that we can begin to imagine the global order along a non-imperial trajectory.

23 In very recent work Tully has also re-focused more specifically both on what he sees as the limitations of the conventional constitutional mind-set and the structures to which this refers (see J. Tully, 'The Imperialism of Modern Constitutional Democracy' in M. Loughlin and N. Walker (eds) *The Paradox of Constitutionalism* (Oxford: Oxford University Press, 2007)) and on the priority of reforming the EU from below rather than from above (see J. Tully 'A New Kind of Europe? Democratic Integration in the European Union' (2007) 10 *Critical Review of International Social and Political Philosophy*). For a less sceptical view of 'top-down' constitutionalism in the transnational context generally see, for example, J. Habermas, *The Divided West* (Cambridge: Polity, 2006,) ch.8; and in the EU context see N. Walker 'A Constitutional Reckoning' (2006) 13 *Constellations* 140–150.

24 Above n2.

Chapter 9

Imperialism and Constitutionalism

Gavin W. Anderson

Introduction

Jim Tully's major contribution to constitutional thought has been to provoke discussion over its appropriate bounds. His most renowned argument is that the predominant western conception of a constitution as founding a homogeneous nation-state which exercises self-governance through 'a set of uniform legal and political institutions'[1] is necessarily a partial account of the historical record. Against this 'empire of uniformity', he juxtaposes the 'hidden constitutions' of indigenous societies, based in conventions of mutual recognition, and whose survival attest to the rich diversity of contemporary constitutionalism.[2] His claim that constitutionalism should no longer be seen as inexorably tied to the institutions of the modern state has been influential in developing pluralistic notions of constitutionalism, for example in the context of the supranational constitutionalism of the European Union.[3] This theme of opening up the frontiers of constitutional discourse also informs his normative position in favour of a thorough-going constitutional agonistics. For Tully, it is through extending constitutional argument from debate *within*, to debate *over*, the rules of governance, that the voices of the previously marginalised can be heard, and their interests accommodated.[4]

Tully's chapter on law, democracy and imperialism in the present collection seems to strike a different note, one that resonates more in terms of exclusion rather than inclusion. In place of the vibrant imagery of The Spirit of Haida Gwaii,[5] symbolising the multiple hands on the constitutional tiller 'squabbling and vying for recognition',[6] here we have a more stilted picture, depicting the relative success of imperialism's

1 J. Tully, *Strange Multiplicity: Constitutionalism in an Age of Diversity* (Cambridge: Cambridge University Press, 1995), 41.

2 Ibid. ch. 6.

3 See, for example, J. Shaw, 'Postnational Constitutionalism in the European Union' (1999) *JEPP* 579.

4 J. Tully, 'The Unfreedom of the Moderns in Comparison to Their Ideals of Constitutional Democracy' (2002) 65 *Modern Law Review* 204 at 223.

5 A photograph of *The Spirit of Haida Gwaii*, a sculpture by the late Haida artist Bill Reid, adorns the jacket of *Strange Multiplicity*. The sculpture is a bronze black canoe which contains thirteen characters drawn from Haida mythology which includes *ttsaang* (the beaver) who is 'paddling menacingly amidships,' *ghuuts* (the wolf) who 'sinks his fangs in the eagle's wing' and *ghuut* (the eagle) who appears to be 'attacking the bear's paw in retaliation' (Tully, supra n. 1, 17).

6 Supra, n.1, 24.

homogenising ambitions. Moreover, his account of imperialist discourse closing down the voices of potential critics, drawing them onto its preferred terms of debate, would seem to thwart, at least in part, realising his aim of fostering a more open political debate. How significant is this apparent change of tone, and how does this relate to his previous constitutional writings? In particular, how does it sit with his position that, notwithstanding constitutionalism's chequered history and its role in supporting the colonial enterprise, it can nonetheless be reconceptualised as a positive force for cultural diversity?

One response might be that Tully is entitled to different views on different topics, and that greater pessimism may well be justified in the case of imperialism than with constitutionalism. Tully would likely resist suggestions of discontinuity and regard this essay as elaborating the necessary linkages between constitutionalism and imperialism. Moreover, he concludes that pessimism here is but one part of the story, the other, untold for the moment, being the 'pre-existing and continuing non-imperial forms of life' which underlie western imperialism.[7] I agree that the essay does not mark a wholly new direction, and that in some highly relevant ways it builds on Tully's previous work. In particular, it develops a sometimes overlooked, but crucial, aspect of Strange Multiplicity which focuses on how dominant forms of constitutional (and imperial) knowledge have maintained hegemonic relations of power. But adverting to the constraining effects of epistemological frameworks creates an uneasy tension with Tully's claim that constitutional discourse can also be a means of opening debate over, not just within, the rules – a tension which has led some to cast him as a constitutional enthusiast, others as a sceptic.[8]

In this chapter, I explore the nature of this tension, and its implications for the reconstructive constitutional project. I consider how adverting to the epistemological dimension undermines the case for constitutional optimism. I address this with reference to Tully's objective, restated here, to enter into a co-equal dialogue with the suppressed constitutional languages of indigenous peoples. My argument is that Tully's optimism here, as with normative constitutional theory in general, is only justified by discounting the limitations placed on this enterprise by the prevailing epistemological framework: but it is precisely this framework that militates against achieving this sort of dialogue in practice.

Tully's essay in the context of his constitutional theory

Tully is in some ways an unusual constitutional theorist. While preoccupation with normative doctrinal debate has left many in the field open to the charge of abstraction,[9]

---

7 As such, he distinguishes himself from critics like Michael Hardt and Antonio Negri who would argue that 'there is no "outside" or that everything is empire'. (See Tully, supra 71, n. 8.)

8 Cf. N. Walker, 'The Idea of Constitutional Pluralism' (2002) 62 *Modern Law Review* 317 at 330/1 and E. Christodoulidis, 'Constitutional Irresolution: Law and the Framing of Civil Society' (2003) *European Law Journal* 401 at 408.

9 See R. Hirschl, *Towards Juristocracy: The Origins and Consequences of the New Constitutionalism* (Cambridge, MA: Harvard University Press, 2004), ch. 1.

there is a deep, and welcome, concern with constitutionalism's relationship with power running through Tully's work. This is rooted in his historical account of the rise of modern constitutionalism, and the necessary connections between this and the colonial project. In *Strange Multiplicity*,[10] Tully outlines how the western constitutional tradition became an important means of legitimating the dispossession and subjugation of indigenous peoples. For example, contrasting the organisation of European states into 'political societies' with the supposedly arrested condition of the lands to be settled, was the basis of the *terra nullius* doctrine under which sovereignty could be exercised over areas occupied by Aboriginals without their consent.[11] These doubts over whether constitutionalism is necessarily a force for advancing progressive causes also informs his analysis of contemporary constitutional phenomena. He regards one of the most pressing challenges to constitutional democracy as the rise of a 'global, corporate capitalism' which can 'override domestic and national constitutions' requiring them to relinquish democratic oversight of the market.[12] But he is not starry-eyed about constitutionalism's ability to check corporate power, noting that while human rights may now have a global reach, they still tend 'to favour the rights of private autonomy'.[13]

Here, Tully engages directly with imperialism, and details how its cause has been advanced through its setting the categories of debate in a manner which neutralises potential opponents. This operates first through the construction of a discourse of international relations, premised either on the sovereign equality of nation-states or the cosmopolitan qualities of global governance, which appears to mark a break from, and to invite a welcome contrast with, the imperial past. For Tully what is significant is that this discourse occludes an alternative knowledge of international politics, namely how an 'informal imperialism' perpetuates global inequalities of power, for example by imposing structural adjustment programmes on former colonies. Even more insidious, though, is that even if one recognises this informal imperialism, the terms of apparent resistance thereto are also terms of co-option. Thus, the language of self-determination, rather than providing liberation from colonial rule, was a further means of informal control: under western tutelage, it had in-built limits which ensured the post-colonial state would, for example, not pursue forms of economic development which challenged the imperial system.[14]

When we locate the present essay in the trajectory of Tully's work, this underscores the importance he places on the connection between knowledge and power, and in particular how the acceptance of certain forms of knowledge as common sense has been a useful strategy for the promotion of hegemonic interests. In *Strange*

10 Supra, n.1.

11 Tully notes that for Locke, in contrast with Aboriginals who were 'commonly without any fixed property on the ground', the European settlers ('those who are counted the Civiliz'd part of Mankind') 'have multiplied positive laws to determine Property', for 'in governments the Laws regulate the right of property, and the possession of land is determined by positive constitutions'. Ibid., 72, quoting John Locke, *Two Treatises of Government*, P. Laslett (ed.) (Cambridge: Cambridge University Press, 1981), second treatise, ss. 27, 38, 30, 50.

12 Tully, supra, n.4 at 212.

13 Ibid.

14 Cf. U. Baxi, *The Future of Human Rights* (Delhi: Oxford University Press, 2002), 36, 37.

Multiplicity, he argues that while from one perspective modern constitutionalism can be characterised as a clash between the schools of liberalism, nationalism and communitarianism, from another they share a common language[15] which 'was designed to exclude or assimilate cultural diversity and justify uniformity'.[16] To the extent that this became the dominant idiom, it impeded the development of a broader knowledge of constitutionalism, one drawing on non-European and non-imperialist traditions such as the indigenous forms of government that pre-existed in colonial lands.[17] In more recent work, Tully has extended this line of analysis, for example, to highlight that the construction of corporations in constitutional thought as private persons and not centres of political power has prevented serious inquiry into how their activities can be brought under democratic control.[18]

This willingness to articulate, and question (insofar as they support differential relations of power), constitutionalism's operative assumptions sets Tully apart from the large number of constitutional theorists for whom these are simply a given, and to be defended if necessary. In doing so, he is following a critical tradition which seeks to scrutinise the 'presuppositions of discussion which remain undisclosed'.[19] The manner in which Tully elaborates the relation between knowledge and power in the context of imperialism does not seem so distant from critics such as Pierre Bourdieu and Loïc Wacquant. Their argument that the spread of American cultural imperialism succeeds through the construction of commonplaces, namely 'theses *with which* one argues but *about which* one does not argue',[20] for example neo-liberalism, has obvious resonances with Tully's characterisation say of debates within self-determination. Moreover, they see the ubiquity of these commonplaces, disseminated through academic meetings and publications, and also more popular media such as bestsellers and magazines, as a means of neutralising their contingent historical and political origins.

Now Tully is of course free to agree or disagree with whomever he chooses, but this is in some ways a jarring juxtaposition. Whereas Tully may follow Bourdieu and Wacquant to some degree in terms of their analysis of imperialism, the latter do not readily spring to mind as fellow constitutional travellers for Tully. This provokes a more general question which I explore further below, namely how the critical understanding of the relation between knowledge and power that emerges from our study of imperialism impacts upon the reconstructive constitutional project on which Tully and others are embarked. In other words, is constitutionalism also a 'commonplace' which seeks to constrain political debate within a limited set of culturally specific values?

15 Tully, supra n.1, 62–70.

16 Ibid. 58.

17 Ibid. 37.

18 Tully, supra n.4, 222.

19 P. Bourdieu and L. Wacquant, 'On the Cunning of Imperialist Reason', (1999), 16, *Theory, Culture and Society* 41 at 41.

20 Ibid. (emphasis in original).

Imperialism, the universal and the particular

A helpful starting point in approaching this question is to situate it in debates about the relation between the universal and the particular. Tully's essay here highlights what Judith Butler labels the 'fear' of those on the left that 'what is named as universal is the parochial property of dominant culture, and that "universalizability" is indissociable from imperial expansion'.[21] For Ernesto Laclau, one of the key features of post-Cold War politics is the redefinition of the relation between universality and particularity.[22] Laclau's own account of the universal is premised in the necessary incompletion of the subject: the impossibility of eliminating antagonism means that all identities are 'penetrated by a constitutive lack'.[23] This leads him to regard the universal as an 'empty, but ineradicable place.' Given this 'absent fullness', the content of the universal is made possible through 'a chain of equivalential effects'. This, given the incompletion of the subject, is necessarily drawn from a boundless list of differences. Accordingly, the chain must remain open, but equally it has to be presented in universal terms – however, a universality which can only be expressed in terms of what appears incommensurable, namely a particularity.[24] For Laclau, this is how hegemonic relationships are constituted, as the community is taken to give its tacit consent to those particularities which 'fill-in' the empty space of the universal.[25] But there is always an underlying tension, as although formulated in apparently transcendental terms, eventually these universal principles will 'become entangled in their own contextual particularism and are incapable of fulfilling their universal function'.[26]

Judith Butler's engagement with Laclau's argument brings the discussion back to the relation between power and knowledge in constitutional discourse. For Butler, Laclau's contention that the universal is necessarily a site of contest is compelling, but she notes that the meaning of this contest has not been fully elaborated.[27] She interrogates Laclau's conception of the universal as an empty place, and argues that we should always situate claims to universality within 'a given syntax'. The key point here is that what comes to be recognised as a universal claim depends on 'an establishing rhetoric' and 'a set of norms that are invoked in the recognition of such claims'.[28] In this way, Laclau's empty space is filled in, and so every assertion of universality receives content from being placed in its (local) cultural context.[29] This results in a porous relation between the universal and the particular, where political

---

21 J. Butler, 'Restaging the Universal' in J. Butler, E. Laclau and S. Žižek, *Contingency, Hegemony, Universality: Contemporary Dialogues on the Left* (London: Verso, 2000), 15.

22 E. Laclau, *Emancipation(s)* (London: Verso, 1996), vii.

23 Ibid. 28. As Laclau puts it, '[t]he basic point is this: I cannot assert a differential identity without distinguishing it from a context, and, in the process of making the distinction, I am asserting the context at the same time'. (27)

24 Ibid. 57.

25 Ibid. 43.

26 Ibid.

27 Butler, supra n.21, 34.

28 Ibid. 35.

29 Put slightly differently, 'no universal is freed from its contamination by the particular contexts from which it emerges and in which it travels' (40).

claims cannot be exclusively characterised in terms of one or the other, and indeed, where each is capable of simultaneously depicting the same phenomenon. Thus, for Butler, the universal is always subject to challenge: through the 'perverse reiteration' of its erstwhile exclusionary norms, we can produce unconventional accounts of universality which expose the limited cultural basis of its previous incarnation, while acting as the focus for new political demands.[30] Following Laclau, she highlights the importance of understanding the hegemonic nature of power relations if one wishes to transcend them. In particular, she stresses how power:

> [i]s remade at various junctures within everyday life; it constitutes our tenuous sense of common sense, and is ensconced at the prevailing epistemes of a culture.[31]

Some discourses though work better at producing epistemic openness, as her critique of recent developments in feminist theory makes clear. She finds that where Anglophone feminism makes universalist claims with regard to the various treatments of non-first world women, it fails to see the need to engage in translating this discourse to the norms of local cultures. As such, it fails to see the parochialism of its own norms, and so lends support to the broader universalist project of remaking the world in accordance with the requirements of (US) civility.[32]

An understanding of how the rhetorics employed to establish universalist claims can also stave off potentially destabilising moves has some resonance for Tully's analysis of imperialism. Although the racist and colonialist categories of imperialism have long been challenged as positing false universals, Tully's account shows that this has not prevented imperialism from enjoying a resurgency. An important insight of his essay is the continuing work done by imperialism's syntax in reinforcing its exclusionary norms. For example, the language of self-determination may appear a promising vehicle to prompt, in Butler's terms, 'antagonistic speculations'[33] over who the subject of international relations should be, and through this speech act subvert the discourse of colonialism by giving voice to the previously excluded. However, in practice debates over self-determination have been informed by an imperialist syntax which privileges a very singular conception of the subject: this is the rational self-maximising individual of classical liberalism who can only perceive the exercise of self-determination as functioning to integrate their country into the global economy.

Tully's point is that this did not just happen – rather, self-determination was inscripted with these limitations by its (imperialist) authors from the outset. I want to suggest that this can be developed into a more general point, viz. that imperialist discourse has succeeded in constructing commonsensical terms of debate which present various ideas as external challenges to imperialism and its false universals, but which are in practice informed by its internal syntax. Moreover, these terms of debate are designed to ensure that the deep grammar of imperialism – such as the practices of informal imperialism, or the exclusionary nature of self-determination – is not articulated, and so not subject to Butler's 'perverse reiterations'. Accordingly,

---

30 Ibid. 40.

31 Ibid. 14.

32 Ibid. 35.

33 Ibid. 38.

any new claim which seeks to challenge the exclusionary nature of the established discourse has to effect change at the level of this deep grammar. But the message of Tully's analysis is that it is by drawing potential critics to work *within* the field constructed by imperialism that the latter's account of the universal has remained relatively uncontaminated.

The limits of constitutional discourse

We now consider how this reading of Tully's analysis of imperialism impacts upon his efforts to reformulate constitutionalism so that it is conceived of as an 'intercultural dialogue' whereby citizens negotiate their forms of governance according to conventions of 'mutual recognition, consent and continuity'.[34] We can characterise this contribution to the debate as an attempt to expose and disturb the (contingent) universal of modern constitutionalism by valorising other particularisms, notably indigenous constitutional traditions, thereby moving to a new universal. But to return to the opening question of whether there are differences between his analyses of imperialism and constitutionalism, it would seem that Tully has to convince us that there is a discontinuity here, and that efforts of him and others to shift the underlying basis of constitutionalism will fare better than those critics of imperialism who have not only failed to do so, but been co-opted in the process.

Tully himself is aware that a deep grammar is at work in constitutional discourse. His account of the rise of the three dominant schools details how the language of modern constitutionalism was held in place 'in spite of, and even as a result of, the continual challenges to aspects of it, by customary linguistic useage, normal activity and institutionalisation'.[35] The enmeshing of this conventional language in society's institutions makes it very difficult to challenge, and so move to a more inclusive basis for constitutional recognition. As the concluding chapter of *Strange Multiplicity* makes clear, Tully believes that the task of remaking constitutionalism is not only a worthwhile endeavour, but also one that is being realised in practice. However, the real test for Tully is not so much whether normative arguments regarding the constitutional aspirations of aboriginal peoples can now be heard within constitutional discourse, but whether they can change the nature of the rules which excluded them in the first place. Accordingly it is important to consider how aboriginal constitutional claims have been received in practice.

According to Tully, the constitutions of contemporary society can be characterised not by a 'comprehensive representation', but instead by 'participation in a practical dialogue where limited and complementary stories are exchanged'.[36] Moreover, these constitutions advance cultural, legal and political pluralism rather than upholding the empire of uniformity.[37] In part support, he refers to jurisprudential developments in negotiating cultural conflict such as the *Sparrow* case, where the Supreme Court of Canada upheld the Musqueam Nation's claim that they possessed

34 Tully, supra n.1, 184.

35 Ibid. 40.

36 Ibid. 183.

37 Ibid. 183.

fishing rights, which pre-existed the colonial settlement, and so could be exercised without obtaining a fishing licence (licences would still be required in the case of non-aboriginals).[38] For Tully, this is an example of rights being taken seriously, and of impartial reasoning on the part of the Court as it does not discriminate against cultural identity. To this we could add cases like *Baker Lake*, where the Supreme Court held that Aboriginals enjoyed pre-settlement rights to hunt and fish which could be asserted against proposed developments on their land.[39]

Certainly, constitutional dialogue with aboriginals has come some way since they were systematically excluded from the conversation, but what is less clear is that the advances that have been made disturb modern constitutionalism's universalising tendencies to the extent that these have been significantly undermined. Instead, what we have here are new styles of syntax, but which still operate within the same deep grammar. Constitutional recognition has been accorded most prominently with regard to 'way of life' rights such as fishing, but Michael Asch argues there has been 'no progress with respect to fundamental political rights'.[40] He suggests that starting from the premise that Aboriginal societies are the political equal of the Canadian state would raise difficult questions including 'how wealth would be shared "fairly"' or how federal and provincial jurisdictions should be redistributed to take account of aboriginal sovereignty. But, as Asch observes, merely to pose these questions underlines the impossibility of their being taken seriously.[41] In other words, debate over the rules would require us to address the consequences of the exclusionary founding acts of the colonial state; but it is by maintaining debate within rules which speak in terms of diversity and accommodation that such questions are avoided, while the legitimacy of the colonial state is preserved, and even enhanced.

It is not just with regard to aboriginal peoples that constitutional discourse limits the parameters of debate while appearing to hold out the prospect of change. To take another example discussed by Tully, there has been much interest recently in reconceptualising constitutionalism in response to the rise of private power. While constitutionalism has traditionally regulated the institutions of the state, a number of scholars have sought to extend its reach, whether by focusing on the nexus between the state and private actors, or the relevance of constitutional guarantees to laws that govern private relations.[42] As with the previous example, the jurisprudence is not always unreceptive to these arguments, and courts have held that the state has positive obligations to ensure rights are protected irrespective of who may be

38 *R v. Sparrow* (1990) 70 DLR (4th) 385.

39 *Hamlet of Baker Lake v. Canada* (1980) 107 DLR (3d) 513.

40 M. Asch, 'From *Calder* to *Van der Peet*: Aboriginal Rights and Canadian Law, 1973-96' in P. Havemann (ed.) *Indigenous Peoples' Rights in Australia, Canada and New Zealand* (Auckland: Oxford University Press, 1999), 428 at 438.

41 M. Asch, 'First Nations and the Derivation of Canada's Underlying Title: Comparing Perspectives on Legal Ideology' in C. Cook and J. D. Lindau (eds.) *Aboriginal Rights and Self-Government: The Canadian and Mexican and North American Perspective* (Montreal and Kingston: McGill-Queen's University Press, 2000), 148 at 166.

42 See, for example, A Clapham, *Human Rights Obligations for Non-state Actors* (Oxford: Oxford University Press, 2006).

infringing them.[43] However, again these developments operate within rather than challenge the deep grammar: while there may be discussion, say over the extent to which private conduct is engaged through legislative inaction, what is not brought into question is why state bodies are regarded as centres of political and legal power, but corporations are not.[44]

Conclusion

The historic mission of modern constitutionalism, as Tully's work has helped establish, has been to prevent key aspects of constitutional knowledge being opened to debate. Recent developments might seem to suggest some broadening out of constitutional discourse, whether to accommodate cultural diversity or reach private action. But in each case, the core of constitutional knowledge has remained in place. What we are highlighting here is the work of powerful rhetorics in filling out the empty space of the universal, and presenting liberal constitutionalism, and its epistemological basis, as the optimum form of governmental arrangement. Rather than being under challenge, this is increasingly regarded as the only viable form of constitutional knowledge, as evidenced by the trends toward global constitutional homogenisation, both at an institutional[45] and jurisprudential[46] level. Moreover, for some there is also a process of epistemological narrowing taking place, particularly with regard to rights, which in Upendra Baxi's words, are being reconceptualised within a 'trade-related, market-friendly [paradigm]'.[47]

These are conclusions which one could draw, I have suggested, by exploring the linkages between Tully's chapter on colonialism in this volume to his work on the historical development of constitutionalism. This highlights a disjuncture in Tully's constitutional theory: to the extent that the above analysis directs us to how constitutional discourse has achieved epistemic closure, this makes his claim that constitutional argument can go all the way down unconvincing. But this disjuncture is not solely interesting in terms of how we read Tully, but raises a point of fundamental importance for those engaged in the reconstructive constitutional project. Tully's constitutional enthusiasm would seem justified only by putting his account of the epistemological constraints of constitutional discourse to one side, and this is precisely what happens when constitutional argument moves into normative mode. Tully wishes to provoke a debate over the rules, and so effect changes to constitutional discourse from outside, but in 'going normative', he becomes subject to the gravitational pull of constitutionalism's deep grammar, and so is debating

43 See, for example, *Plattform 'Ärzte für das Leben' v Austria* Series A no 139 (1991) 13 EHRR 204 & *Vriend v Alberta* [1998] 1 SCR 493.

44 I develop this point more fully in Gavin W. Anderson, *Constitutional Rights after Globalization* (Oxford and Portland, OR: Hart, 2005) ch. 7.

45 See Hirschl, supra n.9.

46 See D. Beatty, *The Ultimate Rule of Law* (Oxford: Oxford University Press, 2004).

47 See Baxi, supra n.14, 144–152.

within its assumptions.[48] Tully may object that his is a more broadly conceived normativity, one that, for example, is not court-centric and avoids the public institutional bias of many theorists. But what is important is not his motivation, but how his contribution will be received and interpreted, and so long as this occurs within constitutional discourse, the originary acts of exclusion on which the latter is based – whether a hierarchical understanding of the relation between European and aboriginal societies, or the exclusion of economic activity from the domain of the political – remains safely 'ensconced' in the epistemes of society.

Tully draws our attention to how the commonplaces of knowledge have advanced hegemonic imperialism. It follows that it is the urgent task of critical theory to effect a shift at the epistemological level if one wishes to construct different hegemonic relations. According to Butler the 'ultimate' question is: 'which specific content has to be excluded so that the *very empty* form of universality emerges as the 'battlefield' for hegemony?'[49] What I have sought to demonstrate in this chapter is that much of this content consists of the taken for granted assumptions of constitutional discourse which are not brought into play in normative debate. Tully closes his essay on a more optimistic note, finding the prospect of an anti-imperial future lying in starting a dialogue with surviving non-imperial languages. This is an ambition which many can share. There is though the suggestion that such an endeavour is something which can wait for another day. But so long as the route to that future lies in reconceptualising constitutional discourse, this is a day which may never come.

---

48 As Loughlin notes, normative approaches 'highlight law's adjudicative and control function and therefore its rule orientation and its conceptual nature' so reflecting 'an ideal of the autonomy of law'. M. Loughlin, *Public Law and Political Theory* (Oxford: Clarendon, 1992), 60.

49 Butler, supra n.21, 137 (quoting Žižek).

PART 3
Public Law and Proceduralism

Chapter 10

Constitutionalism as Proceduralism: A Glance at the Terrain

Frank Michelman

I. A Question Posed: A Political-theory-proof Logic of Constitutionalism?

Can we possibly envisage constitutionalism as a discrete [discursive] sphere, hermeneutically closed off or self-standing, subject to its own proper logic, which can be described without the deployment of categories of political theory?[1] That is the Question posed to me – by law professors, it may not be amiss to observe – to which what follows is a response.

I have read this as a question about the actual or possible freestandingness of certain technical discourses, centrally including legal ones, vis-à-vis a certain set of canonical debates in the forum of western political ideas. Thus I take constitutionalism here – not especially idiosyncratically in today's legal-academic milieu[2] – to refer to practices having to do with the establishment, determination and interpretation of bodies of positive law, distinguished in their legal systems as higher or supreme in relation to ordinary statute law and common law. Correlatively, I take political theory to refer to that parallel field of normative speculation that constantly, for better or for worse, is tempting the attentions, energies and devotions of scholars of constitutionalism.

What are the human interests served by politics? What is justice, politically speaking? Which is prior, the individual or the group? Which is prior, freedom or equality (or maybe dignity)? What is the best interpretation of the value of freedom? Of equality? Of dignity? Of community? How does society in the large, or how do social forces, most fundamentally serve or gravely threaten these values? Who or what is rightly sovereign? Which is prior, rights or democracy (or self-government)? What is the best understanding of rights? Of democracy? The list of such topics in political theory – as the field not infrequently is called – could go on.[3] Participants discuss them in terms of Aristotelian, Augustinian, Machiavellian, Hobbesian, Lockean, Humean, Rousseauean, Sièyesean, Kantian, Madisonian, Benthamite,

---

1 Prospectus for a seminar series at the Faculty of Law of the University of Edinburgh, 2005, see Chapter 1 of this volume at 1.

2 See, for example, the writings collected in Norman Dorsen, Michel Rosenfeld, Andras Sajo and Susanne Baer, *Comparative Constitutionalism: Cases and Materials* (St Paul, MN: Thompson/West, 2003), (examining constitutionalism in countries on five continents).

3 Pick up at random a few numbers of the journal *Political Theory* and you will see it all there.

Schmittian, Arendtian, Ungerian, Derridean, and so on, ideas about political and legal ordering in relation to morality, justice, the good and the human condition.

A shared feature of debates in this field, and one that no doubt helps give the field its unity, is that these are debates that seem to many to have an important bearing on direct evaluations of the merits of social choices embedded in acts of legislation, perhaps especially including any we class as constitutional, and of related legal interpretation. These, in other words, are political-theoretic debates that have a capability to invade constitutional-legal discourses. They are capable of replaying themselves both within and upon the legal-ordering practices that in many countries are non-controversially understood to be established, in part or in whole, by what is called constitutional law. But sometimes, and hereby will hang my tale, they strike us rather as controversies, *the procedures for the* pro tempore *institutional settlement of which* it is the office of a constitution to provide – the constitution's own design being necessarily, therefore, conceived as somehow removed to a locus or a plane standing safely beyond these controversies' always potentially corrosive reach.

Back now to the Question: how to envisage constitutionalism as a discrete sphere, subject to a distinctive logic, which can be described without the deployment of categories of political theory? If 'which' refers to a sphere undergoing description ('sphere … which can be described'), then I think there is no answer to how any sphere remotely identifiable with constitutionalism can aptly be described without deploying political-theoretic categories.

For suppose we adopt an external-observer stance. If our aim is to catalogue and classify constitutions or forms of constitutionalism, we are already in the thick of political-theoretic categories (republicanism, for example). Of course we could always put ourselves to a quite different task, say that of describing – or it could, if you like, be that of imagining – the extent to which insiders to constitutional-legal discourses conduct them, or seek or profess to conduct them, or conceivably might conduct them, without overt or direct reference to speculative concerns about legal ordering in relation to justice and human interest, and perhaps without any focused thought to such concerns. We envision these constitutional-legal insiders as pure technicians, wielding as their technique a code-book called Constitutionalism. (Perhaps the book centres on ingrown notions such as 'proportionality' having no exact counterparts in political theory at large. Perhaps when it uses words like 'freedom', 'equality', 'law' and 'order', it uses them in a strictly discourse-relative way, heedless of any connotation that political theory might happen to assign to them.) One could go further, still from an external standpoint, and undertake to show how the fact of such reflexivity in the discursive field of constitutionalism – or the full achievement of it, if it be not yet a fact – is or might be advantageous, or at least not disadvantageous, to a civilising project of legal ordering.

Nothing could be plainer than that neither such a descriptive/imaginative account of what goes on inside constitutionalism, nor such an appraisal of what is described or imagined as going on, is conducted without reference to categories of political theory. To the contrary, it is the raconteur's own reference to certain such categories, including at least the ones he sees as elided by the object discourses, that gives point to what he tells us about the discourses. What is more, an account thus directed would always itself be instinct with a normative inflection, and one that points irrefragably toward a pending contribution to political theory, insofar as any demonstration that discourses of legal constitutionalism have developed, or could develop, into freestandingness from political-theoretic debates cannot help but prompt evaluative and prescriptive queries: Does such an evolution comport with human interest? If so, how?

I think we do better by the Question if we understand that what it putatively fences off from political theory is not discourses of constitutionalism, but rather is the 'proper logic' of such discourses ('logic, which can be described').

As noted, constitutionalism can refer to a practice of using a constitution – a kind of a law – to regulate the methods by which other, value-laden social choices are resolved in the medium of law. Given that those other choices often implicate issues of substance of the sort addressed by political theory, we may perhaps arrive at the following construction of the idea of constitutionalism as a sphere governed by a logic sealed off from political theory. By the logic proper to constitutionalism we might mean a logic of *the procedural*. It would be a logic differentiated, somehow, from logics of the substantive, where 'substance' means the first-order contested merits – about which political theory always seems poised to say something, directly or inferentially – of the social choices embedded in acts of legislation and legal interpretation. Accordingly, the question would become whether *that* distinction – the one between the logic of the procedural (or say the constitutive) and the logic of the substantive – is one that can be made to hold water. If the answer to that question is yes, then perhaps we can build from there a robust claim about a logic proper to constitutionalism, which is or might be sealed off from political theory.

The idea of a procedural logic that is distinctly non-substantive would seem to map nicely onto John Rawls's bifurcation of procedural-justice claims into those he calls claims of 'pure' procedural justice and those he calls claims of 'perfect' or 'imperfect' procedural justice. In pure proceduralism, the justice claim does not refer at all, in any way, to properties of distributive or other social outcomes. Rather, the justice (or one might want to say here the fairness) inheres strictly and solely in the operations by which outcomes are produced. Any complaints about an outcome, not strictly reducible to complaints about the procedure, are deemed to be misdirected, a sort of category mistake. If an outcome is the product of a performance of a procedure deemed fair, it is absolutely closed to complaints of injustice. We voted, and a majority chose what it chose. That's fair. What more do you want?

If there is more that I want, then either I am denying the intrinsic fairness of the procedure at hand for making a decision on the pending social dispute, or else I have in mind some trumping measure for a materially just social outcome, meaning a measure referring directly to attributes of the outcome independent of the procedure that yielded it. Examples of such a measure would include: everyone ends up with shares of the same size; or the worst-off representative person comes out as well-off as possible; or people's rights are secured and respected; or verdicts of guilt and innocence line up properly with the true facts and the true law. Suppose it is on such a ground of injustice in outcomes that I complain. Suppose further that agreement is universal on my proposed standard for justice in outcomes for cases of the kind in question. It does not follow that procedure goes out the window. Others still might defend the outcomes of which I complain by pointing to the procedure employed to get them. That can happen when direct application of our agreed, relevant criterion of justice in outcomes is impracticable, intractably controversial, or unacceptably costly. Outcomes then may be defended by a claim that the procedure used to obtain them is one that is structurally guaranteed to yield outcomes that match the substantive criteria – 'perfect' procedural justice: you cut the cake in two, I'll have the first pick; or that it is as well designed to do so, granting some inevitable misfires, as any feasible and affordable procedure we know of – 'imperfect' procedural justice: the due-process regulated criminal trial.

On some views, the proper logic of constitutionalism is that of imperfect procedural justice.[4] On those views, the logic of constitutionalism is obviously, irretrievably suffused with political theory. Such a logic necessarily incorporates some definite conception of a materially just social outcome, and the critique, defence, and clarification of such conceptions is very much grist for the mills of political theory. But now consider that there are views in which *pure* procedural justice is the telos of constitutionalism rightly understood.[5] Suppose we embrace such a view. Would we then have gained a clear sense in which a logic proper to constitutionalism is or might be sealed off from that of political theory?

My answer is going to be no, or at any rate not yet. We are going to approach it in stages, taking from contemporary liberal political theory some specimens of variably – more and less radically – proceduralised notions of the proper office of constitutions and constitutional law. By way of preparation, though, we shall need to get in mind a widely influential motivation for the proceduralist turn in the precincts of liberal thought we'll be examining.

II. Liberalism Meets Pluralist Disagreement: Toward the Proceduralist Turn

According to a widely held liberal view, it is very much in the moral and other interests of everyone that the following should be possible on some set of practically attainable conditions:

> that inhabitants of a country are morally justified in collaborating with coercion in support of demands for compliance by everyone with all the laws that the judges in that country treat as validly in force, regardless of doubts that they or anyone may hold about the true rightness-on-the-merits of any such law.

Call that the Justified Collaboration Thesis

The Thesis certainly does not hold for all countries at all times. For liberals, though, the possibility of its holding for some countries at some times is a matter of surpassing moral import, because only where and when it does hold can inhabitants partake of certain great 'goods of the political'.[6] Countries in which the Thesis does in fact

4 For an example see Part IVA.

5 For an example see Part IVB.

6 See Rawls, *Political Liberalism* (New York: NY: Columbia University Press, 1993) at 139, 156–7, 168–9, 209 (on 'the very great goods of the political').

hold – assuming that is possible, and there are any – are morally and otherwise well-ordered in a way that other countries are not. Without society's known and proven readiness to step in as necessary to insist on compliance with the law regardless of differing views of its merit, a country's practice of government by law, by which the moral goods I speak of are produced, could not reasonably be expected to hold together. Thus do liberals believe, whether following Thomas Hobbes or Immanuel Kant.[7] On the other hand, no one's moral interest is served by having these goods redeemed by morally reprehensible means. In order, then, for our moral interests to be served, *it would have to be the case that it is not, in our country now, morally reprehensible to collaborate in demands for compliance with unjust laws.*

Liberals take for granted that the possibility of legal ordering, or call it government by law, is a very fine thing, morally speaking. Government by law prevails to the extent that inhabitants of a country are predominantly disposed (a) to conform their conduct to rules and principles pronounced to be law there by some distinct class or classes of officials, (b) to organise their activities with a view to compatibility with such official pronouncements, and (c) to support, or at least to accept, the use of social pressure and, where necessary, force to secure compliance in general with such pronouncements. Government by law, liberals feel certain, carries with it the potential for incalculable benefits to everyone, achievable in no other way: call them social peace and cooperation, call them civic friendship and community, call them justice.

The taken-for-granted supposition, to be clear, is not that any current governmental or legal order cannot stand vast improvement from the standpoints of justice, morality and efficiency. At its most expansive, the claim will be that 'our kind' of governmental order makes available to everyone involved those mentioned, inestimable goods of the political, when the baseline for comparison is a world without government by law. Liberals easily think of these great goods of the political as *moral* goods, on the understanding that everyone shares in the increase to them that results from any decent practice of government by law. Again, it would be excessive to suggest that *any* world in which government by law prevails must be better for everyone in it, or rank higher on the scale of what is right and fair, than might any realistically

7 On Kant, see Jeremy Waldron, 'Kant's Legal Positivism', *Harvard Law Review* 100 (1996), 1535–66. On Hobbes, see, for example, John Rawls, *A Theory of Justice* (Cambridge, MA: Harvard University Press, 1971) 240, endorsing 'Hobbes's thesis':

> ... [E]ven in a well-ordered society the coercive powers of government are in some degree necessary for the stability of social cooperation. [Even assuming citizens] know that they share a common sense of justice and that each wants to adhere to the existing arrangement, they may nevertheless lack full confidence in one another. They may suspect that some are not doing their part, and so they may be tempted not to do theirs. The general awareness of these temptations may eventually cause the system to break down. The suspicion that others are not honouring their duties and obligations is increased by the fact that, in the absence of the authoritative interpretation and enforcement of the rules, it is particularly easy to find excuses for breaking them. ... The role of an authorized public interpretation of rules supported by collective sanctions is precisely to overcome this instability. ... Given the normal conditions of human life, some such arrangements are necessary.

conceivable world from which this condition is absent. Liberals do take for granted, though, that the claim holds true of many historical and contemporary instances of such worlds. The expected flow of universal benefit can provide a moral motivation to collaborate in social pressure and public force as required to ensure compliance by all with approximately each and every law that issues from a currently established governmental system.[8]

Thus when John Rawls, invoking Hobbes[9] (but it might have been Kant[10]) endorses the proposition that, given men and women as they are, arrangements for authorised public interpretation of rules supported by collective sanction are 'necessary', he means they are *morally* necessary – necessary to achievement of a morally compelling end by morally acceptable means. The moral end is the stability of social cooperation on terms that are 'well-ordered' political cooperation 'on the basis of mutual respect'.[11] The moral means is motivation of compliance by reasons everyone has *apart from avoidance of the pains of legal force* – reasons born of regard for the freedom and equality of persons, but also reasons whose cogency turns out to depend on the known availability of the force of law when needed.

The view, in sum, is this: No practice of government by law can succeed in delivering its vaunted moral goods without the persistence in society of general compliance with the laws and official legal interpretations that issue from the practice.[12] Such compliance cannot reasonably be expected to persist among humankind unless persons experience pressures to comply with law as such. It will not persist in a morally acceptable way unless those pressures are geared to morally compelling reasons for compliance that everyone has. Persons won't in all truth have those reasons in the absence of warranted expectation on the part of each participant that the others – most of them, most of the time – will more-or-less abide by *all* the laws that issue from the specific regime of legal government that currently is established in the country, not picking and choosing which ones they'll respect and which they'll trash. And, finally, such a warranted expectation depends on visible and credible guarantees of institutional backup.

All of this probably sounds right enough to most readers. True, not everyone believes it,[13] but liberals do. So consider, then, the consequence when you add to the picture the kind of deep, intractable, normative disagreement that recent liberal theory posits as endemic in modern political societies. To speak, as John Rawls does, of a plurality of clashing comprehensive ethical and metaphysical views is not quite fully to describe our predicament. Owing in part to what Rawls calls burdens

---

8 We can easily leave room for contained occasions of civil disobedience and conscientious refusal, without disturbing the argument. See generally Rawls, *A Theory of Justice* 319–43.

9 See note 7.

10 See note 7.

11 Rawls, *Political Liberalism*, 156.

12 See, for example, H.L.A. Hart, *The Concept of Law* (Oxford: Clarendon Press, 2nd ed. 1994), 189.

13 See, for example, Robert Paul Wolff, *In Defense of Anarchism* (New York: Harper & Row, 1970).

of judgement,[14] our reasonable clashes of 'view' extend to any number of major, morally fraught, public policy choices that have to be resolved in one and only one way for everyone, typically by enactments or interpretations of the law – for example, under what, if any circumstances, may or shall the state kill a human being, punish abortion, or compel taxpayer support of religious schools?[15] The consequence, then, of our attachments to government by law is that we all become collaborators in webs of social practices that exert coercion and pressure upon persons to uphold and comply with bad, wrong and unjust laws.

Do not doubt it. Day in, day out, by countless little, nameless, unremembered acts of compliance and collaboration with our country's governmental regime, we, with little compunction, involve ourselves in a social mobilisation of pressure and force against others to comply with sundry laws and other legal acts with which they do not agree. And not only acts with which they don't agree, but acts that they confidently judge to be quite bad and wrong, and from what they sincerely and credibly take to be a public and not just a self-interested point of view. And since judgements of the public merits of legal acts rarely will be unanimous, and disagreements about this often will be not only intractable and sharp but also honest and reasonable on all sides – or so some liberals insist – we may as well say that the benign and urgent aims of government by law require our willingness to join in subjecting others (not to mention ourselves) to pressures and compulsions to abide by legal acts that, so far as they (or we) honestly can tell, simply *are* wrong, *are* destructive or unjust, objectively – 'you'd better believe it'[16] – and not just according to their (or our) own personal assessments.[17]

---

14 'Burdens of judgement' encompass sundry causes of obdurate disagreement about justice among persons who, as reasonable, all observe and report honestly, argue cogently, and share a 'a desire to honour fair terms of cooperation' Rawls, *Political Liberalism*, 55. Among these causes Rawls lists the likelihood that 'the way we assess evidence and weigh moral and political values is shaped by our total experience, our whole course of life up to now; and our total experiences must always differ. Thus, in a modern society with its numerous offices and positions, its various divisions of labour, its many social groups and their ethnic variety, citizens' total experiences are disparate enough for their judgements to diverge, at least to some degree, on many if not most cases of significant complexity.' Ibid. at 57. See also Thomas Nagel, 'Moral Conflict and Political Legitimacy', *Philosophy and Public Affairs* 16 (1987), 215–240 at 234–5.

15 Compare Rawls, *Political Liberalism*, 36–7 (describing a reasonable pluralism of comprehensive ethical and philosophical views) with Jeremy Waldron, *Law and Disagreement*, 105–16, 112–3, 152, 158–9 (pointing out the inevitable, resulting persistence of reasonable disagreement over the demands of justice regarding matters of public policy, including at the constitutional level).

16 See Ronald Dworkin, 'Objectivity and Truth: You'd Better Believe It', *Philosophy and Public Affairs* 25 (1996), 87–139.

17 It matters not if the legal system's recognitional norms are understood by all to include a filter requiring every ostensible legal act or utterance to pass a test of 'not unjust' as a condition of recognised validity. See Frederick Schauer, 'The Limited Domain of the Law', *Virginia Law Review* 90 (2004), 1909–56, at 1935. The problem then will arise from disagreement about when, in truth, any such filter is engaged.

In the liberal view I am describing, our situation is that we don't know and can't demonstrate – in fact we don't believe deeply or, more likely, believe at all – that all of the laws whose coercive enforcement we help to sponsor are clear of serious injustice.[18] Nor would we be free of problems if we could and did. Even when *we* are convinced that some particular law in question is perfectly morally okay, insisting on *our* view *coercively* against others whose disagreement we find reasonable is to pay them a sort of disrespect that liberals cannot find comfortable.

No liberal thinks you must forbear from forming or voicing considered opinions on the moral and other merits of laws, just because you know your views clash head-on with those of others whom you feel committed to treat with respect. But with legal coercion more is at stake. You connive in exertions of pressure, and maybe force, against recalcitrants to support and abide by laws they consider badly wrong or maybe execrable, or at any rate you condone the conduct of others who do. You owe the recalcitrants, your civic fellows, an explanation for your stance. Suppose you say, by way of self-justification: 'Those laws are right, they are what they ought to be'.You won't then simply be reporting your own personal opinion, with which you consider other people perfectly free to differ. You rather will be conveying a yes-no judgement that *you* have decided is to count *for them* (as well as for you) as a sufficient justification for your readiness to see *them* coerced.

Apparently, that will not do. A clear sense that a different sort of justification is needed is what drives liberals to posit a gap between judgments of a legal rule's *legitimacy* – the moral supportability of collaborating in its enforcement against the reasonably dissentient – and judgements of its first-order *rightness* on the merits.

But then in what could a rule's legitimacy consist if not in the rule's rightness on the merits? An answer found by many liberals is: something about the general regime or system of government and lawmaking then and there in place, from which the rule in question has issued. The rule's legitimacy then will depend on whether that *regime* is, as I shall say, 'respect-worthy' or 'legitimation-worthy'.[19]

---

18 Note that the claim here is neither that there are no right answers to questions of political justice nor that anyone ever need lack conviction about what those answers are. The problem is that there are no publicly established answers to many of these questions, and aren't likely to be, in real political time, as long as 'reasonable pluralism' is true of our countries. See Jeremy Waldron, 'The Irrelevance of Moral Objectivity', *Law and Disagreement*, ch. 8, 164–81.

19 Some may say the case I have just posited is an impossibility, because a regime that insists on enforcing laws that really are unjust is *ipso facto* incapable of deserving respect. I offer here no case against such a view, except to insist that a rejection of it is not a conceptual confusion. (Compare David Estlund, 'The Insularity of the Reasonable: Why Political Liberalism Must Admit the Truth', *Ethics* 108 (1998), 252–75, at 274: 'It is not a conceptual confusion to think that obligations can sometimes be grounded not in true justice but in a conception which, whether or not it is true, is authoritative for other reasons, such as that it is the only conception that is acceptable to all reasonable citizens'.) My point is simply that the thought that people in a state can somehow be justified in supporting the state's enforcement of bad and immoral laws is one that many liberals feel pressed to accept and explain, for reasons I have presented.

Can you see *constitutions* and *constitutionalism* now entering the picture? Here we are, lending our support to the venture of government by law and thus implicating ourselves in a social mobilisation of pressure and force against ourselves and others to comply with legal acts almost certainly including some that are any or all of witless, vicious, and unjust. For that collaboration in coercion, liberals want justification, and 'legitimate' is its name. 'Legitimate' – or perhaps 'constitutional'? – is what I plead in response to a fellow-citizen's complaint against compulsion to comply with a legal act that he believes to be wrong on the merits and I cannot demonstrate to be right, and maybe don't even believe to be right, or at any rate not with much conviction. In making the plea, I do not take myself off the hook for supporting enactment of a wrong and bad law (supposing I did support it). I only take myself off the hook for supporting compulsion against him to comply with the law – which, presumably, I do out of regard for the moral and other practical goods of the general social venture of government by law and for the sake of that venture's success.

Liberals concerned about unjustified coercion in settings of reasonable disagreement thus hope to liquidate or get past such disagreement about the first-order merits of laws by refocusing on the question of the respect-worthiness of the lawmaking system ('constitution'?) whence those laws issued. That shift of the moral-critical gaze is a first, major manifestation of a contemporary liberal quest for a *procedural* (always as opposed to substantive) criterion on which to base judgements of legitimacy. As Joshua Cohen remarks, 'it is natural to suppose that by excluding a comprehensive consensus on values the fact of reasonable pluralism leads to a procedural conception' of legitimacy.[20]

III. Distinguishing Procedure from Substance

Suppose the question before the house is how to test for the legitimacy of a rule of law or a contested application thereof. If we have taken the proceduralising step of letting rules springing from a respect-worthy constitution be deemed legitimate ipso facto, the question will be how to test for the respect-worthiness of a constitution. (Remember, 'legitimacy' in a legal rule or application means the moral supportability of collaborating in enforcement of that rule or application against the reasonably dissentient.) Suppose someone proposes a test such as the following:

20 Joshua Cohen, 'Procedure and Substance in Deliberative Democracy', in Seyla Benhabib, (ed.), *Democracy and Difference* (Princeton: Princeton University Press, 1996), 95–119, at 96; see Stuart Hampshire, 'Liberalism: The New Twist', *New York Review of Books* 12 August 1993, at 44 ('Within different moralities, … the fairness of an actual outcome of a conflict will be evaluated differently, even though both sides recognize the fairness of the adversarial process. Outcomes are by their nature open to dispute, but processes need not be'.).

> The rule is legitimate, or the constitution is respect-worthy, if it can meet with the assent of all citizens in a discursive process of lawmaking that in turn has been legally constituted.[21]

> The rule is legitimate, or the constitution is respect-worthy, if it is one to which all possibly affected persons could agree as participants in rational discourse.[22]

Tests like these are said to reflect a 'proceduralist' understanding of law and particularly constitutional law.[23] In what sense and to what end are these tests and others like them called 'proceduralist'?

We may start by asking what a non-procedural – thus, a substantive – test would look like. Here are some standard examples of undoubtedly substantive tests: The rule is legitimate, or the constitution is respect-worthy, if it is consonant with divine utterance or the divine will; or if it conforms to right reasoning from certain postulates about the human condition, timeless and universal ('natural law'); or if it conforms to the comprehensive liberalism of Mill, or of Kant.[24] But it seems we must *not* include in our list of disfavoured, substantive tests: '. . . if it measures up to a Habermasian discourse-theoretic conception of constitutional democracy' – that latter having been expressly tendered as a procedural-not-substantive account of legitimacy. But *why is it*?[25]

Now you may say right off that there's an obvious answer to that question, which is that the tests classed as substantive are all *sectarian* in ways that those classed as procedural are not. That would be to many a highly debatable proposition,[26] but we need not debate it here. Here it will be enough to notice that *that* difference, granting that it exists, is not at all what is conveyed by the terminological opposition of the procedural to the substantive. 'Procedural' cannot be equated to nonsectarian unless you are going to maintain that there can be no nonsectarian propositions of normative substance, which is not the way most people talk, not even most academics. 'Wanton infliction of pain on a sentient being is wrong' is neither a sectarian nor a procedural proposition.

What, then, *is* conveyed by the procedural/substantive opposition as applied to tests for the legitimacy or respect-worthiness of legal rules or constitutions? Consider this possibility: We are pointing to the difference between (a) deciding for oneself the rule's or constitution's consonance with certain criteria having reference to normative content, and (b) right now actually running the rule or constitution through a set of test operations *that operate independently of the criterial judgement of anyone in particular* – a 'procedure' to wit – to see whether the rule or constitution comes through the procedure unscathed.

---

21 Compare Jürgen Habermas, *Between Facts and Norms: Contributions to a Discourse Theory of Law and Democracy* (Cambridge, MA: MIT Press, 1996), 110.

22 Compare ibid. at 107 ('Principle D').

23 See, for example, Habermas, *Facts and Norms* at 390–1.

24 For John Rawls's rejection of these liberalisms as unfit for legitimacy testing, see, for example, Rawls, *Political Liberalism* at 37.

25 In Part IVB, we put the same question to a test drawn by John Rawls, from the political conception of justice as fairness.

26 See, for example, Michael Sandel, *Liberalism and the Limits of Justice* (Cambridge University Press, 1972).

That cannot be the meaning intended by anyone who would class as procedural the Habermasian tests laid out above.[27] Those tests are *not* instances of what John Rawls calls 'pure procedural justice', in which an actual run of some non-judgmental operation – a series of cuts of the deck, for example – is allowed to determine the social outcome by force of some fairness-virtue perceived to lie within the operation itself.

A test of *actual*, unanimous acceptance of a rule could be pure-procedural,[28] but these Habermasian tests are not that. They are cast in terms of *hypothetical* unanimous accept*ability*, not actual unanimous acceptance. What is more, they contemplate a unanimity of a highly qualified and decidedly non-empirical sort – a unanimity among those who have taken part in 'rational discourse' (whatever that may mean, but it surely means something important, and something that is not always or automatically guaranteed, and maybe even something that cannot ever be realised in actuality), or in a 'legally constituted' discursive process of lawmaking (ditto). These, thus, are substantive tests by any normal usage of the term. They require whoever applies them to take note of the tested rule's substance, its content; for how else could you judge the rule's acceptability to others defined, counterfactually, as non-coerced or as conditioned by participation in some discourse? These tests, moreover, are obviously motivated by a trans-procedural – I would call it a distinctly liberal – claim regarding the essence of right and justice, or what we owe to each other: namely, to begin with, reciprocal recognition of each other as free and equal rational and moral agents.[29]

So then what *does* differentiate these so-called 'procedural' tests for the acceptability of legal rules and constitutions – I don't mean differentiate them *as liberal* (which they surely and commendably are), but differentiate them *as procedural-not-substantive*? Consider this possibility: A procedural test can be rendered in the form of what Rawls calls a 'procedure of construction' – a hypothetical reflection on what would issue from an imaginatively constructed collective-decision procedure, were such a procedure to take place. It would be a Rawlsian original position, or a Habermasian ideal speech situation, or something along those lines. Sorry, but that cannot give us the clear differentiation we are looking for between procedural and substantive tests. The right-reasoning or natural-law test (which would seem to be substantive if any test is) can be constructivistically recast as what a conclave of right reasoners from such-and-such postulates about the human condition would conclude about the rule. The test of the rule's or constitution's conformity to divine will can be recast as what the divine would say about it in the event the divine would speak. And so on.

To that, you might respond that those recastings I've just mentioned are inferentially too close to their respective, companion substantive tests to count as procedures of construction or provide the sort of 'gap' for critical reflection that such a device is meant to provide. To ask you what you judge the divine would say about a legal rule or constitution is no different, really, from asking you your opinion regarding the content of the divine will. By contrast, to ask you what principles (if any) for the basic structure of society would emerge by unanimous agreement

27 In the text at notes 22, 23.

28 See Part IVC.

29 See, for example, Habermas, *Facts and Norms*, 7–9.

from a Rawlsian original position – veil of ignorance, and so on – seems rather distant from asking you, directly, what you would regard as a justice-serving set of constitutional essentials. This matters for Rawlsian constructivism, because the distance (as it were) between those two questions is what sets us up for the back-and-forth, checking-and-revising process of critical reflection that Rawls commends as the quest for 'reflective equilibrium'. So maybe what differentiates a procedural from a substantive legitimacy test is the amenability of the former to being recast as a procedure of construction that is capable of imparting some sense of 'distance' or 'second opinion' to judgements of legitimacy and respect-worthiness.

No doubt that way of differentiating proceduralist tests from others is philosophically trenchant and important. It certainly is if constructivism is a valid form of moral reasoning and argument, because what we are doing here, in effect, is equating proceduralism with moral constructivism. Alas, such an equation is beside the point of our current inquiry. Constructivist forms of moral argumentation are no more insulated from the controversies of political theory than are hypothetical-contract forms. Indeed the two forms of argument are close cousins, and both issue in *contributions to* political theoretic debates, not levitations above or beyond them.

Two further possibilities for differentiating procedural from substantive tests for legitimacy and respect-worthiness raise questions about whether I have misunderstood what the proceduralists (or some of them) have in mind. Consider, firstly my account of the alternative to a true, or 'pure' procedural test of legitimacy. The latter, you'll recall, I defined as '(b) right now actually running the rule or constitution through a set of test operations *that operate independently of the criterial judgment of anyone in particular* – a 'procedure,' to wit – to see whether the rule or constitution comes through the procedure unscathed' – implying that no theorist in the field actually proposes *that* (an implication we'll soon be refuting[30] but not just yet). At the same time, I posed, as the inevitable alternative, '(a) deciding for oneself the rule's or constitution's consonance with certain criteria having reference to normative content'. But of course that is not the inevitable alternative. There is also the possibility of (a2) deciding for oneself the rule's or constitution's consonance with certain criteria *having reference to the rule's or constitution's procedural provenance*. In a tabular form, the array of possibilities looks like this:

Table 10.1 'Procedural Tests'

	criterial-judgement test (a)	**pure procedural test (b)**
substantive criterion	does the content of the rule measure up? (a1)	
procedural criterion	does the procedural origin of the rule measure up? (a2)	run the procedure, accept the result

30 See Part IVC.

Perhaps what distinguishes a procedural from a substantive test of a legal rule's legitimacy, or a constitution's respect-worthiness, is that, while both kinds call for a criterial judgement, a procedural test is one that calls for a judgement of type (a2) as opposed to a judgement of type (a1) .

One certainly can accept that as a true account of some strains in the proceduralist literature. However, one cannot accept (a2) as an *adequate* account of a mode of testing for the legitimacy of legal rules or the respect-worthiness of constitutions, and the reason is that the account fails conceptually. Here I can only indicate summarily how it fails.[31] Presumably (for theorists of democracy), the test will be whether the legal rule in question issued from an adequately *democratic* constitutional order. In order to decide, one will need a sufficiently robust conception of what a democratic constitutional order *is* – of what features are required of an institutional setup, forms for collective decision making, and background institutions in order to qualify the full practice as democratic. That conception – that criterion – of democracy will itself require defence. The defence may be rooted in some conception of justice and right that is substantive in the sense that it seems ought to be crucial here – that is, it is contestable in the ways that substantive normative claims are generally deemed to be contestable. Alternatively, the defence may be procedural, meaning that the favoured conception of democracy gains its favour by having issued from an adequately democratic procedure. But now we face a choice: Either we are launched on an infinite regress of claims to democratic pedigree, or the regress comes to rest at some point on a substantive (and correspondingly contestable) theory of political justification.[32] It comes to rest on a 'foundation'.[33]

Now, here is another possibility to consider. Maybe I have misunderstood in a more fundamental way what Jürgen Habermas, at least, means by a procedural test for legitimacy. Maybe he is not talking about any sort of criterial-judgement test at all, but really means a pure procedural test. Maybe he means a test not of hypothetical acceptability but of actual acceptance – actual passing of muster through a set of collective-decision making operations that in fact has been run. The Habermasian texts on the point are ambiguous. Some of them speak in terms that demand to be understood as hypothetical and substantive: 'Only those statutes may claim legitimacy that can meet with the assent of all citizens in a discursive process of legislation that in turn has been legally constituted'.[34] That 'can meet' has to be

31 For fuller treatment, see, for example, Frank I. Michelman, 'Human Rights and the Limits of Constitutional Theory', *Ratio Juris* 13 (2000), 63–76.

32 Compare Alessandro Ferrara, 'Of Boats and Principles: Reflections on Habermas's Constitutional Democracy', *Political Theory* 29 (2001), 782–791, at 785:

> [T]he adjective 'democratic' strictly speaking becomes a *legal*, as opposed to merely *moral*, qualification of a certain political practice of will-formation only *after*, not before, a constitution is enacted. Thus, there still cannot be a 'democratic enacting of the constitution', except if we are prepared to use 'democratic' merely as a vague term of praise.

33 Compare Cohen, 'Pluralism and Proceduralism' 592 (speaking of 'a principle of equal consideration that provides the normative foundation' for Robert Dahl's conception of a democratic process).

34 Habermas, *Facts and Norms*, at 110.

read as a hypothetical-subjunctive 'could meet' and not as an empirical-indicative 'do meet', because construed empirically the unanimity test will never in real life be satisfied in the pluralist social conditions with which Habermas is concerned. But Habermas also writes that 'the democratic procedure for the production of law ... forms the only postmetaphysical source of legitimacy' for legal rules,[35] and that 'the democratic process bears the entire burden of legitimation',[36] and he is construed by highly competent readers to mean by these remarks precisely that democratic procedures, actually executed, are a *sine qua non* for legitimacy.[37]

How to reconcile these contrary tending signs in the Habermasian texts? Here is one tempting answer: Legitimacy depends first of all on getting a criterial judgement *right*: the rule indeed is one to which everyone could agree, and so on. However, no such judgment can be sufficiently reliable to bear the weight of legitimation if made in isolation from democratic debate, actually conducted. The democratic debate thus is prerequisite to legitimacy, but for collateral, epistemic reasons.[38] For example:

> Individual private rights cannot be adequately formulated, let alone politically implemented, if those affected have not first engaged in public discussions to clarify which features are relevant in treating typical cases as alike or different, and then mobilized communicative power for the consideration of their newly interpreted needs.[39]

Suppose that is correct. How deep a differentiation can it give us between a procedural theory of the legitimacy of laws from a garden-variety substantive theory? Take Professor *B*. *B* maintains that laws are truly just if and only if they are required for the vindication of classical liberal rights of liberty and property, and if they do not infringe on such rights any more than the general vindication of such rights requires. I assume you won't doubt that *B*'s conception of justice is substantive, not procedural. Now suppose *B*, recognising that opinions often will differ about whether a given law does or does not measure up to that substantive, classical liberal requirement, *and also that a successful social order can't abide allowing everyone to act as her own judge*,[40] sees fit to relax his standards to just this extent: A law is *legitimate* (although it may not be just) if it issues from a set of constitutional arrangements that is about as well-contrived as any we can think up to filter out laws that fail to meet the substantive, classical liberal standard of justice. And, adds *B*, that demand is met by a constitution containing both a bill of rights that makes the correct libertarian noises and provision for an independent

35 Ibid. at 448.

36 Ibid.

37 See, for example, Christopher F. Zurn, 'Deliberative Democracy and Constitutional Review', *Law and Philosophy* 21 (2002), 467–542, at 510.

38 On epistemic virtues of democracy, see David Estlund, 'Beyond Fairness and Deliberation: The epistemic dimension of democratic authority', in James Bohman and William Rehg (eds), *Deliberative Democracy: Essays on Reason and Politics* (Cambridge, MA: MIT Press, 1997), 173–204.

39 Habermas, *Facts and Norms*, 448.

40 See above Part II.

judiciary to pronounce authoritatively, for everyone, on questions of constitutionality – provided the judiciary understands and performs its job correctly.[41]

B's legitimacy test is still substantive, isn't it? (Note that it is a case of Rawlsian 'imperfect' procedural justice, not 'pure' procedural justice.)[42] If so, then in what way is Habermas's test not comparably substantive? Or, if not, then what practically workable test for legal legitimacy or constitutional respect-worthiness would you like to propose that is not every bit as much a procedural test as are those of *B* and of Habermas? And what, then, would be the point of labeling one or another test 'procedural?' Why call that cow a black one when all the cows are black?

An answer possibly could be that Habermas offers a 'formal' as opposed to a 'substantive' epistemic account. David Estlund has defined a formal epistemic account of democratic legitimacy as one 'according to which a democratic process is held to have a tendency to get things right from the standpoint of justice or common good *whatever the best conception of those might be*'. Such an account 'makes no appeal to any specific conception of justice or common good'.[43] This comes closer, I think – for those who find it persuasive – to positing a logic for constitutionalism that seals itself off from political theory than any other candidate I know of.

But I suspect it does not get all the way. My suspicion – and that is all I can claim for now – is that the full and adequate specification of a democratic process, *for which a tendency can be claimed of getting things right from the standpoint of an unknown justice*, is never going to be possible without sticking a thumb into that pudding of the unknown and pulling out a few plums of anticipation of the justice waiting there to be gotten right.

IV. Other Procedural Logics of Liberal Constitutionalism

A. Constitutions As Procedures

In order for legal ordering to exist in a country, people have to know – they have to know commonly and publicly – what the institutional and procedural protocols are by which law in the country gets made and applied.[44] Thus, every legally ordered country, by necessity, has a constitution – written or unwritten, enacted or common-law – to supply at least some starting premises and protocols for deriving at least some of those rules.[45] Turning the point around, we can say that a crucial function

41 I have just been summarising a main line of argument in Randy E. Barnett, *Restoring the Lost Constitution: The Presumption of Liberty* (Princeton: Princeton University Press, 2004).

42 See below Part IVB.

43 David Estlund, 'Jeremy Waldron on *Law and Disagreement*', *Philosophical Studies* 99 (2000): 111–28, at 122.

44 Hart says it is sufficient if it is only the class of legal officials who have such knowledge in common, but then it still would be a prerequisite for legal ordering that inhabitants at large know commonly and publicly how to recognise who is not a legal official.

45 See Lawrence G. Sager, 'The Birth Logic of a Democratic Constitution', in John Ferejohn, Jack N. Rakove and Jonathan Riley (eds), *Constitutional Culture and Democratic*

of a country's constitutional law, written or unwritten, is to supply some high-order 'rules of recognition' without which no system of legal ordering can exist.[46] Thus regarded, a constitution (or a body of constitutional law) sets up a *procedure* for the resolution of a certain set of public questions: those regarding what the laws of a state or country are to say from time to time, or (these would typically be rules of judicial jurisdiction) what these laws are to be deemed to say when their applied meanings are disputed.

Is that correct? A constitution sets up a procedure? No doubt a country's constitutional law does set up a battery of tests for the validity-as-law of things claiming to be laws. (More precisely, it provides at least the starting rules for setting up those tests.) However, not all of the legal-validity tests set up by a given constitution need be procedural tests. Consider 'Congress shall make no law respecting an establishment of religion'.[47] With that test in place for the existence of laws,[48] a pronouncement respecting an establishment of religion cannot be law, so anyone who judges a given pronouncement to respect an establishment of religion is barred from according to that pronouncement the force of law.[49] But the test of respecting an establishment of religion is obviously a substantive, not a procedural test.

The constitution still is serving as a procedure. It still supplies a set of operations for testing whether something is law. What strikes us is that the prescribed operations often include a screening of candidate laws for compliance with standards that not only are plainly substantive (not procedural), but also quite foreseeably are going to be deeply controversial in many applications.[50] How does that observation square with our posited motivation for the procedural turn in liberal constitutionalist debate?[51]

B. Rawlsian Constitutional-Procedural Justice: Imperfect Not Pure

In the view of John Rawls, there would be no necessary contradiction between the two. 'Our exercise of political power', writes Rawls – he calls this 'the liberal principle of legitimacy' – is justifiable to others when the exercise is 'in accordance with a constitution the essentials of which *all* citizens may reasonably be *expected*

Rule (Cambridge: Cambridge University Press, 2001), 110–44, at 118–21.

46 See Kent Greenawalt, 'The Rule of Recognition and the Constitution', *Michigan Law Review* 85 (1987): 621–71.

47 US Const. First Amendment.

48 See Matthew D. Adler and Michael C. Dorf, 'Constitutional Existence Conditions and Judicial Review', *Virginia Law Review* 89 (2003): 1105–202.

49 Refinements are necessary, but they are beside the point here. See the careful discussion in Carlos Santiago Nino, 'A Philosophical Reconstruction of Judicial Review', in Michel Rosenfeld ed., *Constitutionalism, Identity, and Difference: Philosophical Perspectives* (Durham, NC: Duke University Press 1994), 285–332, at 291–94.

50 Look in any book on American constitutional law for the materials on religious establishment.

51 Above Part II.

to endorse in the light of principles and ideals acceptable to them as reasonable and rational'.[52]

Rawls thus relies on the idea that there can be constitutions that no one who is reasonable – no one whose hypothetical-expected response counts in the sight of justice – can reject. With that idea in hand, Rawls is able to equate a law's legitimacy with its constitutionality, *given* that sort of constitution. That is one kind of proceduralist gambit. Rawls is saying that any law issuing from a proper set of constitutional arrangements gains from the simple fact of doing so – no further questions asked – the quality of being justifiably enforceable even as against those who conscientiously and respectably maintain that the law in question is seriously unjust, or is seriously fraught with ill consequences for society.

To be sure, only the right sort of constitution could possibly carry this legitimating virtue – could possibly be, in this sense, a respect-worthy constitution. And of course it is clear that a respect-worthy constitution as envisioned by Rawls will be one in which we find constraints on the content of legislation prominent among the prescribed tests for the validity of laws. A Rawlsian constitution thus exercises direct, preclusive control – never mind what current political majorities might decide – over some matters that surely would have to be called substantive, not procedural in any naïve, intuitive division of the categories. It contains a list of 'basic rights and liberties that legislative majorities are to respect',[53] including guarantees against infringements of freedom of conscience, of a right to hold personal property, even of a right of access to certain basic necessities of life.[54]

And yet Rawls plainly regards the constitution as serving a procedural function. He regards it as comprising a set of simultaneous tests for both the validity and the legitimacy of laws, validity (= constitutionality) now serving as a guarantor of legitimacy. What is quite striking, though, is Rawls's view that a constitution can serve thus even though (only if!) it plainly is designed to screen out some laws on grounds that can only be called substantive. If and insofar as Rawlsian constitutional justice is to be viewed as a kind of procedural justice, it seemingly must be of the imperfect variety, not the pure.

Rawls does sometimes say that laws passing a test of constitutionality (under a respect-worthy constitution) are to be deemed 'just whatever they are' – an insinuation of pure procedural justice – but I think we have to take that with a grain of salt. Rawls is very much aware that his test for a respect-worthy constitution – such a constitution contains all and only those essentials 'which all citizens reasonably may be expected to endorse in the light of principles acceptable to them as reasonable and rational' – means that crucial clauses will have to be cast at levels of abstraction ('freedom of conscience', for example) leaving many large and important issues of constitutionality open to reasonable dispute. Such a constitution has to guarantee the state's observance of the clear and indisputable 'central ranges' of certain basic liberties required by justice for everyone, but it obviously cannot guarantee

52 Rawls, *Political Liberalism*, 217 (emphasis supplied).

53 Rawls, *Political Liberalism*, 227.

54 See ibid. (on basic liberties, constitutional essentials, and provision for 'basic needs') (227–9, and so on).

satisfaction of everyone's sincere and reasonable judgements regarding what will count as infringements beyond the obvious core cases. Rawls's view appears to be that a constitution is respect-worthy as long as the institutions it sets up (which we here can assume include judicial review) are strongly geared to the suppression of core infringements and also seem no less well designed than any proposed, feasible alternatives for assurance of sincere and competent public judgements concerning the rest. If that condition is satisfied, Rawls appears to be thinking, official resolutions of cases falling outside the cores but inside the contestable ranges of applications of the basic liberties are to be deemed 'just whatever they are'.

Well, yes, if what you want to mean by justice in a law is all and only that it has issued from a respect-worthy political regime. But to talk that way is *not* to show that you have found a form of pure procedural justice for the politics of a society marked by reasonable pluralism. It is rather to give up hope of doing so by eliding the distinction between pure and imperfect procedural justice.

In the face of what he doubtless would allow is reasonable disagreement, Rawls is quite ready to brand as *unjust* – as contrary to his own highest ranking principles of justice – certain seemingly quite important, relatively concrete rules of American constitutional law. Take for example the Supreme Court's interpretation of the First Amendment to bar quite sweepingly a family of possible political campaign regulations, *some* form of which Rawls maintains almost certainly must be imposed in order to uphold everyone's right to the fair value of the political liberties.[55] The Rawls who argues thus cannot be taken to mean that each and every official resolution of a constitutional-legal question falling within the contestable range is to be deemed *just* whatever it is. He means such resolutions, whatever they are, are to be deemed worthy of our compliance and support even though doubtless sometimes contrary to justice truly understood.[56] (Such resolutions, he cautioned long ago, produce not 'a statement to be believed' but 'a rule to be followed'.[57]) And the reason why is not some transcendent value pumped into one or another particular resolution by the procedure used to reach it – say, the Supreme Court deciding after a full and fair hearing. Rawls does not think that the Supreme Court's ministrations *impart* moral compellingness to a social result in the way that a coin flip may sometimes

55 *Buckely v. Valeo*, 424 U.S. 1 (1976); see Rawls, *Political Liberalism*, 359–63.

56 Without a doubt, Rawls does mean to maintain that a *political practice at the regime level* can be just – although doubtless some subsidiary parts (or laws) are not compatible with what justice requires – as long as that practice qualifies as an instance of imperfect procedural justice relative to the true conception of justice as that would be applied to the subsidiaries. On that understanding, the suggestion that particular outcomes of the system are 'just whatever they are' may be reconstructed to say: 'the system is just (or is consonant with justice) whatever the outcomes are, and so the outcomes are legitimate whatever they are', Rawls's view then would be that the claim in that form holds as long as the constitutional essentials are what they ought to be and they are applied in contested cases in a manner that satisfies the demands of public reason.

57 See John Rawls, 'Legal Obligation and the Duty of Fair Play', in Rawls, *Collected Papers* (Cambridge, MA: Harvard University Press, 1999), Samuel Freeman (ed.), 117–29 at 122.

be taken to do, or a parliamentary deliberation followed by a majority vote.[58] He thinks something quite different: that the system as a whole, including its provision for the ministry of the Supreme Court, is about as good as any we can contrive for getting these questions decided *right* as gauged by procedure-independent standards of rightness.

In sum, Rawls's proceduralist logic of constitutionalism is the logic of imperfect procedural justice. As such, it cannot be – and it very plainly is not – freestanding from categories of political theory.

C. Majoritarian Democracy as Pure Procedural Justice

Consider now a more radically proceduralist view of a constitution's place in a legitimate political regime. Take it as a view designed to attack, *as unjust* (a point not to be missed!), a form of constitutionalism that has been salient in what I have just been writing. Of course I mean the form in which the constitution consists partly in an establishment in the law of certain rights and guarantees, entrenched against revision or repeal by current legislative majorities and available for an independent judiciary to construe and apply against the manifest legislative wills (and apparent interpretive judgements) of current majorities.

We can break the argument down into two claims. Firstly, moral principles of equality and respect for persons demand access for all, on equal terms, to lawmaking resolutions that will have to bind all in conditions of reasonable disagreement about what is to be done. Secondly, decision of major public questions by majorities of constituencies of the concerned and affected, or by majorities of representatives chosen by majorities of them, is the only way to meet that demand. As Jeremy Waldron sums up the case:[59]

> When we disagree about the desired outcome, when we do not want to bias the matter up-front one way or another, when each of the relevant participants has a moral claim to be treated as an equal in the process, then [majority decision] – or something like it – is the principle to use.[60]

It is to be understood that the 'desired outcomes' here, on which reasonable disagreement among moral equals is posited, include questions – and not just minor or marginal ones – about what rights people have and how those rights should be construed and applied. Waldron mentions, as examples, questions about rights respecting 'abortion, affirmative action, school vouchers, ... gay marriage [and] capital punishment'.[61] At the same time, though, the majoritarian-democratic case against judicial review is – at least it is in Waldron's hands – first and foremost a

---

58 See Part IVC.

59 Waldron argues in support of such a case in a series of writings, including *Law and Disagreement*, 'A Right-Based Critique of Constitutional Rights', *Oxford Journal of Legal Studies* 13 (1993), 18–51, and 'The Core of the Case Against Judicial Review', *Yale Law Journal* 115 (2006), 1346–1406.

60 'Core of the Case' at 1388.

61 Ibid. 1349.

case founded on a moral principle and a related conception of justice in politics, giving rise to a claim of right.[62] Waldron's is, to wit, 'A Right-Based Critique of Constitutional Rights'.[63]

And that settles it, you may say. Insomuch as Waldron openly bases his support for a certain form of political constitution – call it majoritarian-democratic parliamentary supremacy – on a certain, controversial conception of justice and morality in politics (compare the differing conceptions of John Rawls[64] and Ronald Dworkin[65]), he obviously is *not* proposing a possible logic-of-constitutionalism sealed off from traffic with political theory.

Before peering a bit more closely at that last conclusion, we should nail down the point that Waldron, unlike Rawls, *is* proposing a constitutional logic of pure procedural justice. The point is important. If it is correct – and if it also is true, as appears, that Waldron's argument trafficks directly with political theory – then we have an interesting and indeed powerful result: Not even a conception of the constitution as an engine of pure (let alone imperfect) procedural justice suffices to seal off the discourse of constitutionalism from frontal, essential engagement with political theory.

Waldron does clearly want, he does clearly seek, a constitutional logic of pure procedural justice. A constitution, in his view, is respect-worthy insofar as it vindicates one, single right or claim: the claim, that is, to a political arrangement that treats everyone as (a) a moral agent and (b) an equal. A constitution can measure up, Waldron maintains, only by being one that submits all public questions to decision by processes of majoritarian democracy; it being understood that 'public questions' includes questions about what questions are public and questions about what (other!) rights the country's laws shall be drawn and construed to respect and protect.

If that is not an instance of pure procedural justice in politics, nothing could be. Pure procedural justice, after all, does not prescind from standards or principles of *justice*: it prescinds from standards of justice *in outcomes*, so as to locate the justice strictly and solely in the procedure. In pure procedural justice, persons do not *lack* a claim to justice, they most emphatically *have* such a claim. They have a claim that some class of decisions in which they claim a stake be decided by procedures measuring up to … what? To some distinct conception of fairness in a procedure for this class of decisions (what else could the measure possibly be?), meaning (what else could these terms possibly mean?) some distinct conception of aptness to relevant moral posits, beliefs, or facts – concerning, for example, human-personal agency and equality.

Such a claim is a claim of justice, and such a claim of justice is exactly what Waldron propounds with respect to constitutions. No doubt his conception of

---

62 See ibid. 1375 where Waldron invokes

> the notion of a *right* to participate, the imperative that one be treated as an equal so far as a society's decision making is concerned, the sense of principle that is at stake when someone says indignantly, 'How dare they exclude *my* say … from this decision, which affects me and to which I am subject?'

63 *Oxford Journal of Legal Studies* 13 (1993), 18–51.

64 See Part IVB.

65 See, for example, Ronald Dworkin, *Freedom's Law: The Moral Reading of the American Constitution* (Cambridge, MA: Harvard University Press, 1996).

constitutional justice rides on the back of a controversial proposition of political theory, but that is what claims to pure procedural justice *do*, it is how they are made. They are made by segregating *one* substantive proposition about justice – the one concerning the aptness of a certain public decisional procedure to the moral facts, beliefs, or posits (for example, persons are to be treated in politics as moral agents and as equals) – from all other such propositions, which latter are left open to be resolved, for public official purposes, by submission to procedures conforming to the former.

But the former proposition, obviously, is always going to be grist for the mills of political theory, and we should note how this is true in two dimensions. Firstly, any slightest attempt to vindicate the proposition will itself be an instance of political-theoretic discourse.[66] Secondly, the proposition will have to be applied to controversial cases. Waldron, for instance, will have to answer the question whether a regime without controls on political campaign spending can qualify as a procedure that is apt to his moral posits about human moral agency and equality. Doing so will land him in political-theoretic debates not very distant from the ones with which we last saw John Rawls entangled.

66 Compare David Estlund's remarks about Rawlsian liberalism in 'The Insularity of the Reasonable: Why Political Liberalism Must Admit the Truth', *Ethics* 108 (1998), 252–75, at 253:

> [P]olitical liberalism must assert the truth and not merely the reasonableness – or acceptability to all reasonable people – of its foundational principle that doctrines are admissible as premises in political justification only if they are acceptable to all reasonable citizens.

Chapter 11

The Crisis of Im/purity

Johan van der Walt

Introduction

The question posed to Frank Michelman in this book concerns the possibility of articulating a logic of constitutionalism or constitutional law that is insulated from the concerns of political theory. The question concerns, in other words, the possibility of a pure theory of constitutional law (*reine Verfassungslehre*) à la Kelsen.

Kelsen's attempt at a pure theory of law (*reine Rechtslehre*) makes short thrift of this question. Since there is no legal norm that validates the legality of real historical constitutions, constitutions are inevitably and irredeemably impure, that is, stained or polluted by political and social concerns. A pure theory of law therefore does not and cannot depart from any positive or posited (*gesetzte*), that is, any real historical constitution. It must depart from a presupposed (*vorausgesetzte*) foundational legal norm or *Grundnorm* that validates all other legal norms. A pure theory of law has to proceed *as if* (*als ob*) there is a foundational legal norm that is insulated from all political and social concerns and therefore purely legal.[1] In other words, a pure theory of law has to pretend that there is a *Grundnorm* that warrants its pureness. A 'pure theory of law' can only pretend to be pure.

Michelman does not take this short route to respond to the question posed to him. He carefully works through various possibilities of what a pure constitutionalism might imply or mean and only then proceeds to answer that none of the contenders for such a pure constitutionalism succeeds. Ultimately, however, he leaves us in no doubt that he basically agrees with Kelsen that a pure constitutionalism or pure theory of constitutionalism is empirically speaking impossible. It only becomes possible with the assumption or presupposition of a transcendental condition that would make it possible.

Michelman's response to the question posed to him in this book does, quite remarkably, not address the question as to whether constitutional theory *should* pretend to be pure, as Kelsen would have it do. The question whether purity is desirable or necessary for the construction of a consistent theory of law and therefore has to be assumed or presupposed for this purpose is entirely absent from his response. I once heard him moot without answering the question whether it is better for lawyers and judges confronted with the need to make Solomonic decisions to pretend that they can rely on purely legal rules or principles, that is, whether pretending that they rely on pure law in the face of Solomonic decisions is better

1 Cf. Kelsen, *Reine Rechtslehre* (1934), 66–7.

than owning up to the element of 'lawless' politics in these decisions.[2] His own characterization of his revered Justice Brennan as a political theorist would suggest that he fully identifies with not only the inevitability of an 'impure theory' of law, but also with the merits of such an impure theory, the merits, that is, of accepting theoretically the political role of judges.[3] One would nevertheless be going too fast should one infer from this recognition of the political role of judges that he does not credit the transcendental pretense of purity and the concern with pure law with some merit. One would be going too fast should one read Michelman's work as a simple 'law is politics' statement of the Critical Legal Studies kind.

A thoroughly considered and researched assertion as to where exactly Michelman stands as regards the respective merits of pure and impure theories of law would clearly take one far beyond what is possible within the limits of this short response. Section II nevertheless briefly points out two publications in which Michelman clearly makes a move that is very similar to Kelsen's presupposition of a foundational norm for the sake of a pure theory of law, but also different from it for reasons of articulating this presupposition almost exactly in the way Kelsen did not want to articulate it. Suffice it to say at this stage that both Kelsen's and Michelman's positions are marked by an acute regard for the impossibility of pure law *and* a recognition of the need for a concept of pure law in legal theory. In this regard they are not all that far from the concern with *im/purity* (purity irreducibly and inseparably linked to impurity) that I elaborate towards at the end of this response, or from the theorists on which I rely to do so. There is nevertheless a clear difference between the direction from which the concern with im/purity is articulated in Michelman and Kelsen, on the one hand, and the direction from which I articulate this concern in what follows. Where Kelsen and Michelman (at least as far as the two articles discussed in section II are concerned) can be said to move from a regard for impurity to an acute concern with purity, I move from a concern with purity to an acute regard for impurity.

I do this in four steps. Section I sketches an overview of the arguments that Michelman elaborates in his essay in this book. Section II briefly points out the two articles in which Michelman 'makes his Kelsenian move'. Section III explores the question what it might mean to have and stress a regard for impurity in constitutional

---

2 On the occasion of presenting the paper 'Constitutional authorship, "Solomonic solutions" and the unoriginalist mode of constitutional interpretation' at the University of Johannesburg (then still the Rand Afrikaans University) in September 1997. For the published version, cf. Bradfield and Van der Merwe (eds), *'Meaning' in Legal Interpretation* (1998), 208–34. In this chapter Michelman incidentally also paid considerable attention to the impossibility of a Kelsenian *Grundnorm* really existing as an exclusively or purely legal norm that is in no way the consequence of some non-legal event or fact, but did so only to show that this insight does not preclude one from adhering to an originalist approach to legal interpretation. The non-legal event or fact could indeed have been a historical decision in the history of a people or legal community to henceforth regard the 'original meaning' of the constitution as it 'existed in the minds of its drafters' to be the foundational norm for all levels of legal validity in a legal system. Michelman of course only embarked on this course of argument to prepare the ground for sounder arguments against originalist legal interpretation.

3 Cf. Michelman, F., *Brennan and Democracy* (Princeton, NJ: Princeton University Press, 2000), 63–5.

theory and in legal theory in general instead of maintaining the pretence of purity. Section IV elaborates the insights gained from section III further with reference to two 'savage regards' for impurity, namely those of Schmitt and Derrida. It should become clear throughout section III and IV that a consistent regard for impurity in legal and constitutional theory, one that also takes proper cognisance of savage regards for impurity like those of Schmitt and Derrida, is indeed desirable and important for a realistic constitutional theory, irrespective of whether such a realistic constitutional theory still aspires to some level or degree of theoretical purity or not. An incisive regard for the impurity of theory need not translate into an impure theory of law. It simply requires that any concern with theoretical purity always remains deeply aware of the impurity in the face of which the quest for purity is undertaken and from which it derives its existential significance. Section V therefore concludes this reply to Michelman with the assertion that constitutional theory inevitably turns on and should in its own best interests indeed also admit to the im/purity of constitutional concerns and thus of constitutionalism as such.

I. The Impossibility of Purity

The question to which Michelman was asked to respond in this book is this:

> Can we possibly envisage constitutionalism as a discrete [discursive] sphere, hermeneutically closed off or self-standing, subject to its own proper logic, which can be described without the deployment of categories of political theory?[4]

For purpose of this response, Michelman reads 'constitutionalism' to refer to

> practices having to do with the establishment, determination, and interpretation of bodies of positive law, distinguished in their legal systems as 'higher' or 'supreme' in relation to ordinary statute law and common law.[5]

'Political theory' he takes to refer to a 'field of normative speculation' within the wide range of which one can expect engagements with the following type of questions:

> What are the human interests served by politics? What is justice, politically speaking? Which is prior, the individual or the group? Which is prior, freedom or equality (or maybe dignity)? What is the best interpretation of the value of freedom? Of equality? Of dignity? Of community? How does society in the large, or how do social forces, most fundamentally serve or gravely threaten these values? Who or what is rightly sovereign? Which is prior, rights or democracy (or self-government)? What is the best understanding of rights? Of democracy?' The list of such topics in legal theory – as the field not infrequently is called – could go on. Participants discuss them in terms of Aristotelian, Augustinian, Machiavellian, Hobbesian, Lockean, Humean, Rousseauean, Sièyesian, Kantian, Madisionian, Benthamite, Schmittian, Arendtian, Ungerian, Derridean, etc.,

4 141.

5 Ibid.

> ideas about political and legal ordering in relation to morality, justice, the good and the human condition.[6]

The question regarding the possibility of insulating constitutionalism from political theory is better understood, proceeds Michelman, not to refer to the discourse of an outside observer assessing and appraising what is at issue within constitutionalism or constitutional theory. Such an outside observer would all too obviously have to rely on criteria outside the practice of constitutionalism for this assessment and appraisal of what is going on inside this practice. No, the question is better understood to refer to the intrinsic logic of constitutionalism to which practitioners adhere or profess to adhere strictly or at least as strictly as possible.[7] We must understand the question to be asking whether the intrinsic logic of constitutionalism can be insulated from the normative speculation characteristic of political theory.

Given the substantive nature of the normative speculation of political theory, one may also understand the question regarding the insularity of constitutionalism to turn on the more specific question whether the logic of constitutionalism is or can be strictly procedural, that is, completely devoid of the substantive considerations that characterise political theory. This is indeed the cue that Michelman follows throughout his essay. And he prepares his readers for a proper understanding about what is at stake with this substance/procedure distinction by first introducing them to the considerations that informed the 'procedural turn' in liberal political theory.

Central to the procedural turn in liberal theory is the concern with 'justified collaboration', that is, the concern with the moral justification for collaborating with state coercion that ensures compliance with all laws in force in a particular jurisdiction, irrespective of doubts that may exist regarding the merits of any of these laws. Liberals believe, following Hobbes or Kant, that collaboration in state coercion of compliance with possibly or debatably immoral or unjust laws is morally justified. Michelman does not spare his reader the concrete implications of this belief:

> Do not doubt it. Day in, day out, by countless little, nameless, unremembered acts of compliance and collaboration with our country's governmental regime, we, with little compunction, involve ourselves in a social mobilization of pressure of force against others to comply with sundry laws and other legal acts with which they do not agree. And not only acts with which they don't agree, but acts that they confidently judge to be quite bad and wrong, and from what they sincerely and credibly take to be a public and not just a self-interested point of view. And since judgments of the public merits of legal acts rarely will be unanimous, and disagreements about this often will be not only intractable and sharp but also honest and reasonable on all sides – or so some liberals insist – we may as well say that the benign and urgent aims of government by law require our willingness to join in subjecting others (not to mention ourselves) to pressures and compulsions to abide by legal acts that, so far as they (or we) honestly can tell, simply *are* wrong, *are* destructive or unjust, objectively – 'you'd better believe it' – and not just according to their (or our) own personal assessments.[8]

---

6 141–142.

7 143.

8 147.

Where do liberals find the justification for collaborating with the coercion of compliance sketched so unflinchingly in this passage? They find it in the notion of fair or respectable procedure. The pluralist or multi-cultural societies in which we live lack substantive criteria that can unite all their members in a free consensus regarding the merits of the laws by which we are governed. Coercion of compliance can therefore not be justified with reference to substantive considerations. The only justification available to those who collaborate in state coercion of compliance must therefore be sought in the fact that the laws that require coerced compliance are the outcomes of procedures that are worthy of the respect of all the members of these pluralist societies, the respect of the coerced members included. At issue in the justification of collaboration with state coercion of compliance with the law is thus not the moral merit or justness of these laws, but the legitimacy that these laws derive from the fully respect-worthy procedures (procedures worthy of the respect of everyone affected) from which they issue. And for these procedures to be fully respect-worthy, they would have to be *purely procedural*, since the moment that some substantive consideration would slip into them and thus into the procedural justification of coercion, they would no longer be worthy of the respect of all affected and thus no longer justify the coercion of compliance.

It should therefore be clear that liberals concerned with justified collaboration with coercion have high stakes on the table as far as the question regarding the insulation of constitutionalism from political theory is concerned, if we suppose the question to turn on the insulation of procedure from substance, that is, the insulation of the procedural concerns of constitutionalism from the substantive concerns of political theory. And Michelman makes it clear that many typically liberal theories of constitutionalism obviously do not make the grade of pure procedure. This is so because it is not only criterial judgements regarding the substantive content of rules (labeled 'a1' in his essay) that render the discourse regarding the legitimacy of rules substantive. Criterial judgements regarding the procedural origins of the rule (labeled 'a2' in his essay) also involve discourses regarding legitimacy in substantive considerations. A theory of constitutionalism that would turn on the 'due procedures' that would ensure the best possible protection of liberal rights of liberty and property[9] or the best protection of liberty *à la* Mill[10] or even the (according to Michelman) completely 'non-sectarian' protection of bodily integrity that turns on nothing more than the proscription of wanton infliction of pain,[11] would clearly turn on substantive considerations. And so would a theory of constitutionalism that would turn on 'principles of democracy', should such a theory not want to fall into the infinite regress of first deciding democratically what would constitute acceptable principles of democracy.[12]

Michelman subsequently considers the attempts at articulating a purely procedural foundation for coercive laws in the work of Habermas, Rawls and Waldron and finds them all wanting. The Habermasian attempts at articulating a purely procedural

9 Cf. Michelman's example of Professor B, 154.

10 150.

11 Ibid.

12 153.

foundation for legitimate coercion fail because of their hypothetical nature. A rule is legitimate, avers Habermas sometimes, 'if it can meet with the assent of all citizens in a discursive process of lawmaking' or 'if it is one to which all possibly affected persons could agree'. The legitimacy invoked in these tests does not turn on the actual assent or agreement of citizens and affected persons but on an assumed possibility of assent or agreement. They thus self-evidently do not turn on procedure but on some or other unspecified substantive criterion regarding the possibility of consent or agreement.[13] At other times, however, Habermas stresses the need for actual democratic procedures to found the legitimacy of coercive rules or of legal rights (which of course also amount to coercive rules). But this emphasis on democratic procedures, argues Michelman, clearly constitutes nothing but a garden variety of the procedural criteria labeled 'a2' in his essay. It must immediately assume some substantive criterion for 'democratic procedures' or fall into the infinite regress of firstly determining democratically what would constitute 'democratic procedures'.

Michelman addresses Rawls' 'procedural' attempts at founding the legitimacy of laws on two levels. He first addresses the procedure invoked in the moral constructivism elaborated in *A Theory of Justice*. According to this moral constructivism, legitimate rules would be those enacted in or derived from principles laid down in an original position behind a veil of ignorance, and so on. Such moral constructivism is, however, just an indirect way of making substantive judgements (all direct substantive criteria, that of natural law or divine will, for instance, can be proceduralised and rendered indirect through a process of moral construction) and although this indirectness may have the merit of allowing for the method of reflective equilibrium in moral theory (the method of moving to and fro between our actual substantive beliefs and what we think we would believe in an original position), it cannot rid moral constructivism of its obvious involvement in and actual participation in substantive political theory.

The second level on which Michelman addresses Rawls' understanding of the procedural legitimacy of coercive rules concerns Rawls' assumption in *Political Liberalism* of the constitution as the procedural foundation of legal rules that renders them legitimate. According to Rawls, the requirement that all legal rules be subject to the criterion of constitutionality provides a procedural way of ensuring the legitimacy of rules. 'Our exercise of political power', he writes, is justifiable to others when the exercise is 'in accordance with a constitution the essentials of which *all* citizens may reasonably be *expected* to endorse in the light of principles and ideals acceptable to them as reasonable and rational'.[14] In other words, legal rules that require coerced compliance will remain legitimate or respect worthy, irrespective of doubts one may have with regard to their moral merit, when they pass the test of constitutionality. Rawls is aware, however, that the test of constitutionality that offers us a basis for legitimacy cannot derive from just any constitution. The constitutionality test can only ensure legitimacy if it issues from the right kind of constitution, and the right kind of constitution, according to Rawls, is one that guarantees a number of 'basic rights and liberties that legislative majorities are to respect'. And these rights will

---

13 151.

14 156 (Michelman's emphasis); Rawls, *Political Liberalism* (1996), 217.

include a right to freedom of conscience, a right to hold personal property and a right of access to certain basic necessities of life.[15]

It is obvious that the same problem that Michelman identifies in Habermas' claim to pure proceduralism plays itself out again in Rawls' proceduralism. Habermas' proceduralism leaves us with the hypothetical criteria of 'possible assent' or 'possible agreement' of 'all citizens' or 'everyone affected' and Michelman responds to this, we saw above, by insisting that as long as this hypothetical procedures are not met by real procedures, that is, real assent and agreement by all affected, they must rely surreptitiously on substantive criteria of acceptability by all. Rawls' position differs from Habermas' only to the extent that he does not play the game of surreptitious reliance. He expressly introduces a number of basic rights, typical liberal rights at that, as criteria for what will count as a constitution that can and must be endorsed by all reasonable people. The cost of this candour is that he cannot expect anyone to believe for a moment (assuming that Habermas could fool some for a while) that his 'procedural' test of 'constitutional legitimacy' is purely procedural. As in the case of the liberalism espoused by, for instance, Mill, Rawls' procedural liberalism obviously relies on substantive criteria of liberty. His test for the legitimacy of coercion must therefore in his own terms count as an instance of 'imperfect proceduralism'. In terms of the classification that Michelman employs in his essay, Rawls' proceduralism relies on criterial judgements of the 'a2' kind. These judgements are not devoid of substantive criteria and can therefore not claim to represent an intrinsic logic of constitutionalism that is insulated from political theory, assuming we take the distinction between constitutionalism and political theory to turn on the substance/procedure distinction. This is the crucial point that Michelman makes with regard to Rawls in view of the question put to him. But it is worth mentioning that there is a second cost to Rawls' imperfect proceduralism that is also of significance for the question whether he can offer us an independent and insulated logic of constitutionalism.

The second cost concerns Rawls' own insight that the substantive criteria embodied in the constitution can only enjoy the endorsement of all reasonable people affected by them as long as they are cast at such a level of abstraction that they cover only a central range of core constitutional values and leave a vast range of more specific questions regarding constitutionality out of consideration and thus subject to on-going dissent and intractable conflict, dissent and conflict that cannot but involve those affected in the substantive considerations of political theory. What really happens here is that the substantive criteria that Rawls puts down to attain to the 'right kind of constitution' are forthwith emptied out again of most of their substance by positing them at a level of abstraction that cannot invite conflict. And the problem that ensues from this move is that constitutionalism only attains some level of independence or insularity from substantive political theory by rendering itself incapable of answering most of the really pertinent questions that it is supposed to answer. In other words, constitutionalism here only attains to some measure of independence from political theory by largely reducing itself to insignificance.

15 157, Rawls, *Political Liberalism*, 227–29.

The last contender for a purely procedural and therefore 'purely constitutional' and 'non-political' constitutionalism that Michelman considers is Waldron's concept of majoritarian democracy. Waldron's theory of majoritarian democracy seeks to construct a theory of pure procedural justice by having all questions of justice with regard to which we have differences of opinion decided by a majority decision that is not 'biased up-front' with any substantive normative criteria and thus allows everyone an equal say in the matter. This is a very real attempt at 'pure procedural justice', concedes Michelman, but he nevertheless maintains that Waldron can ultimately not avoid questions regarding the aptness of the procedures that produce the majority outcomes that he takes as the only criterion for acceptable coercion. These questions regarding the aptness of these procedures (they range from (perhaps) more simple ones such as 'who can vote, everyone or only people above a certain age?'[16] to more complex ones such as 'how much money can people be allowed to spend on influencing the majority decision?') cannot but involve him in substantive questions regarding the nature of equality and moral agency and thus in questions of substantive political theory.

I believe we have now a sufficient outline of the range of arguments that Michelman offers us regarding the impossibility of insulating a pure procedural logic of constitutionalism from the substantive considerations of political theory. On the whole he clearly provides us with a meticulous statement regarding the impossibility of a pure constitutionalism or the 'impossibility of purity', as we have put it here. One can say that Michelman has thoroughly checked up on Kelsen and leaves us with little doubt that Kelsen is quite right to argue that a pure theory of law or constitutional law is something that must be assumed or presupposed. It is not something we can aver to really exist as a separate field of theoretical inquiry that is independent of other fields of inquiry such as political theory. This nevertheless still leaves us with the question whether Michelman deems Kelsen's transcendental assumption of a normatively pure or purely legal *Grundnorm* for the sake of a pure theory of law wise. Section II will point out that we have reason to believe that he does.

II. Michelman's 'Kelsenian Move'

Michelman probably does credit Kelsen's transcendental assumption of pure constitutionalism and pure constitutional theory with significant merit when one considers two articles that he published in 1995 and 1996 as a reflection of his position in this regard. The first of these publications is the essay 'Always under

---

16 And even the apparently simple matter of 'everyone' can become problematic. Should the state spend money to make it possible for prisoners to vote or should one argue that they got themselves into a position that deprives them of the right to vote? Cf. in this regard the decisions of the South African Constitutional Court in *August and Another v Electoral Commission and others* (CCT 8/99) and *Minister of Home Affairs v National Institute for Crime Prevention and the Re-Integration of Offenders* (*NICRO*) *and Others* (CCT 03/04).

law?'[17] in which he sets out to turn around his argument in 'Law's republic'[18] that one cannot 'cleave wholeheartedly and simultaneously to both of the two ideals of higher law and popular sovereignty, without conceiving that the popular sovereign conducts its higher lawmaking in a normative [or jurisgenerative] spirit ... '[19] The second is the essay 'Can Constitutional Democrats be Legal Positivists? Or why Constitutionalism?'[20] in which he basically restates the argument in 'Always under Law?', but nevertheless makes some small changes that are not insignificant.

The way Michelman puts the matter in 'Always under law?' indicates that 'Law's republic' should already according to him be read as making a Kelsenian move, and making it, moreover, in quite Kelsenian fashion: Law's republic posited the notion of a jurisgenerative or normative spirit of higher lawmaking as a transcendental condition for the non-contradictory co-existence of both higher law and popular sovereignty. Kelsen's presupposition of the *Grundnorm* is effectively nothing but a transcendental assumption of a 'normative spirit' of higher lawmaking (where else could a purely normative *Grundnorm* or higher law be imagined to come from?[21]) that dispenses with the need to contend legal theoretically with the pre-normative and therefore non-normative origins of this higher lawmaking in the law-founding initiatives of people who had at the time of their initiative no law to rely on to give these law-founding acts a legal foundation.

Kelsen's reason for dispensing with the need to contend legal theoretically with the pre- and non-normative initiatives to posit a *Grundnorm* is evidently related to his insight that the deficit of normativity in such pre-normative initiatives could only be remedied if one could assume the existence of complete identity and unity among the law-founders and all those affected by their law-founding, both at the time and forever after. And this assumption was for him sociologically speaking just too glaringly impossible to make.[22] This assumption, however, is exactly what

---

17 Michelman 'Always under law? (constitutional democracy)' (1995) 12/2 *Constitutional Commentary* 227–47.

18 Michelman 'Law's Republic' (1988) 97 *Yale Law Journal* 1499–503.

19 Michelman, 'Always under law?', 227.

20 'Can Constitutional Democrats be Legal Positivists? Or why Constitutionalism' (1996) 2 *Constellations* 292–308 (hereafter cited as 'Why Constitutionalism?').

21 Or to put it differently: It makes no difference whether one's pure theory of law assumes or presupposes a purely normative spirit of higher lawmaking or a purely normative content of higher law.

22 Kelsen 'On the Essence and Value of Democracy' in Jacobson and Schlink (eds) *Weimar. A Jurisprudence of Crisis* (2000), 90: 'It seems to be a basic condition of democracy that a *multitude of human beings* becomes a *unity* in it. For democracy, the 'people' as a unity is even more essential, as it is not only, or not so much the object as the ruling *subject* – or should be, according to the idea. And yet, the unity that appears under the name 'people' creates the greatest problems for a study of reality. Split by national, religious, and economic conflicts, that unity is – according to sociological findings – more a bundle of groups than a coherent mass of one and the same aggregate state. Only in a normative sense can one speak of unity. For the unity of the people as a concord of thought, feelings and desire, as solidarity of interests, is an ethical-political *postulate* declared to be real by the national or state ideology by means of a fiction that is generally used and therefore no longer thought about. Fundamentally, only a legal element can be conceived more or less precisely as the

Michelman's argument in 'Always under law?' requires him to make. 'Always under law?' sets out to show that popular sovereignty is not, as it is often taken to be, 'the [people's right] to make the law be whatever in fact they decide, no further questions asked'. It is on the contrary '*the expression of a wish* to believe the opposite', namely, 'that whoever at any time actually does lay down higher law to the country does so in a spirit of answering to some commonly and publicly perceived or commonly and publicly derivable standard of right'.[23] Needless to say, this notion of a 'commonly and publicly perceived or commonly and publicly derivable standard of right' implies the very identity and unity that Kelsen did not want to presuppose. Michelman is well aware that this is where his argument is taking him.[24] This does not mean that *he* believes this identity or unity exists. He is very clear about this: Popular sovereignty is not the expression of this unity or identity, but the expression of a wishful assumption that this unity exists. And once popular sovereignty is indeed thus understood as the wishful assumption of this unity, his argument suggests further, the apparent contradiction between higher law and popular sovereignty need not bother us any longer.

Michelman restates the argument in an apparently somewhat bolder fashion in 'Can Constitutional Democrats be Legal Positivists? Or why Constitutionalism?'. What makes this second statement appear bolder is the replacement, at least at one point in the argument, of the notion of popular democracy as 'an expression of a wish' by the notion of an *unavoidable necessity* among participants in American constitutional democracy to suppose a pre-existing idea of political morality and right. As he puts it:

> According to the view I hold, participants in American constitutional democracy *cannot help but suppose – or imagine* – that the American people, enacting or amending constitutional law, are engaged in an exercise not of sheer, arbitrary will but rather of judgment under a pre-existing idea of political morality and right.[25]

---

unity of the people: the *unity* of the *state's legal order*'. Cf. also the incisive discussion of the debate about the role of political unity between Kelsen and Schmitt (who did rely on the existential unity of the people in his constitutional theory) in Lindahl 'Constituent Power and Reflexive Identity: Towards an Ontology of Collective Selfhood' in Loughlin and Walker (eds) *The Paradox of Constitutionalism* (2007), 9–24.

23 Michelman, 'Always under law?', 227.

24 Michelman, 'Always under law?', 237: 'We need to say, then, what it is we think confers political identities on empirical human aggregates, identities of a sort that allows us to check for the sameness of the identities of the People who lay down constitutional law and the People to whom it is laid down. What do we think this people – constituting, identity-fixing factor could possibly be? Must it not finally come down to an attitude of expectation or commitment shared by constituent members of the putative capital-P People? Of expectation of the presence among them of some substantially contentful normative like-mindedness, or at the very least of commitment to searching out the possibility of this? An expectation of, or commitment to, some cultural or dispositional or experiential commonality from which they can together try to distil some substantially contentful idea of political reason or right?'

25 Michelman, 'Why Constitutionalism?', 297.

One could note that the notions of 'publicly perceived' and 'judged under commonly and publicly derivable standard of right' are also replaced here by that of a 'pre-existing idea of ... right', but this is not so significant in view of the fact that the notions of 'publicly perceived' and 'commonly and publicly derivable' and the concomitant implications of social unity and identity (or at least an aspiration towards unity and identity) remain central to and expressly return (in almost exactly the same words) in the restatement of the argument in the second essay.[26] What is more significant and more bothersome about this second statement is Michelman's conviction that participants in American democracy *cannot help but suppose or imagine* constitutional democracy in the way he describes. One cannot imagine that there are no participants in American constitutional democracy who do so only strategically (for what it is worth), and do not suppose or imagine it to be what Michelman imagines it to be.[27] Michelman would have done better by retaining the notion of an 'expression of a wish' throughout the second essay and by having avoided the notion of 'all participants in American democracy'. One can accept many such participants to be sharing in the wish that constitutional democracy be what Michelman (or the constitutional democrat that he has in mind) wishes it to be, but, surely not all.[28] As such, the notion remains but a wishful assumption of a more or less pure constitutional theorist and likeminded normative spirits and I shall treat it thus in what follows. After all, his express return to the notion of 'popular sovereignty' as an 'expression of a wish' towards the end of 'Why Constitutionalism?' suggests that he himself is ultimately more comfortable with this notion than that of 'popular sovereignty' as an 'inevitable presupposition' or 'inevitable assumption'.[29]

Be that as it may, Michelman's position in both these essays is surely not all that different from Kelsen's.[30] Unlike 'Law's Republic' which located the

26 Michelman 'Why Constitutionalism?', 302.

27 The evident lapse in this articulation is that of understanding the law exclusively from the vantage point of an internal perspective, as Hart called it. It is well known that Hart took Austin to task for reducing the concept of law to the external perspective of those who only experienced the coercion of the law and not its normative purport. Less well-known or at least more often forgotten is Hart's call for a realistic jurisprudence that understands the law from the vantage point of both an internal and external perspective and thus also of those who only exact or experience its coercion. For a more extensive discussion of this point, cf. Van der Walt, *Law and Sacrifice: Towards a Post-Apartheid Theory of Law* (2005), 25–27.

28 If the so called Texas-mafia (George W. Bush, Alberto Gonzales, Donald Rumsfeld, Dan Bartlett, Harriet Miers, Lewis 'Scooter' Libby, John Ashcroft, Andrew Card, Karl Rove, Ari Fleischer, John Bolton, Paul Wolfowitz) that participated so vigorously in 'American constitutional democracy' in recent years that they can be said to have given an unprecedented meaning to this concept can still be said to have been engaged (or to have understood themselves to be engaged/or wished to be understood to be engaged) 'in an exercise not of sheer, arbitrary will but rather of judgment under a pre-existing idea of political morality and right', the meaning of this expression must clearly accommodate such a wide spectrum of possible interpretations that it forfeits all claims to any distinct meaning.

29 Cf. Michelman 'Why Constitutionalism?', p. 306.

30 Except for a contemporary (post-modern if you wish) twist in the tail in Michelman's argument that one cannot expect to find in Kelsen. If instances of higher lawmaking such as constitutional amendments (or writing new constitutions) are also matters of *judgement*

reconciling link between popular sovereignty and higher law, quite like Kelsen in the assumption or presupposition of a normative spirit, 'Always under law?' and 'Why Constitutionalism?' locate it in the assumption of a unity or identity among the founders of law and all those affected by this founding in a way Kelsen did not want to do. But it ultimately makes little difference (at least at this stage of human history) whether one locates the wishful assumption that conditions the possibility of a pure (always under law) theory of law in an empirically or sociologically unwarranted notion (the existence of social unity) or a logical impossibility (the existence of a normative order that normatively warrants it own normativity).

If Michelman's position in 'Always under law?' and 'Why constitutionalism?' indeed constitutes a Kelsenian move towards a pure theory of law, as I have argued here, it surely evinces a degree of tension with the position regarding the impossibility of a pure or politics-free constitutionalism that his essay in this book articulates. But the tension is not an irreconcilable one. It is not necessarily an indication that he has moved away from his earlier position. I have stressed that the earlier essays do not take 'pure constitutionalism' (constitutionalism that is always under law) as an empirical condition but assumes it as a transcendental condition that allows one to ignore, for the sake of a consistent or pure theory of law, all the political impurities that infiltrate the law at the level of popular democratic higher lawmaking. The essay in this book, in pointing out so meticulously the impossibility of a pure constitutionalism and pure constitutional theory, need not and I believe should not be read as a move away from the need to assume pure constitutionalism as a transcendental condition for a consistent theory of *law*. It should be read as a confirmation and explication of the need to do so. Or at the very least could be read to do so.

This reading rids us of what could have been a puzzling tension between the essays discussed here, but surely not of all the puzzling tensions in Michelman's work. The first such tension that still comes to mind is the one between the essays discussed here and the endorsement of the political role of judges in his characterisation of Justice Brennan that I pointed out at the beginning of this response. I shall not deal further with this tension in what follows, or in any case, not directly so. Suffice it to say

in terms of and therefore of *interpretation* and not *creation* of an idea of pre-existing right and not of arbitrary exercise of political will, why can a relevant constitutional court not review the soundness or constitutionality of such constitutional amendments? Michelman's answer: Because contemporary linguistics and hermeneutics have taught us not to ignore the *performativity* of all *constatation*; and because the level of *performativity* (indeed of *creation*) may well be exceptionally high or just a bit too high in the *constatations* that issue from the judgement and interpretation of matters of higher lawmaking, we should reserve jurisdiction for these judgements for the people's court (parliament) and not allow a bench of unelected judges to pass judgement here. Cf. 'Always under law?', p. 243: '[There are] practical doubts that interpretation of higher-law norms can always be held securely distinct from selection or identification of the norms themselves, or, in other words, practical doubts that acts of interpretation can always be held securely distinct from acts of legislation'. And then 'Why Constitutionalism?' 304: '[I]n constitutional- democratic thought, constitutional amendments are, ideally, not *purely* acts of interpretation, any more than they are purely acts of norm origination. Rather they are both. And they are both in such a way that criticism of them is no proper business of the judiciary'.

that I do not regard these tensions in Michelman's work as simply 'puzzling'. I take them to be hugely significant pointers to the legal and political theoretical concern that I address in what follows. What follows should therefore be understood as an endeavour, not to take leave of the place of Kelsen's and Michelman's thinking, but to approach it from another side in order to highlight and emphasise what remains understated in their thinking. At issue in what follows is, in other words, not a changing of place but a drastic change of direction. Instead of moving with Kelsen and Michelman from a regard for the undeniable impurity of law to an acute concern with a pure (or transcendentally purified) theory of law, I shall explore and expound a return from the concern with pure law and legal theory to an acute regard for the irreducible impurity of law. The reason for doing so stems from the conviction that it is not wise to deny or suppress or repress or underestimate transcendentally or methodologically what one has to deal with on a daily basis.

III. The Regard for Impurity

The concerns that Michelman identifies as those of political theory that a pure constitutionalism would have to exclude from its concerns, we saw above, included the following:

> What are the human interests served by politics? What is justice, politically speaking? Which is prior, the individual or the group? Which is prior, freedom or equality (or maybe dignity)? What is the best interpretation of the value of freedom? Of Equality? Of dignity? Of community? How does society in the large or how do social forces, most fundamentally serve or gravely threaten these values? Who or what is rightly sovereign? Which is prior, rights or democracy (or self-government)? What is the best understanding of rights? Of democracy?

To be sure, Michelman's list of the concerns of political theory includes these mentioned here, but he stresses that the concerns of political theory are not limited to these. 'The list of such topics in political theory could go on', he writes. Be that as it may, the concerns Michelman lists can be assumed to represent the kind of 'impurities' of political theory that one might want to exclude from the concerns of a pure theory of constitutionalism, but cannot, as he has shown us so thoroughly in his essay. I shall therefore take this list of impurities as a point of departure to come to grips with the essential reality of impurity that can be said to underlie, prompt or precipitate all the various impurities that may come to haunt or tempt constitutional theory and constitutionalism.

The origin of the words 'pure' and 'purify' points us directly to the nature of the essential impurity that haunts, tempts and often infects the affairs of humanity and thus impresses upon this humanity a daily urgency to deal with this impurity in the various forms that it may take. The words 'pure' and 'purify' can be traced back to the Latin *purus* and the Greek πυρ.[31] They can therefore be said to have their

31 Cf. Valpy *Etymological Dictionary of the Latin Language,* [1828] Baldwin and Co, London, 381: 'pūrus is properly pure as (ἀπὸ πυρὸς) by fire'.

historical roots in the notion of purification through fire, a notion that goes to the heart of ancient sacrificial rituals and actually denoted the format or method of most of these rituals, namely, *immolation*. The law was as such always closely related to these sacrificial rituals and has in modern times come to replace most sacrificial rituals with which it shared the task of the purification of the social order in earlier societies.[32]

The essential impurity from which ancient sacrificial rituals and ancient law had to purify the social order was the impurity that resulted from miasmic doublings or ambiguities that confused and unsettled the social order and ultimately threatened to tear it completely apart by precipitating the eruption of circles of escalating vengeful violence. Vengeful violence seeks to destroy ambiguity through the destruction of one of the contradictory elements that informs it, but its lack of agreed upon measures of just or justifiable revenge renders it highly susceptible to perceptions of excessiveness that simply restore the ambiguity it sought to destroy and thus reignite the potential for ever more violence.[33] To put the matter more concretely: Society cannot allow the uninterrupted and unsanctioned co-existence of the perpetrator and the victim of an injurious crime, tort or delict without becoming normatively and hermeneutically ambiguous and depriving the members of the means to make sense of their lives.[34] The same or a similar ambiguity would arise in any case where a state or political authority is alleged to have committed a constitutional wrong. Allowing victims to take revenge in these cases is one way of restoring social sense and eliminating social ambiguity, but it is a precarious way of doing so that risks simply turning victims into perpetrators and vice versa and thus inviting an endless return and escalation of violence. Seen from this perspective, the point of law and sacrifice was to prevent or resolve social ambiguities and thus to prevent or terminate the violence these ambiguities precipitated by means of established institutional practices that had a broad enough social claim to measure, exactness, or appropriateness of whatever kind.

The essential impurity that underlies the political impurities that according to Michelman cannot be eliminated from the concerns of constitutional law thus inheres in the fundamental social ambiguity that the law is called upon to resolve in order to prevent escalating circles of vengeful violence. Questions regarding the priority of individual or group or freedom or equality or the best interpretation of freedom, dignity or community, and so on, can all be traced to the sudden eruption (or educational and academic institutionalisation) of social ambiguities that bring these questions to the fore. Individual and society, freedom and equality, different

32 Cf. Van der Walt *Law and Sacrifice*, 227–31.

33 It is not just the level or degree of vengeful violence but the very act of vengeful violence that fuels continuing and escalating circles of revenge. Once one enters the logic of revenge, every act of revenge seeks to 'square' things, but cannot do so without destroying the victim's sense of already having squared things and thus inviting just another and ever more rounds of having to square things again. Hence, according to Girard, the need for an arbitrary (in terms of the logic of revenge) termination of the circles of revenge by means of solemn rites of law or sacrifice. Cf. again Van der Walt *Law and Sacrifice*, 227–31.

34 This is the real crisis that abolitionists of capital punishment have to address. Cf. Van der Walt *Law and Sacrifice*, 101–20.

understandings of freedom or dignity, and so on, regularly live or exist 'shoulder to shoulder' in a civilised and civilising fashion until a sudden miasmic *doubling of claims to justice* emerges from two irreconcilable claims to the same social benefits (or until educational and academic institutions such as law schools and departments of political theory begin to thematise such irreconcilable claims) and renders a particular social context fundamentally ambiguous.

However, an incisive regard for the essence of the impurity that ultimately haunts or tempts constitutional law in this way requires that we also take a closer look at the phenomenon of miasmic doubling as such. One way of explaining the phenomenon of miasmic doubling that sporadically endows the impure concerns of political theory with renewed urgency in questions of law is to attribute or reduce them to simple hermeneutic or semantic failures, that is, by deeming one of the parties involved in a dispute as simply cognitively mistaken with regard to a matter that is really not ambiguous at all. This is what theories of law or adjudication do when they insist that there is one right answer to a legal dispute and simply judge the claim of one party to the dispute to be deluded or wrong.[35] This explanation of the emergence of social ambiguity is unconvincing for reason of its failure to address the passionate and obsessive concerns that turn a 'merely semantic' ambiguity or cognitive disagreement into a dispute that is serious enough to produce the kind of social ambiguity that really requires judicial intervention.

The 'error' of someone who is merely 'mistaken' with regard to an unambiguous legal situation is bound to evaporate in the face of the costs and ordeals of litigation when that 'error' is not informed and driven by passionate and obsessive concerns. And the imaginable but rare cases in which a foolhardy insistence on an 'incorrect' understanding of law in the absence of passionate and obsessive concerns is pursued through litigation are bound to be thrown out of court on procedural grounds (failure to disclose a cause of action, absolution from the instance and/or failure to appeal successfully against any of these) and disappear from the radar screen of the legal system and legal theoretical inquiry, unless some judge or legal theorist discerns in the 'error' of the merely dispassionate and foolhardy litigator a potential doubling of passionate social concerns that the foolhardy litigator himself was not able to discern and experience. It should be clear that the latter case is almost too fantastic to warrant serious consideration.

The inverse is, however, not the case. The ascent of equity and general principles of fairness in modern legal systems makes it very unlikely that serious grievances, be they individual or collective, will not eventually come to enjoy full judicial and incisive academic attention, despite the fact that these grievances might not initially

35 Dworkin's position regarding 'one right answer' is well-known, but one may have forgotten how far he sometimes went to make the point regarding the delusion of the losing litigant. Cf. Dworkin, *Taking Rights Seriously* (1978), 290: 'Some readers will remain unconvinced. Surely it *cannot* be that in a genuinely hard case one side is simply right and the other simply wrong. But why not? It may be that the supposition that one side may be right and the other wrong is cemented into our habits of thought at a level so deep that we cannot coherently deny that supposition, no matter how skeptical or hard-headed we wish to be in such matters'.

appear to warrant attention in terms of existing legal rules and judicial rulings.[36] This is so because of the potential social divisiveness of serious social grievances that remains unattended too long by judicial and scholarly attention. And to invoke notions of mere 'cognitive error' to explain (away) the ambiguity of these latter cases, is simply to be oblivious to how the legal system actually recognises a certain 'correctness' of these claims by deeming it necessary to address them. The 'correctness' that is at issue here does not concern correspondence with the cognitive content of existing law, but the 'correctness' of the insistence that the matter is socially serious enough to warrant the attention of the law. What ultimately happens to the notion of 'cognitive correctness' in view of the considerations that are really at issue here, need not concern us here. Suffice it to say that it is a notion that is simply too shallow to address what is really at issue when a court of law decides a dispute is serious enough to warrant its attention.

The *doubling of claims to justice* and the concomitant social ambiguity that come to the fore in every serious legal dispute therefore require that we look beneath the surface of mere hermeneutic or cognitive failures and probe much deeper to find out what is really at issue when social ambiguity comes to disrupt the 'regular' course of human interaction. Only then shall we be able to also move towards an incisive understanding of the impossibility of pure constitutionalism that Michelman brings to bear on constitutional theory and of the impossibility of ridding procedure from substance with reference to which he explains the impossibility of pure constitutionalism. And this deeper scrutiny requires that we also shift our focus away from the kind of normative considerations that Michelman lists as the concerns of political theory that inevitably pollute constitutionalism and constitutional theory and render them impure. These normative considerations – which is prior, individual or society, freedom or equality; which interpretation of dignity, liberty, equality or community is correct? – are all still predominantly informed or guided by the notion or ideal of a cognitive or hermeneutic correctness and mostly deeply oblivious to the passions and obsessions that inform them. To be sure, they are closer to or more in tact with these passions and obsessions than strict principles or doctrines of constitutional law such as 'due procedure', 'proportionality', and so on, hence the impurity with which they already tempt, haunt and inevitably pollute constitutional law. They are, however, themselves procedurally removed and purified by doctrinal thresholds of normative political theory in a way that eclipses the fundamental impurities, passions and obsessions from which they stem. If one would ask a political theorist whether her discipline is typically concerned with the dynamics of sexual repression, she would most certainly refer one to a psychoanalyst or psychiatrist. Yet, the suggestion

36 Cf. Van der Walt 'Horizontal Application of Fundamental Rights and the Threshold of the Law in view of the *Carmichele* saga' (2003) 19/3 *South African Journal on Human Rights* for a discussion of how English and American procedural law incorporated the principles of equity into the common law by means of the Judicature Acts of 1873 and 1875 and the Field Code enacted in New York in 1848 and similar codes in other states; and how South Africa is still sadly stuck with procedural law that smacks of the writ-based procedural law that it imported from England before the time of the Judicature Acts. I am indebted to Karl Klare for pointing out to me that the Field codes are hardly the high point of the development away from formalism in American procedural law.

offered here is indeed that the regard for the political and political theoretical impurities that Michelman brings to bear on constitutionalism and constitutional theory should be expanded into a regard for the deeper or baser impurities of political theory itself, that is, into a regard for the passions and obsessions that give political theory its existential purchase on the deep and dark reality of human co-existence. These deeper, darker and baser concerns of human co-existence, I wish to argue, cannot be dismissed as ultimately having no impact on constitutionalism and constitutional theory itself. The point is that they ultimately also permeate the domain of constitutionalism and constitutional theory, be it through the slightly more purified passage or channel of 'more or less proper' politics and political theory, be it through short circuits that are hardly fathomable (finding and re-channeling these unruly short circuits are perhaps the infinite *raison d'être* of analytical theoretical inquiry).

The point that I wish to bring to bear on Michelman's essay with these suggestions is ultimately this: The regard for the 'impossibility of pure constitutionalism' ultimately leads to a regard for the impossibility of purity as such. It leads to an understanding of the disciplinary confines of scholarly disciplines as nothing more than markers that theoretical inquiry lays down in its traversal of a vast field of tensions between purity and impurity. This field of tensions, moreover, is not merely traversed by various disciplines of theoretical inquiry, but constituted or co-constituted by these theoretical traversals. Traversing, and constituting by this very traversing, fields of tension between purity and impurity are the ancient abodes of sacrifice and sacrificial rites in the cultural practices of humankind.[37] As already mentioned above, the law used to traverse these fields of tension between purity and impurity alongside and in close proximity to the sacrificial rites of religion. In modern societies it has largely come to replace them. Be that as it may, the regard for the impurity of constitutionalism ultimately leads one to a regard for sacrifice, a regard for the intrinsic relation between theory and sacrifice, law and sacrifice, politics and sacrifice, and so on. The regard for the impurity of constitutionalism ultimately leads one to the regard for constitutionalism as the apex of a sacrificial system. This sacrificial system cannot rid human existence and co-existence from its fundamental ambiguity and impurity, hence the survival of this ambiguity and impurity all the way up into the apex of the system. The sacrificial system is the human way of living with ambiguity and impurity.

IV Savage Regards for Impurity

Michelman himself opens the door for or to the impurities beyond 'proper political' theory. The passage quoted above offers us a second list, a list of perspectives or ideas on the basis of which the above listed concerns of political theory can be expected to be addressed. Participants in political theory, we saw, discuss the listed concerns of political theory in terms of

37 Cf. Van der Walt *Law and Sacrifice*, 129–31.

> Aristotelian, Augustinian, Machiavellian, Hobbessian, Lockean, Humean, Rousseauean, Sièyesian, Kantian, Madisionian, Benthamite, Schmittian, Arendtian, Ungerian, Derridean, etc. ideas about political and legal ordering in relation to morality, justice, the good, and the human condition.[38]

At least two of the theorists or philosophers invoked here can be argued to expose political theory to considerations that exceed the typical concerns of proper political theory. And they can be said to do so exactly because their theoretical endeavours at some point begin to understand politics and the political in terms that point our attention to something more fundamental and basic than 'ideas about political and legal ordering in relation to morality, justice, the good, and the human condition'.

Schmitt comes to mind first. Central to Schmitt's understanding of the political is the insight that the political cannot be understood in terms of the normative considerations of humanity such as economics, culture, or religion, despite its undeniable connections with these considerations. The political must according to him be understood in terms of an exceptional *degree of existential intensity* that distinguishes it from normative concerns. Normative concerns may inform the initial spasm of the political, but it is really the degree of intensification that marks this spasm as a political event and endows it with an independent existence beyond its relation to normative concerns, despite the fact that it has no independent content apart from these normative concerns. This degree of intensification is at issue when normative considerations give way to a decision that draws the line between the friend and the enemy.[39]

What is it about the political that moves it to the degree of existential intensity that endows it with an independent existence beyond normative concerns? In short: what is the existential intensity or intensification that marks the political? Derrida, who is the other thinker on Michelman's list who comes to mind as regards the exposure of political theory to considerations that exceed the typical concerns of political theory,

---

38 141–142.

39 Cf. Schmitt *Der Begriff des Politischen* (1932), 27–28. 'Die Unterscheidung von Freund und Feind hat den Sinn, den äussersten *Intensitätsgrad* einer Verbindung und Trennung, einer Assoziation oder Dissoziation zu bezeichnen', 'Die Begriffe Freund und Feind sind in ihrem konkreten, *existenziellen* Sinn zu nehmen'; 38–39: 'Die Politische kann seine Kraft aus den verschiedensten Bereichen menschlichen Lebens ziehen, aus religiösen, ökonomischen, moralischen und andern Gegenständen; es bezeichnet kein eigenes Sachgebiet, sondern nur den *Intensitätsgrad* einer Assoziation oder Dissoziation von Menschen, deren Motive religiöser, nationaler (im ethnischen oder kulturellen Sinne), wirtschaftlicher oder anderer Art sein können und zu verschiedenen Zeiten verschiedene Verbindungen und Trennungen bewirken. Die reale Freund-Feindgruppierung ist seinsmässig so stark und ausschlaggebend, dass der nichtpolitische Gegensatz in demselben Augenblick in dem er diese Gruppierung bewirkt, *seine bisherigen 'rein' religiösen, 'rein' wirtschaftlichen, 'rein' kulturellen Kriterien und Motive zurückstellt und den völlig neuen, eigenartigen und, von jenem 'rein' religiösen oder 'rein' wirtschaftlichen und andern 'reinen' Ausgangspunkt gesehen, oft sehr inkonsequenten und 'irrationalen' Bedingungen und Folgerungen der nunmehr politischen Situation unterworfen wird*'. (All emphases except the third added.) At issue here for Schmitt is the intensification of cultural, economic, religious and other normative differences to the extreme degree of intensity that turns them into *independent* political differences.

provides us with significant insights regarding the nature of the existential intensity that characterises Schmitt's concept of the political.

Derrida indeed also points our attention to something more fundamental and basic than 'ideas about political and legal ordering in relation to morality, justice, the good, and the human condition'. One might want to take 'justice' off this list in Derrida's case, given the pervasive engagements with the notion of justice in his texts. But one must note that the Derridean concern with justice has always been an idiosyncratic one that seeks to take justice *out of any relation* to the other concerns listed here, that is, *out of any relation* to political and legal ordering and to morality, justice, the good, and the human condition. Justice for Derrida, one must recall, concerns a mad and impossible dream that has only an aporetic relation to political and legal ordering, etc., assuming for a moment that the expression 'aporetic relation' does not already constitute an oxymoron.[40]

What ruins the relation between justice, on the one hand, and political and legal orderings, morality, the good and so on, on the other, for Derrida, and what thus turns his whole theoretical endeavour into 'a love for or of ruins',[41] (a love, it must be mentioned, that can perhaps also be discerned in something Michelman once wrote),[42] is, among other things, his acute regard for the insights of psychoanalysis, that is, the insights of psychoanalysis regarding 'a cruelty as old as and even older than man' (*une cruauté sans âge, aussi vieille et sans doute plus vieille que l'homme*[43]). This *cruelty* that is *older than man* suggests clearly what is at issue here. At issue is something that is doubly 'inhuman'; inhuman because no political theory does and should sit comfortably with a link between cruelty and humanity; and inhuman for reason of it being older than man, older than the human. What Derrida has in mind here is a regard for the insights of psychoanalysis that would also take seriously its mythological discourse regarding the death drive (*son discourse mythologique sur la pulsion de mort*) that conditions and therefore precedes all levels of humanisation and humanity.[44]

It is this psychoanalytic regard for the ancient or pre-ancient cruelty and the mythology of the death drive in Derrida's work that opens up further insights into Schmitt's understanding of the political in terms of a non- or a-normative existential intensification. At play in this intensification are the spasmodic or pulsating tensions between the sub-conscious forces in the economy of subjectivity that existentially condition conscious subjectivity in the first place and thus precede the presence of the conscious subject and all the normative considerations of political theory that typically take the already present or presented subject as their point of departure. At this level of analysis, Freud tells us, an irreducible ambiguity and equivalence

40 Cf. Derrida, *Force de Loi* (1994).

41 Cf. Van der Walt, *Law and Sacrifice*, 190, 197 for a more extensive discussion.

42 Cf. Michelman, *Brennan and Democracy* (fn. 3) 8: 'It does mean we never let ourselves forget that any of society's goals respecting democracy, self-government, and a rule of law or of reason must be ones of approximation, of holding in check the misfortune of how things are, of choosing among necessarily compromised offerings, of necessarily damaged goods'.

43 Derrida, *États d'âme de la psychanalyse* (2000), 70.

44 Derrida, *États d'âme de la psychanalyse*, 77.

between the will to life and the will to death become discernable, an irreducible ambiguity and equivalence from which conscious subjectivity never escapes fully. It is this mess of contradictory passions and psychological drives – in the domain of which the experience of life is both invigorated and functionally disrupted by the experience of death – that the ancients called the sacred or *sacer* and with regard to which sacrifice played a double role; the role of putting ordinary life ritually in touch with the sacred (sacrifices of fusion or sacrifices that bind) and the role of ritually shielding ordinary life from the sacred (sacrifices of separation and of alleviating ambiguity or sacrifices that cut).[45] It is this deep ambiguity and equivalence, this non- or unrestricted economy of the sacred that informs the existential intensification in Schmitt's understanding of the political. The political decision that draws the line between the friend and the enemy puts us in touch with this deep ambiguity. All of this involves "*political* 'subjectivity'" in an economy of psychic or psychological forces that precedes subjectivity. And Derrida takes Schmitt to task for never grasping that his theory of the political and the sovereign exception took him far beyond the limits of subjectivity. Schmitt's theory of the sovereign exception, he contends, remains stuck in a philosophy of subjectivity.[46]

The important thing to recognise here is nevertheless that this pre-subjective and pre-normative economy of deep ambiguity, this deep impurity, revisits the law right up to the level of constitutional review. It revisits the law every time legal 'subjects' pursue a dispute passionately enough to subject it to the ordeal of litigation. No one goes through the sheer death of litigation unless this death somehow turns into the driving force of life (in some respects similar to the way the brush with death in 'extreme' or *frisson* activities such as cliff- or bridge-jumping invigorates the sense of being alive for some people[47]). To assess this process or event exclusively in terms of a dispute regarding the internal or pure normativity of law is simply to misunderstand a significant part of what is going on in litigation. It is not the dispassionate cognitive perception that the law is different from the interpretation given to it by an opponent, but the crossing of a threshold of obsession with this cognitive perception that causes the doubling of justice claims and makes the law ambiguous.[48] Hart's distinction between the certain core and uncertain penumbra

45 Derrida, *Résistances de la psychanalyse* (1996), 51: 'Alors tout se passerait peut-être entre ... le sacrifice qui *noue* et le sacrifice qui *tranche*'. (Everything would come to pass between the sacrifice that binds and the sacrifice that cuts.) There is an interpretive elision in the way I cite the passage here. Derrida's full statement actually concerns the future distinction or 'distinction to come' between sacrifice and non-sacrifice that is in the interim of its approach (*dans l'approche*) still suspended between the sacrifice that cuts and the sacrifice that binds.

46 Cf. Derrida, *Politiques de l'amitie* (1994), 86–87.

47 The obvious difference which makes litigation in some sense 'more extreme' is the fact that it is accompanied by a real sense of the matter as not or no longer being a matter of frivolous choice (to jump or not to jump), but of utmost necessity and normative correctness.

48 And it would still be a simplification to say that the crossing of this threshold of obsession ensues from the cognitive perception that the law is or may be different from what another takes it to be. The cognitive perception may well also ensue from the libidinal or morbid desire to occasionally cross the threshold of obsession. Or both the cognitive perception and

of legal rules is not a matter of innocent semantics. To the extent that it becomes an existentially significant distinction, it is always an ambiguous matter of life and death, an *ambiguous* matter of life *and* death. *Hence* the impurity which, as Michelman shows us so meticulously, pollutes the law right up to the highest level of constitutional law.

A responsible theory of politics and law must take seriously the insights of psychoanalysis, writes Derrida.[49] The insights of psychoanalysis concern the way the pre-human cruelty of man prefaced, kept on and keeps on determining the history of humanity.[50] Freud related these insights with the narrative of the reincarnation of the 'father's cruelty' in the 'cruelty of the sons'. It is a narrative of sexual repression, sexual repression inflicted first by the father on the sons, then self-inflicted by the sons themselves. It is this story that Derrida suggests responsible legal and political theory take seriously. It should be clear that the level of impurity that he is talking about is of a different order than that of the normative impurities that Michelman brings to bear on constitutionalism and constitutional theory. Derrida, one can say, brings to bear on our thinking a level of impurity that renders the very distinction between the pure and the impure hugely unstable and deeply questionable.

Is this just another instance of the French, following that old Austrian again, getting down and dirty? Or is this perhaps the only way of getting to the bottom of things, the only way of articulating a really incisive and realistic theory of politics and ultimately of law and constitutionalism? Should a *theory* of constitutionalism not indeed thus get to the bottom of its own impurity before it moves, on the more superficial level of *methodology*, to the question regarding the desired level of separation and 'interrelatedness' (in view of inevitable contagion or infection) between disciplines such as constitutional theory and psychoanalysis? Should one indeed wish to separate *meaningfully* (albeit inevitably only *partially*, as Michelman shows us), constitutionalism from the impurity of politics, had one not better maintain a clear regard for what these impurities really are so as to not be caught unawares or at least not fully unawares by them while thinking one is safely surfing purified or partially purified waters?

It is with these questions in mind that I believe it is important to maintain a clear regard for the relation between the impurities listed by Michelman and those darker ones invoked by Derrida's call for legal theory to attain to and maintain a

---

the desire to cross the threshold of obsession may inform and nourish one another in such a fundamental way that it is impossible to say which precipitates which.

49 Derrida, *États d'âme de la psychanalyse*, 77–78, C'est en ce lieu difficile à cerner, dans l'espace d'indécidabilité et donc de decision ouvert par la discontinuité de l'indirect que la transformation à venir de l'ethique, du droit et de la politique devrait *prendre en compte* le savoir psychanalytique *(ce qui ne veut pas dire y chercher un programme).* (It is in this space that is [so] difficult to delimit, in this space of undecidability and therefore of the decision opened up by the discontinuity of the indirect [impact of psychoanalysis] that the transformation to come of ethics, politics and law should take into account the knowledge of psychoanalysis – which does not mean to go and look there for a programme.)

50 Cf. The incisive discussion of Freud's views concerning the 'great crime' that initiated society, but also had to be repeated again and again so as to maintain society, in Fitzpatrick, *Modernism and the Grounds of Law* (2001), 11–36, especially 21–25.

regard for the insights of psychoanalysis; a clear regard, that is, for the relation between Michelman's list of rather humanistic and normatively speaking already rather purified political impurities, on the one hand, and the raw inhuman and non-normative impurities that Derrida invokes, on the other. And the crucial question that this regard leads one to ask is this: To what extent are the former indeed just puritan repressions and superficial edifications and therefore cover-ups of the latter and to what extent can one truly regard or begin to regard the former as being truthful and meaningful purifications (albeit partial and incomplete purifications, granted) of the latter? And the point of this question would be to move towards an understanding of 'true' or 'truthful' and therefore existentially significant 'purity' ('purity' of constitutionalism, political theory, or whatever) as something that always stands in a relation of irreducible tension with the impurity from which it is extracted or abstracted. The point of the question would be to move towards a regard for an irreducible im/purity that does not allow for either purity or impurity in the strict and exclusive sense of the word.[51] It is this im/purity rather than exclusive or sheer purity or impurity that should concern us whenever and wherever the concerns of a real or realistic humanity are at stake, and not just the claims of a superficial humanism.

The regard for im/purity may lead us even further down the road of interdisciplinarity (or indiscipline, as Kelsen might have wanted to put it). It may lead us, in fact, from political theory to psychoanalysis to neuro-physiology and theology. The question regarding the im/purity of constitutionalism may thus become this: To what extent can the road from the quagmire and ancient marshes of sexual repression and aggression and sheer cruelty, through the *more* (sometimes only barely more) 'enlightened' normative struggles at issue in political conflicts, to the ultimately *most* enlightened concerns of constitutionalism be regarded as a progression through which the rational processes of the prefrontal cortex managed to emancipate itself from the primitive memories of the amygdala?[52]

Should we wish to put the question in this way, we shall do well to remember the instruction of neuro-physiologists that the amygdala is always quicker on the draw; that the rational and reasonable frontal cortex is always the slow late-comer. It has been suggested that religion may offer ways of slowing down the trigger-happy little man at the base of the brain,[53] but it has indeed been religion that has lately again made us so painfully aware of what trigger-happiness is all about. As we saw above, Schmitt had a significant bit to say about the existential thickening or quickening that constituted the political, the emergence of a firing line (irrespective of whether the firing actually begins or not) between friends and enemies. Existential intensification he called it. This intensification, he argued, attains a life of its own and ultimately separates politics from the normative concerns of religion. But he also recognised that the concepts of politics and political theory are predominantly secular versions

---

51 Bataille, who took the quest for pure impurity just about as far as one can imagine, was aware of this. Cf. Bataille, *L'Érotisme* in *Ouvres Complètes X* (1987), 68–72.

52 Cf. Van der Walt, 'Interrupting the Myth of the Partage – Reflections on sovereignty and sacrifice in the work of Nancy, Agamben and Derrida' (2005), *Law and Critique*, 296–8.

53 Cf. Connolly, *Why I Am Not a Secularist* (1999), 28–9. I am indebted to Peter Fitzpatrick for this reference.

of theological concepts, hence his understanding of politics as political theology.[54] We may be dealing with inversions of political theology in the world in which we live today. We may be dealing with versions of 'theological politics'. This inversion does not change much. It still leaves us in the same old mess, that is, with the ancient libidinal and morbid smell of rotting marshes all too pungent in the air we breathe daily. Freud again: Religion is another expression of our deepest pathologies.[55] The regard for the political im/purity of constitutionalism had better also be a regard for the theological im/purity of constitutionalism, irrespective of the question whether we had better integrate this regard consciously or expressly into the 'logic' of constitutionalism or pretend à la Kelsen to keep it as far as possible out of this 'logic'.

V. 'Immimanence' and the Crisis of Im/purity

The question about the possibility of insulating constitutionalism from the concerns of political theory is a question about the possibility of the *immanence* of constitutionalism. It is a question about the possibility of constitutionalism being or becoming fully immanent to itself, fully insulated from the *imminence* of politics, that is, from the always imminent threat of transcendent political and political theoretical concerns. The dynamic of this question, I have argued above, repeats itself on the level of politics and political theory. Politics and political theory that would seek to limit itself to its own normative concerns can only do so by excluding from its scope of attention the always imminent threats of 'baser' human concerns to this rather idealistic and humanistic empire of strictly normative politics.

It is important to stress that the threats of concerns 'foreign or alien to' the intrinsic concerns of constitutionalism or political theory are indeed instances of *imminence* and not just adjacent fields of *immanence* that neatly, peacefully and unproblematically border one another. The 'relations' between these fields are ones of always imminent impact, affect or infection. And it is surely this sting of imminence that moves and informs all existentially significant attempts at pure theory, moves all existentially significant theoretical attempts at constructing pure domains of constitutionalism, pure politics, and so on. In the absence of the sting of imminence, in the absence of this threat from outside, this threat of *the other* and *otherness*, theoretical attempts at disciplinary insulation and purification end up being little more than 'ivory tower' or edifying compartmentalisations, devoid of any significant or existential purport. This response to Michelman is an argument in favour of a constitutionalism and constitutional theory that would not do so. It is an argument for a constitutional theory that would not only be attentive to the neat normative concerns that constitute their 'intrinsic' or 'immanent' domains, but would also be constantly alert to the always imminent existential crisis that political

54 Schmitt, *Politische Theologie* (1922).

55 Freud, *Die Zukunft einer Illusion* in *Gesammelte Werke XIV* (1999) 325–80. In view of the logic of ambiguity pursued here, it is of course also the expression of our highest state of health (which, at least as far as law and legal theory is concerned, is not necessarily a good thing).

and other even 'baser' concerns of life bring to bear on constitutionalism, the always imminent existential crisis which, for better or for worse, keeps constitutionalism and constitutional theory alive. It is thus an argument for a complex conjunction of immanence and imminence that one can, for the sake of economy, denote by the neologism *immimanence*. At issue in this response to Michelman is then an argument for an *immimanent* constitutionalism and *immimanent* theory of law.[56]

It is thus definitely not an argument in favour of sheer imminence, assuming for a moment that something like sheer imminence (imminence that exists in itself and not as a threat to immanence) is possible. Schmitt and Derrida, I have shown above, alert us to the existential moment of imminence. They alert us to the existential moment in which there is no longer a fully conscious and autonomous subject that, guided by clear norms or standards of action, determines in advance what will be. They alert us to a moment in which normative guidance loses its grip on the subject, loses its grip, moreover, on a disintegrating subject. They alert us to a moment in which the by now 'already former' or 'late' subject enters a zone of deep ambiguity in which anything can happen. They alert us to this moment of imminence and Derrida even calls us to be hospitable to this moment for the sake of a future that could be significantly different from and not just a normatively pre-determined extension of the present.[57] But neither Schmitt nor Derrrida can be said to be simplistic proponents of imminence. They only alert us (and ask us to be hospitable) to the imminence that real life will in any case not spare us, the imminence without which the law becomes a lifeless and irresponsible (responding to nothing) concern with its own logic. Both alert us thus against the background of the 'sheer imminence' that Benjamin invokes with his notion of divine violence that transcends the circle of law constituting and law preserving violence. For Schmitt, there is no such thing as sheer political violence that breaks completely with law. Political violence always takes place in order to preserve the law or to found new law. This also applies to states of emergency. They constitute no pure break with law, but a suspension of law in order to preserve law. Schmitt thus also offers us an 'always under law' argument of sorts. As Agamben explains well, the state of emergency is for Schmitt the moment in which the application of the law is suspended in order to preserve the validity of law. It is the moment of the greatest distance in the relation between the content of a rule and its application, not the severance of this relation.[58]

A similar concern is evident in Derrida's response to Benjamin in *Force de loi*. The decision concerned with justice requires a judge to follow and not follow a rule.[59] It does not and cannot require her to simply take leave of rules. The decision (κρίσις) registers the critical junction between the imminence of deciding and the defined

56 For a more extensive exposition, cf. Van der Walt '*Immimanence*; Law's Language Lesson' (2006), *Law Culture and the Humanities*, 2–16.

57 Cf. Derrida *Spectres de Marx* (1993), 57.

58 Agamben, *State of Exception* (2005), 36 referring to Schmitt's *Die Diktatur* (1921) and *Politische Theologie* (1922). There is evidently a significant difference between the position Schmitt took vis á vis Kelsen and the position he took vis á vis Benjamin that merits a more extensive discussion than can be undertaken here.

59 Cf. Derrida, *Force de Loi*, 50–51.

immanence of the rule. The decision thus *constitutes and absorbs* the interface of purity and impurity. It simultaneously *marks and effaces* the lacerating slash in the crisis of im/purity, the lacerating slash that is also the binding slash between life and law. And the dynamics of this lacerating bond is irreducibly and inevitably that of sacrifice.[60] This, I believe, is the existential deep end of the intersection between substance and procedure that Michelman brings to bear on political and constitutional theory. The presence of a clear Kelsenian streak and an absence of references to the Schmitts, the Freuds, the Derridas and the Agambens of this world in Michelman's work (this is not a reproach or a point of criticism, but a bona fide and respectful observation of obvious difference) would suggest that there may well be some difference of opinion between Michelman and myself regarding the extent to which a healthy or partially healthy constitutionalism should seek to consciously sound its own dark depths, but I do not think we differ with regard to the question whether these depths exist. Frank Michelman's normative liberalism is far too frank and honest for me to think otherwise.[61]

60 Cf. again note 45 above: Everything comes to pass between the sacrifice that binds and the sacrifice that cuts…

61 Cf. again note 8 above as well as Van der Walt 'Frankly befriending the Fundamental Contradiction. Frank Michelman and Critical Legal Thought' in Botha et al. (eds.) *Rights and Democracy in a Transformative Constitution* (2004).

Chapter 12

Between Engagement and Disengagement: Two Concepts of Civility

Ioannis A. Tassopoulos

The proceduralist project in liberal constitutional theory goes far beyond 'a political compromise, as in a modus vivendi';[1] it is not satisfied with 'a community of purpose which consists simply of a shared desire to avoid reciprocal destruction'.[2] According to Frank Michelman, proceduralism requires 'a shift of the moral critical gaze'.[3] As developed by Rawls, proceduralism takes citizenship to be an ideal that imposes the moral 'duty of civility – to be able to explain to one another on those fundamental questions how the principles and policies they advocate and vote for can be supported by the political values of public reason'.[4] The lure of proceduralism lies in its association with the ideas of *rational discourse* (in Habermas) or *public reason* (in Rawls),[5] which are supposed to provide sufficiently strong *internal* (as opposed to external) reasons[6] for endorsing the liberal-democratic constitutional order and for maintaining a critical stance towards the problem of legal coercion. Proceduralism aspires to fulfill the 'hope to liquidate or get past such disagreements about the first-order merits of laws'.[7] The duty of civility supplies the normative grounds for the disaggregation of public law and political theory. Civility is crucial for the ideal of self-government between citizens who pursue fundamentally different conceptions of the good.[8]

The focus of this chapter is on two concepts of civility[9] and their implications for constitutional law: the Rawlsian, already mentioned above, and the Smithian,

1 See J. Rawls, *Political Liberalism* (New York: Columbia University Press, 1993), 218, 146.

2 See L. Fuller, 'The Forms and Limits of Adjudication', in *The Principles of Social Order* (Durham NC: Duke University Press, 1981), 102.

3 See F. Michelman, *Constitutionalism as Proceduralism: A Glance at the Terrain*, in this volume.

4 See Rawls, supra n. 1, at 217.

5 See F. Michelman, *Constitutionalism*, supra n. 3, par. III and IV-B.

6 See B. Williams, 'Internal and External Reasons', in *Moral Luck* (Cambridge: Cambridge University Press, 1981), p. 101.

7 See F. Michelman, *Constitutionalism*, supra n. 3.

8 Rawls, *Political*, supra note 1, at 218.

9 I owe to Prof. Michelman the emphasis on the notion of 'civility', in the course of the discussions held at the Faculty of Law of the University of Edinburgh. See on the notion

associated with the important ethical tradition of moral sentiments;[10] it ends with some thoughts from a comparative perspective on the proceduralist attempt to separate constitutional law from political theory.

Rawlsian civility occupies the space between personhood and citizenship. The one end of the spectrum, that is, citizenship, involves the exercise of coercive collective political power and is limited to the values of the liberal-political domain, while the other concerns the comprehensive doctrines that citizens may hold individually, qua persons who have to reconcile according to their liberty of conscience the political values and the values of their comprehensive doctrine.[11] In this context one must note that though we 'think of citizens as free and equal persons',[12] nevertheless there is Rawls's assumption that 'citizens have two views, a comprehensive and a political view; and that their overall view can be divided into two parts, suitably related'.[13] Rawls's account of reasonable comprehensive doctrine is deliberately loose, avoiding the exclusion of doctrines as unreasonable 'without strong grounds based on clear aspects of the reasonable itself. Otherwise our account runs the danger of being arbitrary and exclusive'.[14] Nevertheless, Rawls, in the context of his response to the objection 'that the avoidance of general and comprehensive doctrines implies indifference or skepticism as to whether a political conception of justice can be true as opposed to reasonable in the constructivist sense',[15] recognises that 'in affirming a political conception of justice we may eventually have to assert at least certain aspects of our comprehensive religious or philosophical doctrine ...'[16] Moreover, he accepts that distinguishing 'between those questions that can be reasonably removed from the political agenda and those that cannot' may be 'controversial, at least to some degree'.[17] What is crucial, however, is that the proceduralist liberal tries to avoid discussion on the true philosophical or religious merits of the doctrines involved, to the extent that such discussion is 'unnecessary and may interfere with the practical aim of finding an agreed public basis of justification'.[18] Civility at the same time bridges and divides personhood and citizenship.

Furthermore, the really divisive issues are relegated from the front-line of the political to the social as the 'background-culture' of civil society, according to Rawls.[19] In a way, a citizen should screen his claims on society and restrict them to

---

of civility, E. Shils, *The Virtue of Civility* (Indianapolis: Liberty Fund, 1997), 17, 70, 335–8; J. Starobinski, *Le remède dans le mal* (Paris: Gallimard, 1989), 11 (the first chapter: Le mot civilization).

10 See, in this respect, K. Haakonssen, *Natural Law and Moral Philosophy* (Cambridge: Cambridge University Press, 1996), 1–14, 129, for the place of the Scottish Enlightenment in the history of ideas, and for the relation between A. Smith's and Kant's view of morality.

11 See Rawls, supra n. 1, at 140.

12 See ibid. at 19.

13 Ibid. at 140.

14 Ibid. at 59.

15 Ibid. at 150.

16 Ibid. at 152.

17 Ibid. at 151.

18 See Rawls, supra n. 1, at 153.

19 Ibid. at 14.

those that are consistent with reasonable pluralism and can be adjudicated within a well-ordered society's shared point of view on justice.[20] While it would be inaccurate to say that civility is apolitical, nevertheless the field wherein civility develops and operates is already constrained and is separated from the political.[21] Civility requires a lot of self-regulation, for a person to behave reasonably and honour the fair terms of social cooperation.[22]

A key element for the understanding of civility is that free and equal citizens cannot and indeed should not fully identify with their democracies to the extent that we should not think of a democracy as a community, but as a well-ordered society.[23] Otherwise we mistake 'the kind of unity a constitutional regime is capable of without violating the most basic democratic principles. A zeal for the whole truth tempts us to a broader and deeper unity that cannot be justified by public reason', as Rawls says.[24]

Another interesting point is that civility originates in a situation of social and political engagement,[25] when people are confronted with the irreducible conflict of comprehensive doctrines. The attitude of civility implies that one reacts to the fact of irreconcilable comprehensive doctrines by developing a certain disengagement and detachment from politics, a kind of withdrawal from pressing on with the boldest claims that express contested conceptions of the good. Civility shows the distance we cover in going beyond the crude fact of divisive and irreconcilable doctrines. By submitting the fact of deep disagreement to reflection and scrutiny, we ultimately come to rely on a moral sense of reciprocity between free and equal citizens who establish their social union on a shared public conception of justice. Proceduralism concerns precisely this mode of rationalising the fact of deep political disagreement. As developed by Rawls, it includes various stages, both stricto sensu intellectual[26] (related to rationality) and moral (related to reasonableness), through which free and equal citizens define and endorse the various kinds of autonomy that are available to them in a well-ordered society.[27] Proceduralism accounts for the distinctive features

20 Ibid. at 35.

21 Ibid. at 35.

22 Ibid. at 305.

23 Ibid. at 42.

24 Ibid. at 42–43.

25 Ibid. at 147, 'The political conception of justice is itself a moral conception' and 'an overlapping consensus, therefore, is not merely a consensus of accepting certain authorities, or on complying with certain institutional arrangements, founded on a convergence of self- or group interests. All those who affirm the political conception start from within their own comprehensive view and draw on the religious, philosophical, and moral grounds it provides'.

26 The idea that one goes beyond the facts and intellectualises them comes from P. Strawson, 'Freedom and Resentment', in G. Watson (ed.), *Free Will* (Oxford: Oxford University Press, 1982), 78–79.

27 See Rawls, supra n. 1, at 78: 'Justice as fairness emphasizes this contrast: it affirms political autonomy for all but leaves the weight of ethical autonomy to be decided by citizens severally in light of their comprehensive doctrines'. See also, ibid. at 306: 'Full autonomy includes not only this capacity to be rational but also the capacity to advance our conceptions

of civility qua relative disengagement that marks the specific kind of political liberalism that we discuss. The reserved attitude of civility shows how far away proceduralism takes us from a conflicting account of politics towards a neutralised view of politics.

One may argue, however, that the attribution of disengagement to Rawlsian civility is at least unfair, if not outright wrong. Rawlsian civility has a moral quality and it is sharply distinguished from other cases of scepticism about politics (for example, the scrupulous austerity of self-righteous persons who do not mingle with worldly matters, or the 'cool and trendy' way of modern consumers). With regard to the more particular objection that the Rawlsian account of civility is prone to detachment and disengagement, Rawls explicitly clarifies that: 'Of course, that certain matters are reasonably taken off the political agenda does not mean that a political conception of justice should not provide the grounds and reasons why this should be done. Indeed, as I note above, a political conception should do precisely this'.[28] The Rawlsian passion in politics would not be expressed in the form of emotional over-enthusiasm but rather as thoughtful, sincere and informed judgement based on strong and convincing reasons. Against the charge of intellectualism or of philosophical elitism, it should be pointed out that the Rawlsian concept of civility is profound. The disengagement that the Rawlsian concept of civility seemingly elicits appears so only to one who disregards that procedural liberalism does not turn on abstract theorising of the good; far from lacking empathy, it has clear sight of how intertwined is our conception of the good with our character and personality, how much it permeates our life and our reflections. This being so, one comes naturally to see how pertinent are the boundaries in political liberalism that separate the private, the social and the public: we may fall in love or feel strong affections and we choose whom to marry or whom to associate with. In a sense and in many respects, people choose us and we choose them. But when we turn to the polity, we have the sense that *here* there is no room for choice between persons. By choosing between different versions of the good, the polity would run the risk of choosing between different persons. Empathising, confronted with the normal condition of politics (the clash over the good), liberalism refuses in principle to choose between different persons and thus sets out for the process that leads to justice. As such, the Rawlsian concept of civility is one of humanism, both political and philosophical. And yet something is still missing and the picture still appears incomplete.

The uneasiness does not regard the destination, political liberalism, but the route, proceduralism. One may fully identify with the Rawlsian project of extending the principles of toleration from equal liberty of conscience to philosophy itself, leaving thus 'citizens themselves to settle the questions of religion, philosophy, and morals in accordance with views they freely affirm';[29] and yet at the same time one may feel anxious that this liberal 'movement of thought',[30] as Rawls calls it, pulls us inward too

of the good in ways consistent with honouring the fair terms of social cooperation; that is the principles of justice'.

28 Ibid. at 151–2, n. 16.

29 Ibid. at 154.

30 Ibid. at 154.

strongly and tends to generalise the account of an individual's religious conscience into a theory of how to conceptualise relational matters about society and politics. Gently resisting that pull inward may not be merely a question of idiosyncrasy or temperament, a cinematic contrast between two types – the introvert, the dweller of the inner self, the diver, and the extrovert, the outgoing, the surfer; rather it is about how the two complementary qualities of respect for the others with adequate responsiveness towards them are combined in our own liberal character.

The proceduralist pull inward calls upon us to be conscientious and respectful. Respect for the other co-exists, however, with disengagement towards the stranger, the familiar figure of our urban environment. As liberal persons committed to pursuing their own plan of life, we mindfully guard ourselves and do not easily accept the personal cost that comes with the further step of involvement and engagement beyond our field of interest.[31] Such are reasonable attitudes that reflect the moral and social psychology of ordinary, daily life. Gently resisting the proceduralist pull inward may show reluctance to disregard how precarious is the balance between the respect for the other and the disengagement towards the stranger: Respect and disengagement are mutually undermining and their interplay may be the source of the 'liberal's anxiety'[32] to which Michelman has alluded. Procedural liberalism may provide a template for proper interpersonal relations but does it properly meet demands of responsiveness? The essence of the liberal's anxiety may be understood as failing the demands of responsiveness towards the other. It is not so much the theoretical objections to procedural liberalism but rather the weakness of its account of social responsiveness or, if you like, its relatively low esteem for the factor of personal and social psychology, of moral sentiments that enhance our motivation and guide our reactions.[33] What may be missing from the proceduralist-liberal's account of civility is the element of compassion. Compassion is the countervailing force that balances the proceduralist pull inward; it is the thrust that drives us outward, stabilising thus our moral personality and helping us to keep our moral equilibrium. The social and benevolent affections serve as a catalyst for our moral health.[34] Without their effect, the liberal soul oscillates between a state of cold disengagement and the fever of overwhelming social and personal responsibility entailed by true respect for the others. A Smithian view of civility interjects sociability into civility, centering the concept itself on the dimension of responsiveness.

Civility may be grounded on a personal psychology of moral sentiments, such as that developed by Smith, who argued that we begin 'to examine our own passions and conduct, and to consider how these must appear to them [to other people],

31 See A. Smith, *The Theory of Moral Sentiments* (Amherst NY: Prometheus, 2000), 16.

32 See F. Michelman, 'Relative Constraint and Public Reason: What is "the Work We Expect of Law"', 67 *Brooklyn Law Review* (2002), 963.

33 See Rawls, supra n. 1, at 86, for his discussion of moral psychology. See especially ibid. at 87: 'The difficulty is that beyond the lessons of historical experience and such bits of wisdom as not relying too much on scarce motives and abilities (say, altruism and high intelligence), there is not much to go on. History is full of surprises'.

34 See e.g., Smith, supra n. 31, at 52, 53.

by considering how they would appear to us if in their situation'.[35] Instead of the Rawlsian duality between comprehensive and political views, Smith offered a different division of the self, in two persons, the examiner and judge and the person whose conduct is examined and judged. The former is the spectator and the latter is the agent.[36] Instead of the distinctly intellectual processes that lead to the development of the relatively disengaged civility of procedural political liberalism, we would have the reverse process of experiencing 'reactive feeling and attitudes which belong to involvement and participation with others in inter-personal human relationships',[37] to quote Peter Strawson. One, however, cannot normally express such feelings, for example, resentment, in a violent way but has to exercise self-control, screen and refine them according to complex and elaborate standards of social behaviour, of civility and mutual respect for the differences, of appeal to common sense through reasonable argumentation.

Both the Rawlsian and the Smithian accounts of civility share the main objectives: reasonableness, aversion to the use of force in politics, mistrust towards 'the man of system' (that is, the zealot of a comprehensive doctrine), awareness of the individuality of each person and of the distinctiveness of her principles. Smith, however, associates civility with substantive social conditions of generalised prosperity, where poverty is easily avoided, and connects the public spirit with a benevolent personal character.[38] The contrast with procedural liberalism's intellectualising process that sets the boundaries of 'politics qua public' is striking and puzzling. Shaftesbury, one of the earlier writers in the tradition of moral sentiments, is quite explicit and illuminating in this respect:

> A public spirit can come only from a social feeling or sense of partnership with humankind. Now there are none so far from being partners in this sense, or sharers in this common affection, as they who scarcely know an equal nor consider themselves as subject to any law of fellowship or community. And thus morality and good government go together. There is no real love of virtue without the knowledge of the public good. And where

35 Ibid. at 164.

36 Ibid. For Rawls's position on the judicious spectator, see J. Rawls, *Lectures on the History of Moral Philosophy* (Cambridge MA: Harvard University Press, 2000), 84; J. Rawls, *Lectures on the History of Political Philosophy* (Cambridge MA: Belknap Press, 2007), 184.

37 See Strawson, supra n. 26, at 66.

38 See Smith, supra n. 31, at 297: 'The general security and happiness which prevail in ages of civility and politeness, afford little exercise to the contempt of danger, to patience in enduring labour, hunger and pain. Poverty may easily be avoided, and the contempt of it, therefore, almost ceases to be a virtue'. Ibid. at. 342: 'The violence of the party refusing all palliatives, all temperaments, all reasonable accommodations, by requiring too much, frequently obtains nothing ...' 'When [the man whose public spirit is prompted altogether by humanity and benevolence] cannot conquer the rooted prejudices of the people by reason and persuasion, he will not attempt to subdue them by force...' As, Smith notes (ibid. at 342–343), 'the man of system, on the contrary... goes on to establish his own ideal plan of government completely and in all its parts, without any regard either to the great interests or to the strong prejudices which may oppose it'. 'In the great chess-board of human society, every single piece has a principle of motion of its own, altogether different from that which the legislature might choose to impress upon it'.

> absolute power is, there is no public'.[39] [Referring to the Britons he notes:] 'We have the notion of a public and a constitution, how a legislative and how an executive is modeled. We understand weight and measure in this kind and can reason justly on the balance of power and property … Our increasing knowledge shows us every day, more and more, what common sense is in politics, and this must of necessity lead us to understand a like sense in morals, which is the foundation.'[40] 'For the opposite of sociableness is selfishness'.[41]

In these very interesting passages the public is inextricably related with the social. Far from being conceptualised as two separate zones, where access from the social arena to the procedurally restricted area of the public is legitimate only for the holders of a valid passport of non-comprehensive doctrines, the public is socially embedded and ultimately depends on moral character and on the appropriate attitude of sociability. The social and the public form a continuum, a field of interaction, engagement, political and moral conflict between sociability and selfishness. Within such a context, the role of reason is not procedural, aiming at intellectualising disagreement. Rather, reason should control passions. 'The only poison to reason is passion' and reason is 'the best antidote' for passion.[42] We cannot understand human nature without having a real appreciation for the power of passionate enthusiasm to inflame the heart and the mind. In addition, enthusiasm is easily transmitted from one another and therefore it presents a sociopolitical phenomenon of the first magnitude. 'The combustible matters lie prepared within and ready to take fire at a spark, but chiefly in a multitude seized with the same spirit'.[43] Our response to the challenge posed by the potentially ruinous impact of extreme passions and enthusiasm upon our personal and social life is absolutely crucial. At first, it would be a serious mistake to try to suppress or eradicate enthusiasm. 'Enthusiasm is wonderfully powerful and extensive'.[44] 'To forbid men's natural fears and to endeavour the overpowering them by other fears, must needs be a most unnatural method'.[45] According to Shaftesbury, the best response to enthusiasm is a combination of 'good humour', self-knowledge and tolerant attitude: '[t]he knowledge of our passions in their very seeds, the measuring well the growth and progress of enthusiasm, and the judging rightly of its natural force and what command it has over our very senses, may teach us to oppose more successfully those delusions which come armed with the specious pretext of moral certainty and matter of fact'.[46] The tolerant policy of the ancients was most

39 See Shaftesbury, 'Sensus Communis, an Essay on the Freedom of Wit and Humour', in L. Klein (ed.), *Characteristics of Men, Manners, Opinions, Times* (Cambridge: Cambridge University Press, 1999), 50.

40 Ibid. at 50–51.

41 Ibid. at 53.

42 Ibid. at 43.

43 See Shaftesbury, 'A Letter Concerning Enthusiasm to My Lord', in L. Klein (ed.), *Characteristics of Men, Manners, Opinions, Times* (Cambridge: Cambridge University Press, 1999), 23.

44 Ibid. at 27.

45 Ibid. at 10.

46 Ibid. at 22–23.

appropriate: 'Thus superstition and enthusiasm were mildly treated and, being let alone, they never raged to that degree as to occasion bloodshed, wars, persecutions and devastations in the world'.[47] From the perspective of moral sentiments, our intellectual capacities take a more or less social and behavioural twist, refining our conduct and helping us to understand common sense in politics and morals. As Shaftesbury writes:

> 'It is the habit alone of reasoning which can make a reasoner.'[48] 'All politeness is owing to liberty. We polish one another and rub off our corners and rough sides by a sort of amicable collision. To restrain this is inevitably to bring a rust upon men's understandings. It is a destroying of civility, good breeding and even charity itself, under pretence of maintaining it'.[49]

Civility requires our understanding that 'the lovers of mankind respect and honour conventions and societies of men' and that 'it is a breach of the harmony of public conversation to take things in such a key as is above the common reach, puts others to silence and robs them of their privilege of turn'.[50] Civility regards our knowledge of how to strongly disagree without showing disrespect and animosity towards our interlocutor, of how to be adamant in the face of abuses of power or office, of how to indulge those who for some reason lose their temper or are taken by enthusiasm. Finally, civility reflects our basic human decency, our reaction to offensive lack of compassion and ruthlessness, to moral indifference and to ethical paralysis. The Smithian civility then is the display of our sociability and of our personal performance in the interplay between reason and (com)passion.

Rawlsian civility is associated with what Bernard Williams has called a 'rationalistic conception of rationality', 'which impose[s] on personal deliberation and on the idea of practical reason itself a model drawn from a particular understanding of public rationality. This understanding requires in principle every decision to be based on grounds that can be discursively explained'.[51] Free and equal citizens who are both reasonable and rational derive the principles of justice and reconfigure accordingly the domain of the political, setting inclusiveness as its distinctive feature. By the very rationality of the project, philosophy – public and political – occupies an important if not a privileged place fully developing, analysing and systematising the various intellectual steps that lead to the procedural reconfiguration of politics according to the principles of Rawlsian justice. Rawls's is a universally applicable, constructive

47 Ibid. at 11. For the importance of 'good humour' see Shaftesbury, *Sensus*, supra n. 39, at 59–69.

48 Ibid., at 33.

49 Ibid. at 31. See also ibid. at 39: "There was a time when men were accountable only for their actions and behaviour. Their opinions were left to themselves. They had liberty to differ in these as in their faces. Everyone took the air and look which was natural to him. But in process of time it was thought decent to mend men's countenances and render their intellectual complexions uniform and of a sort'.

50 Ibid. at 36.

51 See B. Williams, *Ethics and the Limits of Philosophy* (London: Fontana Press, 1993), 18.

and optimistic theory that is based on the inherent capacity of every person for further intellectual growth and enlightenment through the exercise of reason. Being moved by reason alone is a distinctive feature of one's autonomy[52] and the Rawlsian concept of civility is resolutely oriented towards autonomy.

By contrast, the Smithian concept of civility does not develop out of the quest for autonomy, but out of a perseverant effort to meet the challenges of heteronomy.[53] These are not equivalent attitudes. According to the Smithian account, reason is not sovereign in its own territory; rather, the task of reason is to tackle and control the forces that cause and maintain heteronomy, be they internal and psychological, for example, violent passions, prejudice and fanaticism, or external and sociopolitical, for example, the tendency of those who exercise authority to serve their own interests and augment their power to the detriment of their subjects. Depending on the circumstances, personal change, political struggle or a combination of both may be the appropriate response.[54] Unfortunately, however, reason may be defeated and outweighed in the battleground of politics. Power relations are precarious, having uncertain outcome and potentially destructive consequences. Sociability, moderation, common sense and the other bases of Smithian civility enhance the effect of reason in politics.[55] Civility is a primary ethico-political good that is fragile and vulnerable; engagement and commitment to the practice of civility are necessary for its survival. As such, the Smithian civility differs from the Rawlsian one because it does not try to sustain the more ambitious philosophical project of a procedural reconfiguration of politics, but to engage the universal audience of humanity,[56] hoping to shape peaceful and civilised relations between real persons in our real world.

Rawlsian and Smithian civility have a different view of the bond that keeps us together. For the former this bond is primarily public,[57] while for the latter it is primarily social.[58] The two concepts of civility are not incompatible; rather, they

---

52 See J. Rawls, Kantian Constructivism in Moral Theory, in *Collected Papers* (Cambridge MA: Harvard University Press, 1999), 320.

53 See on Shaftesbury, the subtle analysis of S. Darwall, *The British Moralists and the Internal 'Ought'* (Cambridge: Cambridge University Press, 1995), 197–202, and in particular 198.

54 See Williams, supra n. 51, at 47.

55 In fact, politeness and the critique of divine enthusiasm were directed against religious fanaticism; see, L. Klein, 'Shaftesbury, Politeness and the Politics of Religion', in N. Phillipson and Q. Skinner (eds), *Political Discourse in Early Modern Britain* (Cambridge: Cambridge University Press, 1997), 283. See also, N. Phillipson, 'Propriety, Property and Prudence: David Hume and the Defence of the Revolution', in N. Phillipson and Q. Skinner (eds), *Political Discourse in Early Modern Britain* (Cambridge: Cambridge University Press, 1997), 302.

56 See G. Christie, *The Notion of an Ideal Audience in Legal Argument* (Dordrecht: Kluwer, 2000), 3–4, 193.

57 See Rawls, supra n. 1, at 35, 66.

58 See I. Hamspsher-Monk, 'From Virtue to Politeness', in M. van Gelderen and Q. Skinner, *Republicanism: A Shared European Heritage, v. 2, The Values of Republicanism in Early Modern Europe* (Cambridge: Cambridge University Press, 2002), 85, 89.

should be regarded as distinctive and identifiable parts of an enlarged and structured account of civility.

Two of the most prominent features of the public bond are its immediacy and thinness.[59] The public is not mediated by a third factor, external to our common relationship. It is neither the authority of God, nor of the state, not even of nature. Besides, the public depends on rather thin substantive commitments (free and equal persons who are both reasonable and rational). Immediacy and thinness are important to prevent external dependence and over-determination of the public bond. Otherwise some of the citizens who happened to qualify on the basis of the accepted criterion (the high-priest, the absolute monarch or the oracle of natural law) would claim a special and privileged position vis-à-vis the collective power. Even worse, they could be easily tempted to use 'their' power against those who oppose them, in which case civility would break down.

Pertinent, however, for our discussion of the two concepts of civility is a third characteristic of the public bond: its abstraction.[60] This feature complements the immediacy and the thinness as the intrinsic qualities of the public bond. Culturally speaking, civility may have close affinity with the Stoic and the Christian traditions of Natural Law,[61] as they have shaped our idea of individual conscience and the notion that we should realise in life the *logos*, the common touch of nature or God within us. But the public bond transcends all the various movements of thought that have exerted strong influences and have been assimilated in the canvas of our relationship, making civility possible; the public bond retains pure its peculiar normative character, based on the rational and the reasonable. Abstraction illuminates the disengagement and detachment of the Rawlsian concept of civility. Simply stated, a gross violation of the rules of civility is the tendency of turning disagreement into a personal dispute. This attitude is not merely counterproductive; it is also wrong as it lacks respect for the other person. If the disagreement concerns theoretical matters, abstract ideas, then there is nothing counterintuitive in that claim of civility. If, however, the disagreement concerns matters that strongly implicate someone's character, then the disengagement and detachment of Rawlsian civility becomes much more demanding upon us and potentially problematic.[62] In a sense, as persons we are the embodiments of our character. For the most extreme cases, for

59 See Rawls's discussion of doctrinal autonomy in relation to political liberalism, supra n. 1, at 98: 'A view is autonomous, then, because in its represented order, the political values of justice and public reason (expressed by their principles) are not simply presented as moral requirements externally imposed. Nor are they required of us by other citizens whose comprehensive doctrines we do not accept'.

60 See Rawls, supra n. 1, at 46.

61 See, for example, Haakonssen, supra n. 10, at 4.

62 See B. Williams, 'Toleration: An Impossible Virtue?' in D. Heyd (ed.), *Toleration – An Elusive Virtue* (Princeton: Princeton University Press, 1996), 18, 25: 'In the light of this, we can now better understand the impossibility or extreme difficulty that was seemingly presented by the personal value or attitude of toleration. It appeared impossible because it seemingly required someone to think that a certain belief or practice was thoroughly wrong or bad, and at the same time that there was some intrinsic good to be found in its being allowed to flourish'.

example, for Hitler, we may say meaningfully that he was the embodiment of evil. But we accept ordinarily that a person has the right of self-determination and that we should not gel our image of another on the basis of stereotypes that we loosely project upon him. A crucial aspect of respect for someone is the recognition of his power to become something different from what he is now. Abstraction as a quality of the public bond, as a duty associated with Rawlsian civility is related precisely to the fact that 'it is only in virtue of his rational capacities that a person is capable of becoming critically aware of his own will and of forming volitions of the second order', to quote Harry Frankfurt.[63] That kind of freedom is at the root of the Rawlsian concept of civility and of the public bond. Abstraction and disengagement are for the sake of a person's liberty and power to devise, reconsider, rework and change his personal plan of life, to transcend his conditions and to become something different from what he already is.

Smithian civility is more about a person's responsibility[64] for what he has already done or omitted. It addresses primarily our sensibilities and our conscience. It is mostly concerned with our commitments and our reactions. Its focus is on our character, on our attitude towards injustice, pervasive or incidental, and it basically raises the question: 'But, didn't you know?' Smithian civility develops an account of the social bond on the basis of our responsiveness.

In an analysis of civility that integrates both the Rawlsian and the Smithian ideas, love, compassion and respect are indispensable parts. Love without respect can be oppressive; kindness can be disrespectful;[65] respect without love or compassion can be alienating. Culturally speaking, our notion of civility is not in harmony with the melancholy of the declining Hellenistic world[66] or with the theological cosmology of pious Christianity; rather civility relies on the Classical component of our tradition; it has to do with our understanding of what it means to live and grow up in the polis. Notwithstanding the importance of individual conscience and of the inner self, our idea of life has a social and external aspect, or rather a democratic sociopolitical locus and our personal development and human flourishing require the dialogue at the agora of the polis. Civility is the ethos of our polis. The challenge of civility is the creation of a sociopolitical environment that is conducive to each one's opportunity to devise and realise his or her own plan of life; it is a question of cultivating a robust liberal and democratic *paideia.*

The focus of Rawlsian and Smithian civility on the public and the social bond, respectively, elucidates a corresponding distinction that we may draw between the 'politics of the public' and 'the politics of the social'. Likewise, it is possible to

63 See H. Frankfurt, 'Freedom of the Will and the Concept of a Person', in G. Watson (ed.), *Free Will* (Oxford: Oxford University Press, 1982), 87.

64 See with regard to the place of 'desert, responsibility, guilt, condemnation, and justice' in moral life, Strawson, supra n. 26, at 78, and at 76–80.

65 See Smith, supra n. 31, at 181–2: 'In France Despreaux and Racine did not think it below them ... even to treat the good La Fontaine with a species of the most disrespectful kindness'.

66 See in this respect, Cicero, 'De Finibus III', 16–31, 62–64 and the discussion on 'oikeiosis' in G. Vivenza, *Adam Smith and the Classics* (Oxford: Oxford University Press, 2001), 191, 205–06, 210–2 (the Postscript).

conceive constitutional law as being primarily concerned with the legal regulation and entrenchment of the public or of the social. The project of proceduralism in liberal constitutional theory clearly opts for a view of constitutional law as public law, hoping to insulate the legal evaluation of laws from judgements on their true merits. But constitutional law cannot be confined to the deontological and consensual[67] view of the 'politics of the public' without being severely impoverished. The antagonistic and conflicting 'politics of the social' with their realistic account of human nature and of economic relationships within society have greatly contributed to the formation of constitutionalism. In the Federalist Papers the role of passions and interests in relation to factions is well known,[68] while the constitutional organisation of the state according to a system of effective checks and balances owes much to the insight that common sense belies reliance on the good will of those who exercise political authority, because power is 'restless, aspiring and insatiable'[69] and 'il faut que, par la disposition des choses, le pouvoir arrête le pouvoir'.[70] Above all, it is hard to exaggerate the importance of 'political enthusiasm', with its power to assemble the citizens in the central squares of their capital, for our notion of popular government and of democratic empowerment. Finally, the passionate voices, usually dissents,[71] of the Supreme Court's Justices in favour of civility and justice stand more for a jurisprudence of Smithian impartial engagement, rather than of Rawlsian proceduralist disengagement.

Nowhere is the necessity of a theory of constitutional law that covers both the politics of the public and the politics of the social more evident than in Rawls's discussion of subversive advocacy. Rawls asserts that 'historically, the question of when resistance and revolution are justified is one of the deepest political questions' and that 'subversive advocacy is always part of a more comprehensive political view',[72] as a consequence, 'to repress subversive advocacy is to suppress the discussion of these reasons, and to do this is to restrict the free and informed public use of reason in judging the justice of the basic structure and its social policies'.[73] His conclusion is that in a constitutional convention, the delegates who represent the rational interest of equal citizens 'would draw the line between protected and unprotected political speech not (as *Gitlow* does) at subversive advocacy as such but (as *Brandenburg* does) at subversive advocacy when it is both directed to

67 See the discussion of the idea of an overlapping consensus in Rawls, supra n. 1, at 133.

68 See M. White, *Philosophy, The Federalist, and the Constitution* (Oxford: Oxford University Press, 1987), 102.

69 See B. Bailyn, *The Ideological Origins of the American Revolution* (Cambridge MA: Belknap Press, 1967), 56.

70 See Montesquieu, *De l'esprit des lois*, book XI, ch. IV.

71 See, for example, J. Harlan's dissent in *Plessy v. Ferguson*, 163 US 537 (1896). 'But in view of the Constitution, in the eye of the law, there is in this country no superior, dominant, ruling class of citizens. There is no caste there. Our Constitution is colour-blind, and neither knows nor tolerates classes among citizens'.

72 See Rawls, supra n. 1, at 346.

73 Ibid.

inciting imminent and unlawful use of force and likely to achieve this result'.[74] But advocating the violent overthrow of a functioning liberal democracy in favour of a totalitarian comprehensive doctrine can hardly be reconciled with a proceduralistic, liberal theory of legitimacy; the abstract delimitation of legitimate political speech would normally exclude subversive advocacy of totalitarian doctrines that expressly reject the duties of Rawlsian civility and reciprocity.

By contrast, Smithian civility allows that freedom of speech guarantees a social state of tolerance, which may be something quite less than the genuine tolerance of political liberalism, being limited to the legally protected peaceful interaction of persons whose attitude towards the liberal democratic constitution varies from wholehearted support to a rhetoric of violent and intransigent hostility.[75] From the standpoint of Smithian civility, the liberal and democratic polity may have to indulge the totalitarian fanatic as one who has been taken by an aberrant political enthusiasm. Commitment to the practice of civility, recognition that it can be worse for civility to try to suppress and eradicate the revolutionary message than to mildly treat it, knowledge of what is common sense in politics and in morals, all these are grounds to require, in the punishment of subversive advocacy, that 'the influence of the words must be manifested not from inferences from the speech but from action which is additional to, and independent of the fact itself that the speaker knowingly undertook criminal advocacy'.[76] The Smithian account of civility, with its emphasis on social manners and behaviour, is indispensable; it informs the cultural and technical distinction of speech as opposed to conduct, guiding the judiciary in drawing the line between permissible revolutionary advocacy and punishable overt acts of violence, on the basis of external, that is, empirically verifiable factors.[77] But this does not mean that the Rawlsian account of civility becomes superfluous.

'The combustible matters lie prepared within and ready to take fire at a spark', noted Shaftesbury.[78] 'A single revolutionary spark may kindle a fire that, smouldering for a time, may burst into a sweeping and destructive conflagration', pointed out J. Sanford in *Gitlow*.[79] These metaphors present the volatile effect of enthusiasm and of subversive speech on the mind as an irresistible chain of natural causation analogous to that of fire on ammunition.[80] They are dangerously misleading and inapposite, because they disregard the freedom of the will, that is, the rational capacity of a person for disengagement and detachment, so as to become critically aware of his own will. It is a distinctive feature of the Rawlsian account of civility to expound this freedom's true normative import to politics.

The Smithian account of civility shows that civility and mutual respect do not depend on proceduralism. Smithian civility is consistent with passionate engagement

74 Ibid. at 348.

75 See I. Tassopoulos, *The Constitutional Problem of Subversive Advocacy in the United States of America and Greece* (Athens-Komotini: Sakkoulas, 1993), 184.

76 Ibid. at 206.

77 Ibid. at 200–01.

78 See supra n. 40.

79 See *Gitlow v. New York*, 268 US 652, 669 (1925).

80 See Tassopoulos, supra n. 75, 127–9.

in politics in favour of liberal comprehensive doctrines such as those of Mill and Kant, which share the crucial assumption of political liberalism 'that equal citizens have different and indeed incommensurable and irreconcilable conceptions of the good'.[81] According to Rawls, these doctrines adopt 'the ethical values of autonomy and individuality, which may apply to the whole of life, both social and individual, as expressed by the comprehensive liberalisms of Kant and Mill'.[82] Likewise, constitutional theory may be a quest for the ethico-political foundation of the constitution,[83] rather than a theory of public law. The main interpretive sources of constitutional theory may be looked for in the liberal and democratic political philosophies that have influenced our constitutional traditions.

The actual historical impact of a proceduralist account of political liberalism as opposed to a comprehensive ethico-political view varies from country to country. For example, in 2005 France celebrated the centennial of the legal separation between Church and State. The French *laicité* originated in a context of ardent political struggle between the Catholic Church and the Republic.[84] In such a political context, political liberalism tends to take the form of a forceful and full-fledged ethico-political doctrine against the comprehensive claims of religious dogma, rather than the relatively mild and neutral form of procedural political liberalism. The latter is more congenial for societies which have achieved a better balance between the individual and the collective aspects of self-government and therefore are naturally inclined to a more sober and less dramatised view of politics. Actually, this account may be more democratic to the extent that the individual will rarely have to suffer radical disruptions of his personal life-plan for the pursuit of collective plans of action, sanctioned by the authority of popular sovereignty. It may be the case that Europe, in the process of a consensual political integration, becomes more and more prepared for the proceduralist version of political liberalism, overcoming the polarisations between comprehensive ethico-political doctrines and the passionate account of combative politics, which prevailed in the old constitutional tradition of popular sovereignty in the continental nation-states.

A final comparative point, regarding continental constitutional law, and by that I mean the constitutional law whose development is more or less directly associated with the series of events that we usually call 'the French Revolution'. At the end of the nineteenth century, the idea of public law as an autonomous field separated from politics, unadulterated by political philosophy and focused on the analysis of the institutions of the Rechtsstaat, grew out of a disillusionment with politics, a sense that the political does not fulfill the moral hopes generated by the Revolution; rather it undermines essentially both the stability of the state and the security in the exercise

81 See Rawls, supra n. 1, at 303.

82 Ibid. at 78. Rawls, ibid. at 304, emphasises that in political liberalism, 'the social union is no longer founded on a conception of the good as given by a common religious faith or philosophical doctrine, but on a shared public conception of justice appropriate to the conception of citizens in a democratic state as free and equal persons'.

83 See, for example, I. Tassopoulos, *The Ethico-political Foundation of the Constitution* (Athens-Komotini: Sakkoulas, 2001) (in Greek).

84 See Y. Bruley, 1905 *La séparation des églises et de l'état* (Paris: Perrin, 2004) (présentation de D. de Villepin).

of individual rights. Consequently, the fundamental document of the social and legal order was not the Constitution but the Civil Code.[85] The reduction of public law to a separate and autonomous field meant to be a remedy for the inherent unreliability of politics and the contentious nature of political philosophy. Maurizio Fioravanti forcefully captures the gist of the idea, when he says that the prevailing attitude among liberal constitutionalists was that the revolutionary doctrine led to a situation where 'there was too much state within society, but also too much society within the state'.[86] When liberalism as a substantive ethical ideal regresses both socially and politically, proceduralism in liberal constitutional theory may be one more line of defence of the rich tradition of liberal constitutionalism in an effort to constrain overly conservative political doctrines.

Michelman's analysis of the project of proceduralism in liberal constitutional theory invites an inquiry into the constitutional meaning of civility. This chapter discussed two different concepts of civility. The Rawlsian one, being primarily concerned with fanaticism as a menace to liberal pluralism, makes civility the groundwork for propelling rationalism in politics. By contrast, the Smithian concept of civility, knowing that the Roman maxim 'qui tacet consentire videtur' may be sufficient for the effective exercise of authority over people but is haplessly inadequate as a condition for the preservation of political liberty, puts forth civility as a substantive value that should instruct and guide the politics and law of our liberal democracies. Embracing civility as a moral duty, the Rawlsian concept offers a procedurally restricted account of politics. Confronting politics as an inherently open-ended and dynamic social process, the Smithian account submits the claim for greater civility. Perhaps the challenge is to integrate the social and public dimensions into a broader notion of civility; one that better serves a liberal democracy capable of greater altruism and social responsiveness.

---

85 M. Fioravanti, *Stato e Costituzione* (Torino: G. Giappichelli, 1993), 133.

86 M. Fioravanti, *Appunti di storia delle costituzioni moderne – Le liberta fondamentali* (Torino: G. Giappichelli, 1995), 104 ('*troppo Stato nella societá*, ma anche *troppa societá nello Stato*').

Chapter 13

Enabling Proceduralism

Victor Tadros[1]

I Three Challenges to Proceduralism

Frank Michelman's 'Constitutionalism as Proceduralism' develops an account of the motivation behind the move to proceduralism in constitutional theory and its relationship with political theory. Michelman suggests that constitutional theory cannot be detached from political theory. Proceduralism, he suggests, is a solution to two connected problems. The first is that of disagreement. In circumstances of disagreement, perhaps even deep disagreement, about what is substantively just, how should a solution, a way forward, be determined? Secondly, given that any political solution, to be practically effective, will be dependent on coercion of those who disagree with the solution in substantive terms, how can we justify coercion?

We need, Michelman suggests, to justify coercion of those who disagree, or even deeply disagree, about what is just in law. Falling back on a procedure will be justified, Michelman suggests, if it is an appropriate way of resolving disagreements *and* one that can justify coercion of those who continue to disagree.

Michelman then traces two competing accounts of proceduralism: pure proceduralism and imperfect proceduralism. The former suggests that the decision taken through a particular procedure constitutes what is just. On this account justice cannot be determined independently of the procedure through which it is determined. The latter suggests that proceduralism is justifiable in that a procedure constitutes the best method of tracking the content of justice.[2] Whilst there are independent considerations which constitute the substantive justification of a decision, use of the procedure is justified in that, and insofar as, there is no better way to determine what those considerations are such that decisions reached will reflect substantive considerations that obtain in fact. On this account procedure is primarily *epistemic*:[3] it is there as a way of knowing what is substantively just rather than a way of contributing to the substance of justice.

In this response I will suggest three challenges to this account of the terrain. I will suggest that disagreement is at best part of the motivation for proceduralism, and that there are challenges to seeing it as providing a justification of proceduralism at all. The

---

1 Thanks to Zenon Bankowski, Emilios Christodoulidis, Scott Veitch and Neil Walker for helpful comments and discussions.

2 A decision will track the content of justice insofar as it is a decision that is consistent with what substantive justice demands. I leave open whether it is also required on this account that the decision is taken *for those reasons*.

3 At least for moral realists who suppose that there really are moral considerations in the world that can be discovered.

justification depends on there being more likelihood or more reason for agreement about procedures of justice than there is for substantive questions of justice. I will suggest that it is unlikely that there is more reason to agree or that there is more likelihood of an agreement on questions of procedure than there is on substantive questions.

Secondly, I will argue that it is not, or at least not only, *coercion* that we should be attempting to justify. It is important, I suggest, for constitutional scholars to focus on the practices and implications of the law more directly than that. Coercion, I argue, is an unfamiliar remedy for breach of the law. As far as the *criminal law* is concerned it is the justification of *punishment* rather than the justification of coercion that we ought to be seeking. Whilst decisions are to be regarded as binding on those who agree, their bindingness in the criminal law authorises punishment for breach. And that has implications for the status of the procedure.

Thirdly, I will suggest that there is a middle ground between pure proceduralism and imperfect proceduralism that is worth exploring. I will outline two further positions: additive proceduralism and enabling proceduralism. Both of these positions suggest that the substance of the justice of a decision is dependent on the procedure, and hence they are not purely epistemic in the way that imperfect proceduralism is. But they do not indicate that the procedure is constitutive of justice in the way indicated by pure proceduralism; there remain substantive questions of what a just outcome is that are independent of what the procedure does or would decide. I will argue that it is the latter of these positions, enabling proceduralism, that is the most promising, and that focusing on punishment rather than coercion can help us to see that this is so.

II Justice and Disagreement

We disagree about justice in three ways. Firstly, we disagree about substantive issues of justice. For example, we disagree about distributive justice, and consequently the appropriate levels of taxation and how the resources generated through taxation should be distributed. We disagree about corrective justice, and consequently about the grounds of actions in civil cases and their damages. And we disagree about retributive justice, and consequently about what should be a crime and how much and in what ways crimes should be punished. Secondly, we disagree about procedural issues of justice. We disagree about the proper method by which we should come to determine the rules of substantive justice. We disagree about whether there should be democratic processes and what kinds of processes are the right ones. We disagree about the constitution of the demos. We disagree about the division of labour between courts and parliament and we disagree about the proper forum of public reasoning and the style of public reason. Thirdly, we disagree about the relationship between procedural and substantive issues of justice. We disagree about how much the procedure should be constrained by substantive issues, which are placed 'beyond argument', and we disagree about whether what is substantively just is dependent on or independent of procedure.

For some, the first kind of disagreement is more intractable and serious than the second. If we are more likely to resolve disagreement of the second kind than the first, we might generate some procedures that might satisfy some who persist with disagreements of the first kind. If I agree with you about a particular procedure to solve issues of distributive justice, I may agree *to* the outcome even if the outcome is one which I substantively disagree *with*. This kind of justification for procedural justice is hostage to empirical fortune. It works only insofar as there is more agreement about procedural justice than substantive justice.

An alternative is that there is *more reason* to agree with a particular procedure than there is with a range of substantive matters. A particular set of procedures might be justifiable from a number of different ethical perspectives.[4] All can accept processes of public decision making, it might be argued, even if they cannot regard all of the outcomes of public reason as themselves justifiable. In this case, even if there is no agreement about procedures in fact, it is nevertheless justifiable that such procedures and the decisions that are made are backed up by coercive force, in that all reasonable parties *ought* to agree with them.

Of course, it is insufficient justification of a procedure to show that all participants can agree that there should be *some* procedure of rule by law. We can agree, as Michelman suggests, with liberals when they claim that ensuring compliance with the law will be better for if not all, then most, citizens. But it is of course a step from there to the acceptance of any particular set of political processes. And it is in relation to a particular process, rather than the need for some kind of process, that agreement is required. This, incidentally, is a problem for Hobbesians in particular, who can identify the necessity for political authority but lack the motivation to specify any particular content that it should have.

Although this seems to put me at odds with much writing in political theory, my suspicion is that the existence of disagreement about justice does not provide the best defence of political procedures available. As far as the empirical question is concerned, I see little evidence of greater agreement about modes of political procedure, the constitution of the demos or the division of labour between courts and parliament than there is about a range of substantive issues. And it may well be that, if there are deep disagreements in society from different ethical perspectives (something which itself, I think, remains to be demonstrated), disagreements about procedure themselves reflect deeper disagreements about ethics. It is not even clear how we are to quantify the level of disagreement that is relevant here. If we think that a constitutional arrangement is justified only if it can be justified from all reasonable ethical perspectives we put the bar of justification too high.

Furthermore, once we have discovered that those who disagree about what is to be done can agree about a procedure for deciding what is to be done, there is every reason to push for further agreement about the substance of what is to be done, at least in principle. There seems little reason to suppose that there will be agreement about who is to decide political questions and how, but no agreement about the principles that are to be used to decide those questions. In fact, on the contrary, acceptance of who is to decide and how will be warranted only on the grounds that

4 See, for example, J. Rawls *Political Liberalism* (Columbia, 1997) where Rawls argues that the basic institutions of society must be justifiable to a range of reasonable comprehensive or partially comprehensive moral outlooks.

the who and the how are likely to reflect acceptable principles in practice. If we can agree on public *persons* to decide political questions we can agree on public *principles* to decide political questions. For agreement on public persons can only plausibly be generated from some level of agreement about public principles.[5]

Finally, proceduralism doesn't seem especially to be a solution to the problem of disagreement, or at least only to that problem. It's not as though the proper procedures would become redundant were there agreement about the substance of justice. Suppose that we all agree that it should be criminal to *v*. That is not to say that criminalising *v* can be done in the absence of proper procedures. Philosopher kings and colonial masters are objectionable even if they are both wise enough to generate the right answers about substantive questions of justice and they are sufficiently charismatic to persuade citizens of that. Citizens may still rightly object that the philosopher kings are deciding for them questions which they ought to decide for themselves. So even if disagreement is *one* of the problems that proceduralism is a solution to, a full defence of proceduralism would have to move beyond disagreement. As we shall see, this is particularly true when we consider that one of the things that procedures should attempt to justify is not coercion but, at least as far as the *criminal law* is concerned, something more.

III Punishment and Proceduralism

This brings me to an oddity, or at least vagueness, in Michelman's discussion, one that is common in thinking about liberal constitutionalism. Michelman suggests that the central question that liberal constitutional theory addresses concerns the conditions under which rules and principles of law can be developed that will organise the lives of citizens, and which can appropriately be backed up by coercion or force. The problem, a familiar problem in political theory, is how to ensure coordination and cooperation in a manner that is just and fair where, inevitably, force or coercion will be required.

One oddity about this conception is that, as Hart pointed out a long time ago in his critique of Austin, many laws cannot be understood as rules backed up by force, and even the criminal law, which comes closest to this model, is quite distinct from it[6] (perhaps more so than even Hart thought). So one question is why this problem is still seen as the central problem. If laws are not rules backed up by force, but something else, then why would we set the problem for constitutional and political theory as the justification of coercion? Coercion isn't an idea immediately recognisable as central to the law.

But what is recognisable to *criminal* lawyers, in particular, is not the idea of coercion, but the idea of *punishment*. What must be justified, at least as far as the criminal law is concerned, is the existence of rules the breach of which will involve

5 See in particular M. Ridge, 'Hobbesian Public Reason' (1998) 108 *Ethics* 538.

6 *The Concept of Law*, 2nd ed. (Oxford: Oxford University Press, 1961; 1994), 20–25. For an account of why we should not see criminal law in this way, see also in particular R. A. Duff, 'Rule-Violations and Wrongdoings', in A. P. Simester and S. Shute, *Criminal Law Theory: Doctrines of the General Part* (Oxford: Oxford University Press, 2002).

the imposition of punishment. Outside the criminal law, it is not clear what the relevant coercion is. Is it coercive to require the payment of damages in contract law or tort? And beyond that, where the law creates powers rather than imposing liability, Austin's model is even less salient. And yet all of these areas of law are areas which must be decided according to a constitution, and which consequently ought to provide part of the question to which constitutional theory ought to provide an answer. Perhaps (although I doubt that this is uniformly the case) we should see these areas of law as warranting punishment for breach themselves, however, as criminal sanctions are ultimately available to reinforce the requirements of other parts of the law. For this reason, I will focus on criminal law.

This creates a further question, a question which needs an answer before the proceduralism debate can be addressed. Should we expect the same answer to the proceduralism debate with regard to every different kind of law? Is the procedure doing the same work in each case? Or could we adopt different procedures with different standing to substantive justice for different kinds of law? If the problem is set as the justification, through a procedure, of coercion, we assume that all different kinds of law need the same kind of justification. But it is not clear that that is the case, and in fact I suspect that it isn't. The function of criminal law is quite different, I will suggest, from other kinds of law. And to perform that function it is insufficient to refer to the justice of a particular procedure. In the imposition of criminal liability it is always open for courts to reconsider the substance of the offence. That is true in a way that need not be true of every other kind of legal rule.

In order to see why, let's return to the three familiar kinds of justice: distributive justice, corrective justice and retributive justice. There are laws that relate to each of these kinds of justice. Tax law is primarily concerned with enforcing a distributive scheme. Tort law is primarily corrective. Criminal law is retributive (assuming, for the moment, that the best account of punishment will be retributivist).

Now, in most justifications of retributive justice, the punishment that is imposed on the defendant is justified at least in part through the communicative function of the sentence.[7] In imposing a sentence for breaching the criminal law, the criminal law communicates to the defendant, the criminal justice system and the community more broadly that the defendant has perpetrated the kind of moral wrong that is of public concern. The sentence is normally intended to reflect the moral significance of the wrongdoing.

Given this fact, as far as retributive justice is concerned, we need a different conception of the preliminary question than Michelman offers, and one which creates worries for some kinds of proceduralism. Rather than asking what can justify coercing others to obey the laws that the state creates, we should be asking what can justify punishment of defendants *for breaching those laws*. On some accounts of proceduralism, the procedure is required in order that decisions can be made where

---

7 See, for example, A. von Hirsch, *Censure and Sanctions* (Oxford: Oxford University Press, 1993) and R. A. Duff, *Punishment, Communication and Community* (Oxford: Oxford University Press, 2001). For recent exploration in the context of sentencing see A von Hirsch and A. Ashworth, *Proportionate Sentencing: Exploring the Principles* (Oxford: Oxford University Press, 2005).

disagreement persists. The bare existence of the law, which all agree on, does not necessarily reflect agreement about its moral content.

However, as far as criminal law goes, that poses a significant problem with regard to sentencing. Suppose that D is convicted of an offence, O, which legislators A and B agreed should be passed. However, A and B disagree about the moral significance of O. When D is sentenced for breaching O, he is sentenced for his morally wrongful conduct, not for the breach of an agreed rule. The mere existence of a rule would justify only the most trivial penalty. Without determining the wrongfulness of the conduct which the rule prohibits, sentencing necessarily becomes trivial: all that would be available to the court would be the fact that there was agreement that the offence was punishable as a criminal offence, not about the nature of the wrong. And it is the latter that is required to determine the sentence. Without a common understanding of the relevant wrong, achieving retributive justice is severely hampered. If proceduralists are right about the level of moral disagreement about substantive questions of justice, it seems that retributivist justice cannot be effectively delivered.

Furthermore, in justifying punishment *to the defendant*, it seems problematic to refer to the procedural rather than the substantive justice of the law. If the defendant asks why he is being punished (and let us not forget here that criminal punishment, at least in the form of imprisonment, tends to destroy families, deprive the defendant of a livelihood, subject him to further risk of crime and undermine his dignity as well as depriving him of his liberty) it seems utterly inadequate to say to him: because that was what was decided. Rather, the court must refer to the substantive correctness of the rules of the criminal law.

None of this is intended as an invitation to ignore the important justificatory function of the political process. Here's why: the decision to punish must be justified in relation to the content of the wrong: that it is a wrong that ought to be criminal. But as punishment involves *public* condemnation of the defendant's conduct, it must also be the case that such condemnation is *warranted by the public*. In other words, the justification of punishment requires that the defendant has acted in way that *would* justify public condemnation *and* that such condemnation *has been* warranted by the appropriate public process. But the process, here, cannot be referred to as the justification of punishment in isolation. The justification of punishment must come primarily from the content of the wrong, albeit that punishment for the wrong must be ratified by the proper kind of public process.

IV Four Proceduralist Theories

This account will be important in determining the content of proceduralism. Michelman invites us to consider the contrast between two versions of proceduralism: pure proceduralism and imperfect proceduralism.

1. *Pure proceduralism*: the justice of a decision, *p*, is constituted by the procedure by which *p* was decided.
2. *Imperfect proceduralism*: the justice of a decision, *p*, is constituted by substantive features of justice (*x, y, z*) external to the procedure by which *p* was decided. However, the procedure is the best method of ensuring that *p* tracks *x, y, z*.

Were the procedure to be such that *p* was guaranteed to track *x, y, z* we would have 'perfect proceduralism'. But as that is not feasible in the constitutional context we need not consider it as an option.

If pure proceduralism is true, there is no relevant theory of justice about the content of *p* unless *p could not* have been arrived at through the procedure. A potential rule could be called unjust in its content only if it could not have been arrived at through the procedure. Imperfect proceduralism, on the other hand, may (at least sometimes) establish that we should *treat p* as just although *p* may be substantively unjust. *Treating p* as just is required insofar as no better way of establishing whether *p is* just can be found.

There is some middle ground between 1 and 2. It may be that the procedure can contribute to the justice of *p* without entirely determining whether it was just. There are a number of possibilities. Here are two:

3. *Additive proceduralism*: the justice of a decision, *p*, is in part constituted both by *x, y, z*, and by the procedure by which *p* was decided.

On this account, there may be decisions which do not go through the proper procedure, but which are just. The absence of the proper procedure may be an injustice that is outweighed by *x, y, z*. Or it may be that the absence of an otherwise necessary feature of justice, say *z*, is outweighed by the presence of *x* and *y* if the decision is reached by the proper procedure. This leaves open the power of the decision in determining the justice of *p*. It may be that the procedure is given very large or very small weight in determining the justice of *p*.

4. *Enabling proceduralism*: the justice of a decision, *p*, is constituted by features *x, y, z* of justice external to the procedure by which *p* was decided. However, it is also a necessary enabling condition of the justice of *p* that it is arrived at by the appropriate procedure.

On this account, going through the proper procedure is an enabling condition[8] such that *p* could be considered just were it to fulfil *x, y, z*. But it does not contribute to the substantive features of justice. All decisions are unjust, on this account, if the procedure is not followed. But if the procedure is followed it does not supply a further substantive feature that can contribute to justice of *p*. Once the question of justice is enabled by the procedure, it is to be determined entirely by *x, y, z*. This

8 On enabling conditions, see J. Dancy, *Ethics Without Principle* (Oxford: Oxford University Press, 2004).

is the version of proceduralism that I am inclined to defend here. This version, I suggest, escapes the dilemmas of proceduralism that Michelman outlines.

Pure proceduralism, as Michelman suggests, is implausible in the context of constitutional theory. It only appears plausible in cases where there are no substantive concerns about the justice of *p*. If, in all cases, it is just to *v* on heads but unjust to *v* on tails, there are no substantive conditions of justice that apply to *v*. For example, suppose that you and I come across an indivisible good worth £5. We both have £5. We agree that if I have the good I should give you £5 and vice versa and (I stipulate) that would be just. In that case the justice of who has the good and who has the £5 is entirely determined by the toss of a coin. But that is only because in this case there is no substantive feature of the situation that distinguishes the results. If either result would be equally just, what is just is constituted purely by the procedure. But pure procedural justice is, in that case, true only by its triviality. Furthermore, although the justice of *p* is, in this case, determined by the procedure, it can equally be explained on any other of the proceduralist theories above.

The justice of a decision, then, is determined by features of substantive justice, at least in part. Furthermore, there often appears not to be a way of specifying what the proper procedure *is* or whether it has been followed without referring to the substantive features of justice. For example, if we take hypothetical agreements, such as the agreements that could be reached by all reasonable participants, it is difficult to see how we could establish that a particular agreement could be reached by such participants other than by showing that the agreement is substantively just. Were the agreement manifestly unjust in substantive terms, it would be difficult to see why *any* (let alone *all*) reasonable participants would agree to it.

Take the view that a political or moral principle is just only if no one could reasonably reject it as the basis for informed, unforced general agreement.[9] What counts as reasonable rejection, here, surely depends upon a moral theory of the legitimate interests of participants forming such an agreement together. And that is surely because, on this view, the formulation of agreements which properly respect the legitimate interests of participants is central to the best conception of what justice *is*. And that is crucial to ensuring that reasonable participants will respect agreements formed in this way.

Nevertheless, decisions do appear to be just or unjust also according to the procedure by which they come about. Punishment for breach of a criminal law that is substantively just, but which has been arrived at without democratic participation, or some other kind of public warrant, might be considered unjust. Imperfect proceduralism does as though the only reason in favour of designing our procedures in a certain way is to track substantive justice. Imagine that the state were run by Plato's philosopher kings, who are sufficiently wise always to make substantively just decisions. In that case, we would have perfect proceduralism, as the decisions of those philosopher kings would best track what is substantively just, and there would therefore be no claim to injustice. As I suggested earlier, this seems

9 A formulation that is close to Scanlon's influential account of contractualism in moral theory. See T. M. Scanlon, *What We Owe to Each Other* (Cambridge MA: Harvard University Press, 1998), 153.

wrong. Decisions of the state would be unjust even though their outcome would be just. Justice depends on procedures not just because procedures are a good way of discovering what is substantively just, but because, in their absence, otherwise substantively just decisions aren't just (at least in one respect). Decisions to punish require the appropriate public warrant. That follows from the public nature of the criminal law.

If this is right, neither pure proceduralism nor perfect/imperfect proceduralism provides a good grounding for constitutional theory. Pure proceduralism problematically fails to recognise that justice is not merely a question of procedure but of outcome. Imperfect proceduralism treats procedures as only significant instrumentally in their tendency to produce outcomes which are substantively just. They fail to recognise any intrinsic value in procedures.

This leaves us with the task of exploring the relationship between procedure and substance in a theory of justice. I will suggest that enabling proceduralism accords best with a theory of justice. This will be shown in the particular context of establishing the central rules of the criminal law (that is rules which instruct courts when punishments rather than mere penalties are due[10]). This is the area of law where the case for enabling proceduralism is strongest, although I think that it is the best theory of procedural justice more generally. The truth of enabling proceduralism, however, rests in part on the force of the epistemic success of the process in tracking substantive questions of justice. So enabling proceduralism, I suggest, can co-opt the force of imperfect proceduralism.

Why see procedure as making merely an enabling contribution to substantive justice? In order to answer that question, we should return to the justification of punishment. As I noted earlier, when a defendant is punished for a criminal act, the law communicates to him that he has performed a public wrong, a wrong which the public are rightly concerned with. But punishment for a public wrong seems problematic where the content of the wrong cannot be communicated publicly. In justifying punishment to the defendant, and to the community more generally, reference must be made to the content of the wrong. 'Because we decided' is an inadequate justification of punishment. It is inadequate in that the agreement itself does not normally set the conditions of punishment. Whilst it is common for politics to determine a range of appropriate punishments for criminal offences, it would be impossible for courts to specify the proper decision in that range without appreciating the content of the wrong itself.

In addition to this, in justifying punishment to the defendant, the defendant must be able to appreciate that his conduct was wrongful in a way that could justify public condemnation. In deciding which criminal laws to pass, the legislature ought to be debating which behaviour deserves such condemnation, condemnation that all could in principle accept. The wrongfulness of the conduct, this suggests, is prior to the decision to indicate its wrongfulness. The justice of the criminal law normally rests on the wrongfulness of the conduct independently of the decision to declare it

---

10 On the distinction between punishment and penalty, see J. Feinberg, 'The Expressive Function of Punishment' in *Doing and Deserving* (Princeton: Princeton University Press, 1970).

wrong. It is only with *mala prohibita* (if there is such a thing) that this may not be true, on which more in a moment.

For this reason it is difficult to see any decision to create a criminal offence in itself as contributing to substantive justice in an additive fashion. This would be to suggest that whether a form of conduct is worthy of public condemnation is dependent on whether we have decided it to be so. But this makes the debate of the legislature about the creation of criminal laws mysterious. For how can we debate whether to declare a form of conduct criminal when its very *value* as criminal is dependent on our decision? In deciding whether *v*ing is sufficiently wrongful to make it criminal, and hence subject to punishment, we surely do not take into consideration any value that would be added to the wrongness of *v*ing by our decision to make *v* criminal. On the contrary, the legislature should be simply debating what is worthy of public condemnation, not what *would be* worthy of public condemnation were we to decide that it is so.

It might be argued that this is not true when an offence *mala prohibita* is created. Criminal lawyers commonly distinguish between *mala in se* (things wrong in themselves) and *mala prohibita* (things wrong because prohibited). One common formulation of *mala prohibita* is that an offence is *mala prohibita* if the conduct prohibited would not have been wrongful were it not for the fact that it is prohibited, but its prohibition makes it wrongful. This formulation creates a number of theoretical problems. For example, there are some things that are wrong only if they are regulated by rules, but the rules need not be the rules of the criminal law. If they are criminalised, do these things count as *mala in se* or *mala prohibita*? Furthermore, if this is the right formulation, justifying *mala prohibita* is very difficult.[11]

We might skirt round these problems by focusing more directly on the principles of criminalisation. On one influential view, criminalisation of conduct is justified if and only if it fulfils utilitarian goals. It is this that provides the general justifying aim of punishment, distributed on retributive grounds, for breach of the law.[12] Given that utilitarianism is more or less defunct as a moral theory, this theory should be rejected.[13] Perhaps we can substitute other goals (consequentialist or distributive in some other fashion) for utilitarian goals, making this kind of theory more palatable. But even on views of this kind, the justification of criminalisation tracks the interests that would be protected or promoted by criminalization, to which nothing substantive is added by the fact of agreement.

Let me put this another way. Additive proceduralism supposes the following: there are some forms of conduct, *v*ing, which there is some, but insufficient reason

---

11 See particularly D. N. Husak, '*Malum Prohibitum* and Retributivism', in R. A. Duff and S. P. Green, *Defining Crimes: Essays on the Special Part of the Criminal Law* (Oxford: Oxford University Press, 2005).

12 'Two Concepts of Rules' in *Collected Papers*, S. Freeman (ed.) (Cambridge MA: Harvard University Press, 1999), more or less followed in H. L. A. Hart, 'Prolegomenon to the Principles of Punishment', in *Punishment and Responsibility: Essays in the Philosophy of Law* (Oxford: Oxford University Press, 1968). It is Hart who uses the distinction between the general justifying aim of punishment and its distribution.

13 See especially D. N. Husak, 'Guns and Drugs: Case Studies on the Principled Limits of the Criminal Sanction', (2004) 23 *Law and Philosophy*, 437, particularly at 463–5.

(x, y, z) to call publicly wrongful, but which, once we add a further reason, *r*, that is sufficient to call them publicly wrongful. On this account, *r* is the reason *that we have decided.* But equally it is difficult to see how members of the legislature are to decide whether to declare *v*ing criminal. It seems as though there could not be sufficient reason to declare *v*ing to be criminal under such circumstances. For in declaring *v*ing to be criminal, the legislature would increase the range of conduct that is punishable. And why would it want to do that? It would make behaviour which was not worthy of punishment into punishable behaviour. And it is difficult to see how that could ever be rational.

This inclines me to suggest that we should see the procedure as enabling of the justice of the decision. In order to see it as enabling we need to understand a way in which procedure can contribute to the substance of justice and a way in which it cannot. It contributes to substantive justice in that without it considerations of substance cannot make a decision just. Substantive considerations determine what it *would be* just to decide, through the proper procedure. They do not determine what *is* just. If there are substantive considerations for and against a particular decision, the procedure itself cannot tip the balance in favour of one side over the other. But it is only through the procedure that the decision in favour of the heavier side is fully just. Substantive considerations of justice, on this account, need to be 'switched on' or 'warranted' by the procedure. Otherwise, we should see them as at least defective.

On this account, then, reference to the decision in justifying punishment is appropriate, but not in order to show that the defendant perpetrated the kind of wrong that warrants punishment. Rather it is appropriate in showing that there is good reason to believe that the defendant perpetrated a wrong (the epistemic function of procedures) and that the wrong was legitimated by the appropriate procedure (its enabling function). The right to punish for the appropriate kind of wrong was 'switched on' by the procedure.

This shows why, even in relation to *mala in se* offences, it is necessary for the appropriate political procedure to be used even though at least the core of some of those offences, such as rape, robbery and murder, is politically uncontentious. Even in those cases, where there is no disagreement, political procedures are necessary to warrant punishment for a public wrong.

Things may be different as far as *mala prohibita* are concerned. There the justification of punishment for breach rests on the fact of the prohibition itself rather than on the declaration of the wrongfulness of the conduct. But even there, the procedure is best seen as enabling. For, as I noted earlier, even with regard to *mala prohibita* offences, the justification for punishment must rest on some further principles that are independent of the decision itself. The difficultly of finding such principles leads some to conclude that it is difficult to justify punishing for breach of *mala prohibita* offences at all.[14] But breach cannot be warranted simply on the basis of the fact of the decision itself. It must refer to further values that justify the decision such as the importance of cooperation or the wrongfulness of free-riding.

Of course, it might be argued that this does nothing to resolve the disagreements about what should be criminal. But disagreement about that is *just that*: disagreement about what should be criminal. The process is designed to foster debate about

14 See Husak, '*Malum Prohibitum*', n.10 above.

what should be criminal and to make declarations about that. Its conclusions are conclusions about what should be criminal, not conclusions about *the agreement that we could come to* about what should be criminal.

In other words, the procedure itself does have an epistemic function as imperfect proceduralism suggests. Part of the justification for the procedure is its efficiency in attaining knowledge about the substantive considerations of justice. But that is not its *only* justification. Procedure must be both epistemically efficient and otherwise politically acceptable in order to play its enabling function. For it must both lead to just decisions about what the substance of the criminal law, for example, should be *and* be able to legitimise public condemnation for breach.

However, whilst enabling proceduralism has these attractions, it might also seem to some extreme and therefore counterintuitive. Compare decisions in the following two societies:

S1: colonial masters decide to introduce a distributive scheme that is ideal in terms of substantive justice.

S2: democratically elected representatives, despite their best efforts, decide to introduce a scheme that is less than ideal in terms of substantive justice.

Enabling proceduralism, it seems, would suggest that the decision in S1 is not just at all. The substantive excellence of the decision cannot contribute to the justice of the decision at all as it is not enabled by the appropriate procedure. The decision in S2, in contrast, is somewhat just. Its lesser degree of substantive excellence can contribute to justice overall as it is enabled by the procedure.

Of course, the account does not establish that we should always *prefer* S2 to S1. S1 may be preferable for non-justice related reasons. Perhaps we should say that there may be *pragmatic* reasons to prefer S1. But others might disagree. They might want to say that substantive and procedural questions of justice are incommensurable, but that sometimes S1 will be more just than S2, substantive questions of justice outweighing the procedural injustices. I am tempted to defend a pure version of enabling proceduralism on the grounds that citizens of colonies are unlikely to see their situation as just at all, regardless of the fairness of distributions and other questions of substantive justice, as well as concerns about additive proceduralism outlined earlier. But perhaps a less pure version is better, where there is a particular respect in which the decision in S1 is unjust, rendering the substantive justice it achieves at least defective.

V Conclusion

Proceduralism has generally been defended on the grounds that it is the only way in which agreement can be reached under circumstances of disagreement about substantive justice. However, it is not clear that a defence can be provided on those grounds or that such a defence would be necessary for the purposes of the law. Once we appreciate the nature of the criminal law and of punishment, we are encouraged to explore a different role that political procedures might play.

Proper procedures might fulfil a dual function. Firstly, they provide the best method of tracking substantive questions of justice epistemically. They provide the way in which we discover what it *would be* just to do. Secondly, they enable the transformation of what *would be* just to what *is* just. They provide the public warrant that is necessary to justify public condemnation of the defendant for breach of the criminal law. This defence of proceduralism is drawn from different resources than those familiar in political theory. Political theory, I suggest, has wrongly focused on the justification of coordination through coercion rather than of punishment for breach. Justifying the latter does not involve abandoning proceduralism. But it does provide a foundation for it that invites an analysis of it that is quite different from that invited by the presentation of the problem by Michelman. However, given that it *is* punishment rather than coercion that needs justification, at least in respect of the criminal law, I suggest that the terrain is redrawn in this way.

I leave open, here, just what the grounds for accepting particular procedures might be beyond their epistemic success in tracking substantive questions of justice. There are reasons of dignity of citizens, of responsibility, of fairness, of social solidarity, community and of the educative value of participation that might be given, and perhaps many others. These reasons contribute to the motivation to see additive or enabling theories as superior at least to imperfect proceduralism. I don't have space to explore those possibilities here. I suspect that these reasons all have some force and that we need not choose between them. The question that I have tried to address is in a sense more basic than that, the question of the relationship between procedure and substance in justice. Ultimately, that question may only be answered once we have all of the reasons to adopt procedures beyond their epistemic success fully articulated. Michelman's chapter in this book goes some way to achieving that aim.

Index

Page numbers in bold indicate chapters within the book

Aboriginal
    peoples 30, 131, 135, 136, 138
        rights 30, 91n, 136n
Althusser, Louis 64, 97
'The ancients' 182, 195
Anderson, Gavin W. 2, 4-16, 101, 108, **129-138**
Amin, Samir 78
Arendt, Hannah 142, 165, 180
Aristotle 29, 36
Asch, Michael 136
Augustine 141, 165, 180
Authority
    Abuse of 176, 197
    Democratic 104-108, 125, 202-203
    Political 29, 31, 58n, 104-108, 207
    Public 2-4, 30, 38
    Sovereign 22, 30, 86,
Autonomy
    And plurality 111, 112, 127
    'Private' 131
    And 'pure' public law 3, 18, 27-45, 48-60
    And Rawlsian 'civility' 191n, 197, 198n, 202
    Reason as the distinctive feature of 197
    And self-determination 25, 104

Bacevich, Andrew J. 74, 75, 76, 77, 81, 91, 92
Badiou, Alain 62-64
Barnet, Michael 80
Baxi, Upendra 131, 137
Beard, Charles 74
Bentham, Jeremy 142, 165, 180
Bodin, Jean 16, 23, 48
Boundaries
    And the autonomy of politics as 'public' 192, 194
    And the autonomy of public law 36-38
    Political community and spatial boundaries 104, 114-115
    Territorial boundaries in the imperial world 79
Bourdieu, Pierre 31, 33, 57, 132
Bratman, Michael 106, 107
Bretton Woods Institutions 75, 78, 89, 119
Bush, George W. 70, 75, 76, 93, 118, 173
Butler, Judith 133-134, 138
Butler, Major-General Smedley 92

Callinicos, Alex 81
Christodoulidis, Emilios **1-12**, **35-45**, 55, 59-64, 96n
Citizenship
    And civility 190-192, 196, 198
    And governance 15-23, 135, 145n, 200
    And participation 106, 111, 124, 135, 147n, 150, 153, 156, 157, 161n, 168, 169, 200, 207, 208
    Principles of 4, 10, 58, 104, 109, 124, 196, 202, 217
Civil society 57, 59, 126, 190
    European 22
Civility 10, 11, 19, 134, 189-203
Clinton, William 75, 76
Coercion
    Justifications of 10, 11, 144, 147-149, 166-170, 173n, 189, 205-209, 217
    Kant on 86n
Cohen, Joshua 149, 153
Commonwealth 17, 30, 49n
Community
    And Criminal justice 209, 213
    International 78
    Monism/pluralism and 103, 111
    Political 103, 104, 111
    Proceduralism and 141, 165, 175, 189, 191, 194, 217
Compliance
    As social 'good' 145-147, 207
    UN enforcement and 78
    And unjust laws 145, 158
Conant, Charles A. 73, 74, 75
Conflict
    And constitutional order 44, 64, 169, 171n, 184

Cultural 135
And morality 139n
And Political engagement 184, 191, 195
Constituent power 17-18, 24, 37, 39, 49n, 61, 64, 104, 112, 172n
Constituted power 17, 18, 61, 104, 111
Continuity
And autonomy 35-45, 60-61
Informal imperialism and modern global relations 72-57, 121-122, 130
And revolution 125
Courts
Division of labour, with parliament 207
Protection of rights by 136
And punishment 213
Sphere of, distinguished from 'political sphere' 57
Criminal law
And proceduralism 206-217
The Crown 30, 31
Crown-in-Parliament 55
Custom 48, 50, 51, 105, 106
Customary law 79, 97

Democracy
And constitutionalism 38, 44, 58, 124, 141, 167, 172, 173, 175, 191, 201, 203
And law 4, 7, 17, 18, 38, 58, 69-101, 129, 131, 153
And Monism/pluralism 103-115
And 'the political' 62-63, 165
And self-determination 120
Derrida, Jacques 113, 165, 180-187
Force de loi 186
Dialogue
And Constitutionalism as intercultural dialogue 123, 130, 135, 136, 138
And human flourishment 199
And identity 69-101, 103-115
Dicey, Albert V. 64
Dyzenhaus, David 50, 52, 53, 54

Estlund, David 148, 154, 155, 161
European Union
Constitution of the European Union, referendums 22
Member state identity 22
Supra-state model 16, 20, 56, 78, 129
Exploitation
And colonialism 76n, 96, 100
Of conflict 38, 42, 57
And Public law 4, 7, 9, 27-33, 58, 64

Fanon, Frantz 9, 79, 80, 99, 123
Fassbender, Bardo 78
The Federalist Papers 200
Feminist theory 134
Frankfurt, Harry 199
Freedom
And constitutional justice 157, 160, 169, 175, 199, 201
From external influence 19, 20-23, 55
And global markets 92n, 94
And imperial rule 74, 79, 81, 91, 92n, 93n, 98
'Lawless' freedom 86, 87n
And morality and 51
Normative considerations of 61, 62, 142, 146, 176, 178, 201
And participation 97, 124, 125
As politics 63
Freud, Sigmund 181, 183, 185, 187
Foucault, Michael 5, 36, 69, 87, 95, 97, 99, 119
The Subject and Power 95, 104n
Foundation
And the colonial state 136
Foundational moment 8, 17, 18
Kelsen and foundation of law 36, 171, 174
Fukuyama, Francis 88, 94

Gadamer, Hans-Georg 8, 88, 105, 108-114
Gallagher, John 73, 74
GATT 70
Globalisation 15, 20, 21, 47, 82, 89
Governance
And citizens 129, 135
Global 72, 77-82, 84, 89, 119-120, 131
Levels of 24, 97
'Practices of' 69, 71
Territorial 15
Griffith, John 35, 38
Grundnorm 36, 59, 163, 164n, 170-171

Habermas, Jürgen 149, 142, 150-151, 153-155, 167-169, 189
Einbeziehung des Anderen 110, 114
Hardt, Michael 6, 21, 71, 75, 98, 130
(and Negri) *Empire* 6, 75n, 98n
Harvey, David 78, 81

Hay, John 74
Hegel, Georg Wilhelm Friedrich 47n, 48, 51, 83n, 114
Hegemony
Imperial features 9, 90n, 99, 199, 121
Legal 77
Heidegger, Martin 109
Held, David 69, 72, 77, 78, 81, 89, 90
Herder, Johann 87, 88
Higher law 18, 171-172, 174
Hobbes, Thomas 16, 48, 72, 141, 145, 146, 165, 166, 179, 197, 198
Human Rights Act 1998 52
Hume, David 141, 165, 179, 197

Identity
As the conceptual core of the Pluralism/ Monism debate 103-115
Cultural identity, in the courts 136
Kelsen and 171-172
Of 'orders' 41
And social unity 173
And the state 6-8, 17, 22, 30
'Immimanence'
And constitutional imminence/ immanence 185-187
Imperialism
And constitutionalism 131-138
Informal 88-99, 103-104, 118-120, 125-126, 131, 134
Law, democracy and 69-101, 117-128
Indigenous peoples 30, 41, 58n, 80n, 87n, 90, 91, 101n, 130, 131
Rights 30, 91n, 136n
Injustice 143, 148, 199, 211, 212, 216
International Monetary Fund 70, 81, 94
New 69-77, 82

Johnson, Chalmers 74, 91
Judgement
Burdens of 147-149
Criterial judgement 150-154, 158, 167, 169
As 'Higher law making' 173n, 174n
Prudent 16-17
Rawlsian theory and 192, 200
Judiciary 54, 155, 159, 174n, 201
Juridification 16, 33, 47, 76n, 96
Jurisdiction 41, 44, 54, 136, 156, 166, 174n
Justice
Distributive 206, 207, 209
See Injustice
See 'Proceduralism': 'Imperfect procedural justice'; 'Perfect procedural justice'
Retributive 206, 209, 210
Justified collaboration 10, 144, 166-167

Kant, Immanuel 36, 48, 56, 82-90, 91-98, 100, 103, 105, 110, 114, 119, 122, 141, 145, 146, 150, 165, 166, 179, 190, 197, 202
Idea for a Universal History with a Cosmopolitan Purpose 83, 87n
Perpetual Peace: A Philosophical Sketch 83-86, 89n, *110*
Kelsen, Hans 5, 35-36, 43, 59-60, 64, 112, 163-164, 170-175, 184, 185, 186, 187
Kennedy, John F. 75, 93
Koskenniemi, Martti 74, 76, 80, 90, 99
Kutz, Christopher 106

Laclau, Ernesto 133-134
League of Nations 75, 79, 81, 88, 91n
Lefort, Claude 41
Legitimacy
And legality 54, 148-157, 167-169, 201
And political power 2, 3, 5, 9, 94, 127, 136, 201
Liberal constitutionalism
Challenged 1, 135
Coercion and force at the centre of 208
Defended 203
Procedural logic of 155-161
Liberty 58, 154, 169, 178, 190, 192, 196, 199, 203, 210
Lindahl, Hans 2, 7-8, 60, 66, 101, **103-115**, 171
Locke, John 48, 83, 131, 141, 165, 179
Loughlin, Martin 1-10, 15-24, 27-33, 35-45, **47-65**, 69, 71, 74, 75, 82, 97, 100, 101, 112, 128, 138, 171
The Idea of Public Law 43, 47-65, 69n
Sword and Scales 27
Lourdes, Audra 98
Loyalty
And identity 19, 21, 22, 24, 25
Luhmann, Niklas 36-39, 42, 43, 60, 61

Mabo case 30, 58
Machiavelli, Nicolò 16, 141, 165, 179

MacIntyre, Alasdair 12, 39
Madison, James 141
Mala in se 214-215
Mala prohibita 214-215
Mann, Michael 75
Marks, Susan 20, 21, 94, 95
Marx, Karl 30, 33, 40, 64, 69, 73, 83, 86, 88, 100, 186
Michelman, Frank 1, 2, 10-12, **141-161**, 163-181, 183-187, 189, 193, 203, 205, 207-210, 212, 217
  Always Under Law? 171-174
  Law's Republic 171, 173
  Why Constitutionalism? 171-174
Modernity 1, 6, 19, 83n, 96
Monism
  And community 103, 111
  And the methodology of public law 7
  See 'Pluralism': 'Pluralism-Monism debate'
Monroe Doctrine 74, 91, 92
Morality
  And coercion 86n
  Derrida on 142, 166, 172, 173n, 180, 181
  And political reciprocity 113, 160
  And positive morality 16
  Relationship with law 51, 54, 145
  Shaftesbury on 194
Morgenthau, Hans 90

NAFTA 127
Nation-state
  Beyond the nation-state model 6-9, 129
  And decolonisation 80, 93
  And identity 6-8
  And modern sovereignty 19-25, 131, 202
Nationalism 15, 23, 25, 93, 132
Negri, Antonio 6, 21, 64, 71, 75, 98, 130
  (and Hardt) *Empire* 6, 75n, 98n
Neo-liberalism 33, 70, 78, 81, 94, 95, 97, 104, 122, 132

Oakeshott, Michael 19
Orders
  Loughlin's three orders of the political 35, 37-42, 59-64
Orwell, George 32, 33

Parliament
  Crown-in-parliament 55
  Division of labour, with the courts 207
  Parliamentary deliberation 159
  Sovereignty of 15, 160
'The People'
  As constituent power 17-19, 24, 64, 86, 105, 112
  And democracy 69-102
  And the Monism-Pluralism debate 103-116
  And Sovereignty 7, 55, 105, 107
  Status of 58
Pluralism
  Economic 103, 125
  Legal 7, 95, 103-105, 108, 110, 114
  Pluralism-Monism debate 103-115
  'Reasonable' 147-149, 158, 191
  Societal 7, 25
Polanyi, Karl 44-45
'the political'
  And democracy 62-63, 165
  Orders (three) of 35, 37-42, 59-64
Political constitution 35, 38, 43, 44, 54, 160, 170
Popular sovereignty 90, 92, 94, 105, 106, 111, 171-174, 202
Power
  See 'constituted power'; 'constituent power'
  Economic 3, 4, 69n, 73, 93
  'Federalist Papers' on 200
  'Great powers' 70, 73, 74, 76n, 77, 80n, 93n, 120
  Imperial, 74, 75, 77, 79, 81, 84, 93n, 98
  Military 81, 84, 92n
  Political 2, 5, 15, 19, 28, 30, 37, 72, 79, 111-114, 132, 156, 168, 190
Positivism 15-19, 37, 55, 145 171, 172
Proceduralism
  Additive 206, 211, 214, 216
  Enabling 11, 205-217
  'Imperfect' procedural justice 143, 144, 155-160
  'Pure' procedural justice 10, 143, 151, 155-161, 170, 212
Prudence 16, 17
Psychoanalysis
  Insights from, for politics and law 181-184
Pufendorf, Samuel 48
Punishment
  Capital punishment 159, 176n

And civility 201
Justification and 11, 206
And proceduralim 208-210, 213-217
Pure theory of public law
Autonomy of public law considered 15-25, 22-33, 35-45, 47-65
Kelsen on 5
See 'Purity'
Purity
And impurity 11, 163-187
Kelsenian 'purity' 43

Rancière, Jacques 61-62, 64
Rawls, John 10-11, 52, 52, 78, 90, 143, 144, 145, 146, 150, 151, 154, 156-161, 167-169, 189-194, 196-203, 207
A Theory of Justice 52, 53n, 168
Political Liberalism 147, 168, 207n
Reagan, Ronald 70, 75
Rebellion 86
Representation
And imperialism 104
Low intensity 98
And participation 104, 111-112, 135
And public law 8, 17
And statehood 18, 25, 60
Resistance
As 'lawless freedom' 86, 87n
And the 'failed state' 80
Imperialism and 92, 96, 97, 98, 100, 122, 131
'Just' 200
As political reflexivity 107
Respect
And civility 193-201
Constitutional 'respect-worthiness' 148-160, 167, 168
And proceduralism 212
Responsibility 32, 91, 92, 107, 193, 199, 217
Revolution
As emancapatory politics 61-64, 91
And civility 201
Conservative 31, 123, 124
French 202-203
Neo-liberal 33
Ricoeur, Paul 106
Rights 4, 49n, 58, 73, 76n, 98, 136, 137, 141, 143, 159, 175, 187n
Aboriginal/indigenous 30, 91, 136n
'Age of' 28
Basic/fundamental 42, 136, 157, 168, 178n
Civil and political 2
claims 58
Competition 33
Constitutional 52, 108, 160
Human 52, 72, 80, 89n, 94, 131, 153
Individual 94, 203
Liberal 167, 169
Private 154
Property 94, 154
Transcendental 65
Robinson, Ronald 73, 74, 93
Roosevelt, Franklin D. 74, 93
Roosevelt, Theodore 74-76
Rousseau, Jean Jacques 48, 49, 50, 51, 141, 165, 179
Du Contrat Social 48
Rule
Colonial rule 73, 94, 97, 131
Imperial rule 72, 73, 77, 85, 87, 89, 91, 99, 104
Self-rule 7, 82, 91, 94, 103-131
Rule of law 42, 43, 80, 99, 124, 149, 181n

Sacrifice
Law and 49, 176-187
Said, Edward 93, 97, 119
Culture and Imperialism 95, 96n, 97n
Salus populi 27, 31
Schmitt, Carl 39-42, 53, 55, 60, 72, 142, 165, 171, 179-187
Self-determination 104, 108, 112, 119-120, 131-134, 199
Sieyès, Emmanuel Joseph 17
Simpson, Gerry 76, 78, 80, 93
Smith, Adam 29, 189, 190n, 193-194, 196-199, 201-203
Smith, Neil 74, 81
America's Empire 81
Sovereignty
Aboriginal 131, 136
And the autonomy of the political sphere 56-59
As distinct from 'sovereign' 55-56
As foundation of modern public law 52, 55
In Loughlin's *The Idea of Public Law* 15-25
Kant's account modified by globalisation 89

See 'Popular sovereignty'
Schmitt on 40
Space
Constituent 61, 63
Laclau, 'empty space' of the universal 133, 137
Sovereignty and (territorial) 16, 22, 24
Spinoza, Baruch 48
The state
And Identity 6-8, 17, 22, 30
See 'Nation-state'
'State-building' 19, 24, 29, 41, 52, 72, 79, 80, 91
Sub-state nationalism 2, 15, 23-25, 41
Supra-state challenge 2, 16, 20, 21, 25
Struggle 9, 53, 58, 62, 63, 80, 83, 91n, 94, 98, 99, 107, 122, 124, 184, 197, 202
Supreme Court
Baker Lake case (Australia) 136
Of the United States 76n, 158-200
Sparrow case (Canada) 135n

Tadros, Victor 2, 10-11, **205-217**
Tassopoulos, Ioannis 2, 10-11, **189-203**
Tawney, Richard Henry 31-33, 58
Terra nullis 131
Territory
And governance 2, 15
And Kant's universal principles 84, 86
Of former colonies 79
Of supra-state entities 20
And plurinational states 23
Sovereignty relationships within 16, 23, 55, 127
State and nation within 6
Theology 184-185
Tierney, Stephen **1-12**, **15-25**, 55-56, 90n, 96n
Truman, Harry S. 93
Tully, James 1-9, 21, **69-101**, 103-114, 117-128, 129-138
Strange Multiplicity: Constitutionalism in an Age of Diversity 7, 62n, 101, 105, 112, 123, 129n, 130, 131, 135

Unger, Roberto 142, 165, 180
United Nations
Charter 72
And the Declaration of Human Rights 72
And multilateralism 77, 78, 88, 98
And the New International Economic Order 80n
And the Security Council 9, 120, 127
Trustee system 79

Values
Conflict of 10, 124, 141, 147n, 165, 175
Constitutional/political 132, 169, 189, 190, 223
Juridification/marketisation of 3
Of public law 35, 44, 51
Universal values 90
Van der Walt, Johan 2, 10-11, **163-187**
Veitch, Scott 2, 3, 4, **27-33**, 55, 57-59, 205

Wacquant, Loïc 132
Waldron, Jeremy 11, 145, 147, 148, 155, 159-161, 167, 169, 170
Walker, Neil 2, 5, 6, 8, 9, 22, 24, 41, 56, 60, 61, 71, 78, 82, 90, 96, 100, 101, 112, 116, **117-128**, 130, 163, 223
Walzer, Michael 51
War
Cold War 76, 79, 90, 93, 94
'On terror' 70, 76, 79n
Post-Cold War 88, 133
World War II
Post-war institutions 78, 80, 81
Shifts in imperialism studies 89
US wars
with Iraq (2003) 76, 93n
with Philipine nationalists 73
with Vietnam 92n
Wendt, Alexander 80
Westphalia 6, 9, 20, 72, 74, 75n, 80, 126
Williams, William A. 74, 92
Wilson, Woodrow 74-76, 91-92, 94
World Bank 70, 81, 94, 98
World Trade Organization 20, 70, 81n